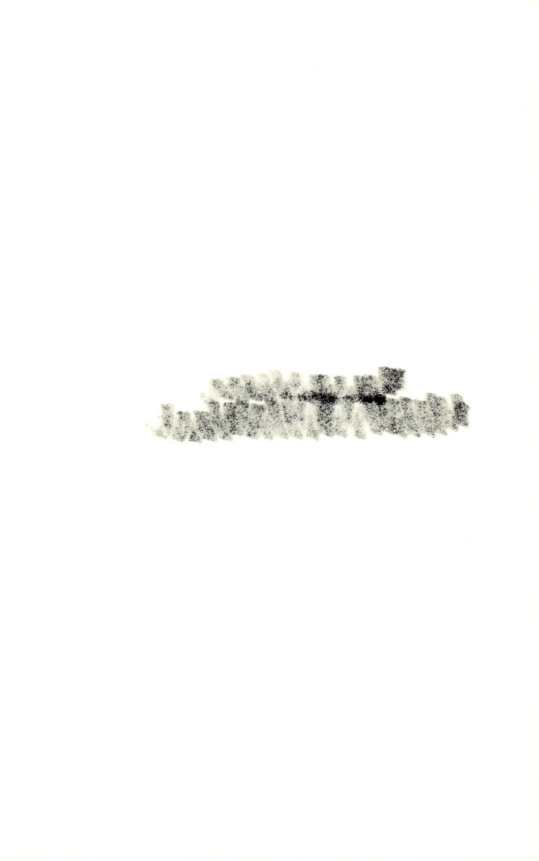

Science Fiction
for Young Readers

Science Fiction for Young Readers

Edited by
C. W. Sullivan III

Contributions to the Study of Science Fiction and Fantasy,
Number 56

Greenwood Press
Westport, Connecticut • London

Library of Congress Cataloging-in-Publication Data

Science fiction for young readers / edited by C. W. Sullivan III.
     p.   cm.—(Contributions to the study of science fiction and
fantasy, ISSN 0193-6875 ; no. 56)
  Includes bibliographical references and index.
  ISBN 0-313-27289-1
  1. Science fiction, American—History and criticism. 2. Young
adult fiction, American—History and criticism. 3. Children's
stories, American—History and criticism. 4. Children—United
States—Books and reading. 5. Youth—United States—Books and
reading. I. Sullivan, Charles Wm. (Charles William). II. Series.
PS374.S35S334 1993
813'.08762099283—dc20   92-26667

British Library Cataloguing in Publication Data is available.

Library of Congress Catalog Card Number: 92-26667
ISBN: 0-313-27289-1
ISSN: 0193-6875

First published in 1993

Greenwood Press, 88 Post Road West, Westport, CT 06881
An imprint of Greenwood Publishing Group, Inc.

Printed in the United States of America

The paper used in this book complies with the
Permanent Paper Standard issued by the National
Information Standards Organization (Z39.48-1984).

10 9 8 7 6 5 4 3 2 1

For my parents
Helen and C. William "Bill" Sullivan, Jr.
readers themselves
whose example and encouragement
opened the treasure house of books
for this one-time young reader

Contents

Preface

The Bookmobile was my salvation, my source of reading matter through my junior high and high school years, my first major supplier of science fiction. In a small town with no library or bookstore and a small central school with a library for only the upper grades, reading matter was scarce. Early, especially when sick or laid up with a broken leg, I had exhausted neighbors' attics and read much of the original Tom Swift, Tarzan, and Hardy Boys series—along with other older series featuring characters with names like Poppy Ott and Jerry Todd or groups like the Radio Boys and the Moving Picture Boys. Whenever we went to the nearest city, some 45 miles away, I checked my favorite bookstore for the latest Tom Swift, Jr., volume.

The Bookmobile (it should be capitalized; it was that important) came every two weeks and parked in the lot across from my family's grocery store. During the summers I foraged there myself, but during the school year my mother was given specific instructions on what to look for: anything by Andre Norton, Robert Heinlein, or Isaac Asimov; anything with the Doubleday science fiction logo on the spine; anything about the future or with a futuristic title. As a result, my reading fare was an interesting mix. A two-week ration might include one of Norton's Time Traders books, Pat Frank's *Alas, Babylon!,* and George Orwell's *1984* (it was a futuristic title then, after all) or Aldous Huxley's *Brave New World*. My reading was enthusiastic. I devoured new books and new ideas with relish—but certainly without guidance.

My easy acceptance of anything futuristic was mirrored by my high school English teacher's automatic rejection of it. My first lesson in science fiction as an unacceptable or "ghetto" literature came when I was handed back a book report on Frank's *Alas, Babylon!*. The opening comment at the top of the page was something like, "Who told you you could do a book report on something like this?" Thereafter, I kept my science fiction to myself, my small town being much too small for anything like a science fiction club. As a final act of defiance, I wrote on Orwell's *1984* for the literature question on my senior New York State Regents' Examination in English (that might explain the grade). My ultimate revenge or justification or foolhardiness (it all depends on your perspective, I suppose) has been an academic career in which imaginative literature, both science fiction and fantasy, has played a major part.

In the years since I was a young reader, English teachers have become aware of science fiction as literature and of science fiction's attraction for young readers—and that brings me to this volume. Although both children's literature and science fiction have attained some stature as areas of legitimate literary inquiry, science fiction written specifically for the young reader has been, by and large, ignored or treated only in passing. Perhaps the thought of joining two such vulnerable subgenres makes such an attempt too risky. Perhaps the presence of so many series books of dubious quality has caused critics to pass by all science fiction written for young readers. Perhaps, in fact, the thought of doing critical work in science fiction for young readers seldom crosses anyone's mind. In addition, science fiction, fantasy, and children's literature have their respective scholarly organizations, the Science Fiction Research Association, the International Association for the Fantastic in the Arts, and the Children's Literature Association, and professional journals, *Extrapolation, The Journal of the Fantastic in the Arts,* and *The Children's Literature Association Quarterly.* Perhaps their existence allows science fiction for young readers to fall through the cracks in between. Still, some excellent work has been done—a look at the selected bibliography will reveal that; but comparatively speaking, there has not been very much directed specifically at science fiction as written for the adolescent market.

Science Fiction for Young Readers is an attempt to provide a collection of essays that will be both a place to start for those unfamiliar with the field as well as a source of new interpretations and ideas for those already working with such materials. Any anthology of essays could be organized in a variety of ways; in this anthology, I have tried to present both a historical and a thematic perspective on science fiction for young readers and on science fiction criticism. To that end, in Part I, there are five chapters dealing with specific individuals considered to have been major shapers in and of the field. Part II contains seven chapters that deal with more recent writers and use a variety of approaches to discuss authors and themes. The last four chapters, Part III, deal with science fiction in which the literature is discussed as almost subordinate to the ideas that the authors may be trying to communicate or that seem imbedded in the fiction. The chapters are followed by a selected bibliography of critical materials.

ACKNOWLEDGMENTS

A collection such as this one cannot really be the product of a single individual. I would first like to thank the College of Arts and Sciences at East Carolina University for a start-up grant that got this project off the ground and for the recent summer stipend that allowed me to finish (more or less) on time. I am also grateful to the individual writers who came up with the ideas, did the work to get them into print, and were understanding about my editorial eccentricities. Tina Moore, former English department graduate secretary, was invaluable in scanning most of the essays onto computer disks for the initial manuscript; East Carolina University graduate student Robin Whaley was equally invaluable in finishing the scanning when Tina moved up to a secretarial position in the College of Arts and Sciences' main office. Marjorie McKinstry, another graduate student and my research assistant, spent many hours in the library checking quotations and running down bibliographic details; she also helped proofread the final manuscript. Laurie Evans, current English department graduate secretary arrived just in time to help with the final bits and pieces of manuscript preparation, was then crucial in turning disparate pages into a whole book, and became, *de facto*, Assistant Editor of this volume. Without all their help, this project would have taken much longer and been less enjoyable.

C.W. Sullivan III

PART I

The Shapers of Science Fiction for Young Readers

Tracing the history and development of science fiction for young readers leads one back to the dime novels, penny dreadfuls, and storypapers of late nineteenth- and early twentieth-century America. The formulaic series structure and the action-adventure emphasis that still hold sway, to some extent, in today's science fiction were first developed in these publications. The form and content of the Tom Swift series and others like it as well as that of the pulp magazines that appeared soon after developed directly from those early mass-market publications. The more literary science fiction of Jules Verne and H. G. Wells became influential only later.

Francis J. Molson's "The Tom Swift Books" discusses a series with a hero who has become a household name, and Molson demonstrates that the Swift series not only aided in the growth of science fiction itself, but also helped develop the audience for science fiction. The series formula and action-adventure emphasis appear in the Swift books almost unchanged from their nineteenth-century print origins and, as Molson chronicles, retain sufficient power to reverberate through three additional series, one currently in production, bearing the name Tom Swift.

Molson suggests that one of the effects of the Tom Swift books was to make young people, especially boys, think about careers as engineers; Robert A. Heinlein took this concept a step further, according to C. W. Sullivan III in "Heinlein's Juveniles: Growing Up in Outer Space," and tried to make young readers comfortable with the rapidly expanding technological world after World War II. In addition, Heinlein created a different kind of series, one that featured different characters in each book but was still progressive, each novel occurring thematically and/or historically subsequent to the ones that had preceded it. Moreover, in most of the novels, there are references to characters and/or events whose stories are told in full in other novels in the series, in other short stories, or in the adult novels.

In "The Formulaic and Rites of Transformation in Andre Norton's Magic Series," Roger C. Schlobin discusses the nature of the formula used in much science fiction for young readers and uses Norton's Magic series as an example of how science fiction—actually science fantasy, in this case—can clarify the rite of passage by depicting it in an alternate world where the value structure is clearer than in the reader's (and, for that matter, the main character's) world. In that other world, the main characters grow in ways that profit them on their return to their own world; the main characters' growth empowers the reader by suggesting that an adolescent can grow, can succeed, and eventually can do things even adults recognize as important. Norton's success with this formula has made her a standard in the field since the 1950s.

Elizabeth Anne Hull's "Asimov: Man Thinking" explores Isaac Asimov's Lucky Starr series and Isaac and Janet Asimov's Norby series as social science fiction rather than hard science fiction—in spite of the famous Laws of Robotics. Both series contain similar political, social, and moral themes, but the two are structured differently. The Lucky Starr series, from the 1950s, is almost vintage series science fiction for young readers; but the Norby series, written some thirty years later, is a sequential series in which each book contains the same main characters but builds, to some extent, on the events in the previous books.

The concept of a series seems to disappear from but still subtly understructures Madeleine L'Engle's fiction as M. Sarah Smedman aptly demonstrates in "The 'Terrible Journey' Past 'Dragons in the Waters' to a 'House Like a Lotus': Faces of Love in the Fiction of Madeleine L'Engle." Characters and events from all of L'Engle's fiction—science fantasy, historical romance, and realistic fiction— appear and reappear to make one enormous tapestry out of seemingly disparate threads, taking the concept of series fiction to what might well be its limits. Except for those specifically written as companions, as in the *Wrinkle in Time* trilogy, each of L'Engle's books may easily be read on its own; however, because characters from the *Time* trilogy appear in other volumes, it may be that, as Smedman implies, the only way to fully grasp what L'Engle is about in her famous science fantasy trilogy is to read everything else she has written as well.

There were certainly other authors who might have been included in this section as shapers of science fiction, but these are the five who have unquestionably taken the series format and added to it; in addition, each author and series has been very popular, making the Tom Swift books, Heinlein's juveniles, Norton's Magic series, Asimov's Lucky Starr and Norby novels, and L'Engle's entire canon enormously powerful influences both on the writers who must compete with them in the marketplace and on the tastes of the young readers who make up that market. The creation of a new Tom Swift series and the current availablity of the other authors' works attest to their importance in the field.

1

The Tom Swift Books

Francis J. Molson

Reading the early Tom Swift books today may elicit one of several possible responses. One is nostalgic, even affectionate, especially for those who in their youth actually read the stories. For these readers, observing again Tom's many exploits and the assurance with which he went about accomplishing them and touched anew by the certitude he displayed about who is good or bad or what is fair play or not, rekindles—for a moment—belief in a value system they now realize is gone forever and actually had been at best naive, if not downright false. A second response is patronizing, amused, uncomprehending, and, hence, incapable of accepting the fact that several generations ago many young readers did actually enjoy fiction, like the Tom Swift series, which featured "cardboard" characters, preposterous situations, and quaint, sometimes even wretched writing. For individuals experiencing the second response, the early Tom Swift books have no significance today and deserve discarding on the rubbish heap of history. A third response is definitely less censorious than the second as well as less sentimental than the first. Genuinely curious, the third response takes seriously the question: What was it in the Tom Swift books of three-quarters of a century ago that spoke so persuasively to youth that hundreds of thousands of copies of the books were published, purchased, circulated, and read? It is the third response that prompts this chapter in which are attempted answers to several key questions. What were the Tom Swift books? Not just the first series or vintage Tom Swift, so to speak, but also the three subsequent series? What accounted for their popularity? What, if anything, did the series, in particular vintage Tom Swift, contribute to the development of science fiction, children's as well as science fiction in general?

* * *

Vintage Tom Swift is the initial series of books—forty volumes long, the first of which appeared in 1910 and the last in 1941—that celebrate the adventures and inventive exploits of Tom Swift, boy inventor extraordinaire. The first 15 titles, clustered in bundles of five as was then customary, were published by Grosset & Dunlap between 1910 and 1912. Subsequently, the same publisher released a new volume each year until 1935 when, forced to acknowledge the irreversibility of the decline in sales that had begun around 1930, the company terminated the series. In 1939 the Whitman Company, which had previously acquired reprint rights to the last ten titles of the series, tested the possibility of a Tom Swift revival by commissioning two new titles, *Tom Swift and His Giant Telescope* (1939) and *Tom Swift and His Magnetic Silencer* (1941), as part of their Better Little Books offering. The hoped-for revival, however, did not materialize, and the first series ended once and for all.

Victor Appleton, the title page author of vintage Tom Swift, is a pseudonym, one of the house names employed by the Stratemeyer Syndicate, which has been until very recently so prominent in the history of American juvenile series fiction. In truth, each Tom Swift story was first conceived and plotted out by Edward Stratemeyer (or his successor)—as was customary in the operation of the syndicate—and then fleshed out by a contract writer, most often Howard Garis, one of the most talented authors in the syndicate's employment. Because Garis was already recognized under his own name and esteemed as the author of the popular Uncle Wiggley series and other books, it is fair to infer that Stratemeyer was sufficiently concerned for the success of the new Tom Swift series that he assigned its actual writing to a proven author. It is also fair to infer Stratemeyer's satisfaction over his editorial decision inasmuch as vintage Tom Swift proved to be very successful, selling at least 6 million copies in the Grosset & Dunlap hardcover editions and, given the strong likelihood that many of these copies were perused by more than one person, read by millions more. Thus, there is every reason to believe that Tom Swift ranks, along with Nancy Drew, Frank and Joe Hardy, the Merriwell Boys, and the Bobbsey Twins, among the most read and admired of heroes in popular juvenile fiction.

Tom Swift, the hero of the series, is a young inventor and self-taught engineer whose inventions, mechanical adaptations, and engineering designs primarily in aeronautics, transportation, and weaponry are the ostensible subject matter of the volumes. The actual plots, however, focus not so much on inventions, adaptations, or designs (and definitely not the process of invention) as on Tom's various adventures involving the products of his genius. One particular focus is the youth's invariably successful attempts to prevent rivals from stealing or tampering with his inventions. Another important focus is the financial success Tom achieves as a result of his inventions and engineering exploits. The latter are in part accounted for by heredity and environment inasmuch as Tom's father, Barton Swift, is himself a successful inventor who always encouraged his son to realize his several talents. Although Tom's mother died when he was only three years old, he still enjoys "mothering" at the hands of Mrs. Baggert, the housekeeper. Tom has two loyal assistants: Sampson Eradicate, or Rad, a "colored" handyman who has attached himself to the Swift household and who unfortunately is allowed to become the butt of many racist jokes; and Koku, a giant South American native prince who had been rescued by Tom and then invited to join the household as its bodyguard. Completing the relatively constant cast of supporting characters are Mr. Damon, an eccentric old man whom Tom saves from a potentially fatal motorcycle accident and who subsequently accompanies the youth on many of his adventures; Ned Newton, Tom's very good friend and eventually his business partner; and Mary Nestor, whom Tom marries after a long "understanding." Not to be overlooked in the cast of characters is the "rival" or "enemy"—in the first books members of a family by the name of Folger and in later stories various unrelated villains—who, despite continually failing to thwart the young inventor's plans and enterprises or steal his inventions, persist in trying to be both difficult and "nasty."

Although the chief protagonist of the series, Tom is flat and static, as are all the characters. There is one exception to this generalization: Tom gradually grows into adulthood, slowly aging over the twenty-five-year span the series lasted. At the height of the series' popularity, he is a young man in his mid-twenties, hence, old enough to marry his "friend" of many years, Mary Nestor. Given Stratemeyer's generally sound understanding of his young audience, it is surprising that he decided to have Tom marry his sweetheart—the wedding occurs at the conclusion of *Tom Swift and His House on Wheels or, A Trip to the Mountain of Mystery* (1929). That decision reflected a failure to think through all the implications of Tom's marriage. That is to say, Stratemeyer neglected to realize that Tom's marrying implied a definite level of behavior and values that did not easily mesh with the decidedly teenage quality of Tom's adventures. As a result, the stories after 1929 became increasingly implausible and difficult for young male readers to identify with. Thus, the wedding, presumably a kind of apogee of Tom Swift's personal happiness and success, ironically marked the beginning of the decline in popularity of vintage Tom Swift.

In addition to being an inventor, Tom is a tinkerer, an improviser, and an entrepreneur, but "young inventor" is Appleton's favorite epithet to describe the hero. Very early in the series his inventions are few, and it is actually Barton Swift who is responsible for the few "big" inventions referred to. As the series caught on, however, Tom became more and more the "big" inventor whose exploits dominated the plots and made him admired, respected, and eventually rich and famous, while his father was allowed to grow old rapidly and retire. Generally speaking, the very titles of the series volumes testify to the nature and extent of Tom's achievements: an "electric runabout," a "sky racer," an "electric rifle," an air glider, a "wizard camera," a "great searchlight," a giant cannon, a "photo telephone," an aerial warship, a big tunnel, a war tank, and so on. As an inventor, Tom does virtually no basic research of his own but develops the initial findings of others. He is not a trained chemist, physicist, or engineer; his professional or "college" background is the proverbial one of "hard knocks." His genius is his method of work—neither hit or miss nor relying on luck, but a commitment to the necessity for extensive design and testing—and a sixth sense that enables him to sense opportunity and immediately decide to capitalize on it. In general, Tom is modest and unassuming about his achievements, although his father and friends are enthusiastic about the youth's accomplishments and anything but restrained in their praise. When Mary, observing the testing of Tom's new tank, exclaims how exciting it is that he "should know how to build such a wonderful machine," Barton Swift points out, "And *run* it, too, Mary! That's the point! Make it *run!* I tell you, that Tom Swift is a wonder" (*Tom Swift and His War Tank or, Doing His Bit for Uncle Sam* 100).

It is becoming commonplace to acknowledge the modest but real contribution of the chronicles of Tom Swift and his wondrous inventions to the development of American science fiction . Yet it is odd that not until the final two volumes, the Whitman Better Little Book titles, were two of the most conventional and pervasive science fiction topics—interplanetary travel and the possibility of extraterrestrial life—utilized. So evident is the absence of these and many other conventional science fiction topics that we cannot but help suspect that the former is the result of a deliberate editorial decision. That is, from the beginning Stratemeyer intended to focus his new Tom Swift series not on conventional science fiction topics but on recent developments in the application of electricity and motor design to contemporary modes of transportation. Consider, for instance, Stratemeyer's advertising for the series that trumpets: These new stories are "spirited tales" that will dramatize "the wonderful advances in land and sea locomotion." Hence, the first five volumes, all published in 1910, feature the excitement of redesigned motorcycles (*Tom Swift and His Motor Cycle or, Fun and Adventures on the Road*), the speed and dependability of motor boats (*Tom Swift and His Motor Boat or, The Rivals of Lake Carlopa*), the existence of the airship, a distinctive but somewhat ungainly combination of biplane and dirigible (*Tom Swift and His Airship or, The Stirring Cruise of the Red Cloud*), a submarine water boat, propelled by a unique tandem of oil-burning engines and electric magnets (*Tom Swift and His Submarine Boat or, Under the Ocean for Sunken Treasure*), and a battery-powered automobile capable of attaining speeds greater than any other vehicle currently in production (*Tom Swift and His Electric Runabout or, The Speediest Car on the Road*). Once the series gained acceptance, Stratemeyer expanded its focus to include air transportation; and advances in aeronautical technology, futuristic and otherwise, became a prominent subject of many of the subsequent Swift volumes.

Additional evidence that Stratemeyer consciously avoided conventional science fiction topics for his new Tom Swift series is the fact that the latter were the focus of his just recently released Great Marvel Series, three volumes of which had already appeared by 1910. In this series, it needs to be recalled, Stratemeyer first sent his young protagonists to the North Pole (*Through the Air to the North Pole or, The Wonderful Cruise of the Electric Marvel,* 1906), the South Pole (*Under the Ocean to the South Pole or, The Strange Cruise of the Submarine*

Wonder, 1907), and underground (*Five Thousand Miles Underground or, The Mystery of the Center of the Earth,* 1908). Then, beginning in 1910, Stratemeyer dispatched his protagonists off Earth as they traveled to Mars (*Through Space to Mars or, The Most Wonderful Trip on Record,* 1910), the Moon (*Lost on the Moon or, In Quest of the Field of Diamonds,* 1911), unnamed planets (*On a Torn-Away World or, Captives of the Great Earthquake,* 1913, and *The City Beyond the Clouds or, Captured by the Red Dwarfs,* 1923), Venus (*By Air Express to Venus or, Captives of a Strange People,* 1929), and finally Saturn (*By Space Ship to Saturn or, Exploring the Ringed Planet,* 1935).

These stories, as is evident from their very titles, fit readily into the Jules Verne tradition of adventurous journeys over vast spaces on and off Earth that futuristic modes of transportation make possible. Further placing the series in the Jules Verne tradition is the cast of characters: Professor Henderson, an adult inventor of a marvelous rocket ship who often times is also seeking to perfect some kind of futuristic weapon, and his assistants, prominent among whom are two youths, Jack Darrow and Mark Sampson. Given the emphasis of inventions, the cast of characters, and an American context, it is also possible to situate the Great Marvel series in the Lu Senarens tradition of invention stories. In other words, the series can be understood as Edward Stratemeyer's attempt to blend the Verne and Senarens traditions into a new type of story specially adapted for an American juvenile audience. It must be kept in mind that Stratemeyer, despite his error in permitting Tom Swift to marry, was quite successful in assessing the reading tastes and needs of American youth. Accordingly, he suspected that the Verne/Senarens traditions, although seemingly played out by the early 1900s, might still be profitably tapped, provided changes in format and merchandising were made. Specifically, Stratemeyer determined to take advantage of new advances in print technology that improved quality while lowering costs—advances that Carol Billman describes in *The Secret of the Stratemeyer Syndicate* (17-35). As he was already doing for some of his other series, he published the Great Marvel stories in hardcover and, more importantly, for just fifty cents instead of the prices customarily charged for hardcover fiction, which could go as high as $1.25. By so doing, he was able to compete in pricing with the available pulps, including those "old" and "dated" inventions stories still occasionally reprinted. At the same time, because his new Verne/Senarens stories would appear in hardcover format, which at that time signaled a relatively high quality level, Stratemeyer prevented their becoming stigmatized as disreputable or shabby reading material—a reputation from which the pulps had always suffered.

For the first three volumes of the new Great Marvel series, Stratemeyer seemed content to combine the Verne/Senarens traditions, as these volumes feature exotic locales, marvelous inventions, specifically in transportation technology, and an adult inventor with his assistants. However, between the publication of the third and fourth volumes of the series, Stratemeyer changed his mind concerning its focus. In the absence of any external evidence, we can only speculate why he did so. Perhaps reader acceptance of his recently initiated Motor

Boys series suggested that the market for stories about motor cars and trains could be expanded. Perhaps the increasing public fascination with inventors like Thomas Edison, as well as over the explosion of technological innovations, justified a new kind of story that would be about the wonderful exploits of inventors. Perhaps the advent of stories about boy inventors—by the year 1910 there were already what looked like the beginnings of three different series— suggested the feasibility of his own series about the boy inventor. In any case, Stratemeyer decided to alter the thrust of the Great Marvel series. Although it would continue, its focus would be even more distinctively the Verne tradition; that is, the exotic locale would definitely be off-earth; the transportation technology, more marvelous and futuristic; and the cast of characters (an adult with juvenile assistants), the same. However, Stratemeyer would not discard the now-deemphasized Lu Senarens tradition. Instead, he would tap it for a new series whose adventures would be restricted to this world and feature more plausible, less futuristic, but still wonderful technological innovations in transportation modes. While Stratemeyer was drawing up his final plans for the new series, he made one other change—in retrospect a most significant one. The protagonist would be an inventor, as in the Great Marvel series, but a youth around whose inventions the plots would revolve. Moreover, the young protagonist would not be passive or relegated to an assistant's position; indeed, he would be very active, in charge, and doing "things" instead of having them done to him. Thus were formulated the essential features of the new series that Stratemeyer entitled Tom Swift.

In all likelihood, the change in characterization, and not the editorial decision to split the Verne/Senarens adventure series into two, accounted for the immediate success of the Tom Swift series and for its long run. Making Tom the protagonist as well as a remarkable inventor went a long way in satisfying a fundamental need of young readers, its intended audience—the desire to identify with a young protagonist and his exploits in order to "feel" that youth too is competent and reliable and, as such, capable of accomplishing important deeds that make a "difference" and elicit praise and respect from grown-ups. The importance of this change in characterization should not be underestimated and perhaps is best appreciated when it is compared to the subsequent major change in characterization and its aftermath; that is, Tom's marriage to Mary Nestor and its deleterious effect on the popularity of the Tom Swift series. When asked to continue identifying with a protagonist who is obviously no longer a "boy" because of his marriage, young male readers, who were uninterested in marriage, had difficulty doing so; gradually they lost interest and switched their allegiance to more credible series that might satisfy their need for identification.

That a youth served as the protagonist and the medium for reader satisfaction underscores the necessity of recognizing that vintage Tom Swift is also series fiction. As such, it is true, the Tom Swift stories exhibit the typical weaknesses of series fiction: uniformity in plot and subject matter, one-dimensional characterization, emphasis on action along with over-reliance on stock situation and coincidence, earnest tone, themes reflective of what has been called the American dream, and pedestrian style. At the same time, it is also true, the Tom Swift stories manifest the strengths of series fiction, specifically its capacity to facilitate reader identification (as has just been stated) and its function as a relatively practical guide to coping with the transition from childhood/adolescence to adulthood. As has been pointed out, the latter function of series fiction has often been overlooked or misunderstood (Lanes 133-34), but apparently not by Edward Stratemeyer, who seems to have intuited that his new series might be successfully marketed as a medium whereby young readers could receive guidance for future career success. Witness these words from the advertising for the first five volumes: "It is the purpose of these spirited tales ... to interest the boy of the present in the hope that he may be a factor in aiding the marvelous development that is coming in the future." Indeed, there is some evidence that vintage Tom Swift may actually have influenced youngsters' career choices. In his study of the Stratemeyer Syndicate and many of its series, *Tom Swift & Company*, John Dizer approvingly cites the words of John W. Donahey: "Stratemeyer certainly built an image of the boy inventor which profoundly influenced generations of young men.... Stratemeyer spoke to his readers at their most impressionable age, and he must have sparked an interest in science in many of the men who are today leading scientists and engineers" (13). To put this another way, vintage Tom Swift is science adventure that is both fantasy (or science fantasy, if you will) and realism. As fantasy, the series celebrated the wondrous inventions and technological adaptations of an incredibly talented and creative youth. As realism, the series both informed youngsters about possible careers they might enjoy as inventors and engineers and encouraged and even inspired them to see themselves not only as possible imitators of Tom Swift but as successors to the great inventors like Thomas Edison, Alexander Graham Bell, or Orville or Wilbur Wright.

One final way of appreciating vintage Tom Swift is to perceive its contribution to the development of science fiction. First, the success of the vintage Tom Swift stories convincingly demonstrated that fiction that dramatized the fascination people felt for technological innovations was adaptable to a juvenile audience and that this adapting could be done without recourse to exotic plot and futuristic paraphernalia. Hence, not only did the science fiction field expand, so to speak, but its putative audience also grew. Second, vintage Tom Swift effectively communicated to young readers the fascination society felt for technology—a "gee whiz" attitude, if you will—and did so through a style that, eschewing artificial language, excessive sentiment, or allusions to moribund literary tradition, was content to state baldly and describe objectively. Witness this passage from *Tom Swift and His Wireless Message or, The Castaways of Earthquake Island* (1911).

There was certainly plenty of machinery in the cabin of the *Whizzer*. Most of it was electrical, for on that power Mr. Fenwick intended to depend to sail through space. There was a new type of gasolene engine, small but very powerful, and this served to operate a dynamo. In turn, the dynamo operated an electrical motor, as Mr. Fenwick had an idea that better, and more uniform, power could be obtained in this way, than from a gasolene motor direct. . . . There were various other apparatuses, machines, and appliances, the nature of which Tom could not readily gather from a mere casual view. (59)

As a matter of fact, for all its weaknesses, the style of vintage Tom Swift signaled the definite waning of the influence the literary fairy tale had on depicting the "wonders" of science and technology in American children's literature. This influence, incidentally, can be observed very much at work as late as 1900 in L. Frank Baum's *An Electrical Fairy Tale*. Here, explicitly utilizing metaphor and imagery from the Arabian Nights, Baum narrated his story about the "wondrous" working of the "genii" of electricity. Third, and lastly, because they were published in relatively inexpensive, hardcover format and not in cheap paper form, the first Tom Swift series showed that not every invention story or science adventure merited classification as "disreputable" fiction. Thus, in all these small but real ways, vintage Tom Swift assisted in broadening the field of science fiction, expanding the audience for science adventure, and generating additional impetus to the process by which a still young American science fiction genre gradually shed the somewhat disreputable reputation it had garnered from its early association with pulp/paper fiction.

* * *

Indulging in a bit of whimsy, John Dizer speculates that shortly before 1954 the Swift family made one of two possible decisions: casting off the mantle of modesty it had voluntarily assumed in 1936 or ignoring government pressure to keep secret the ongoing research and development at Swift Enterprises (57). As a result, there appeared in 1954 five new volumes of Tom Swift stories that celebrate the presumably new exploits of the young inventor extraordinaire. To underscore their newness, these five volumes, as well as all twenty-eight subsequent volumes, were subtitled "The New Tom Swift, Jr., Adventures." This subtitle, however, was somewhat misleading for the term new, it turns out, referred not to a "new" or second series of adventures involving the Tom Swift whose previous adventures had already been publicized in forty volumes but, rather, to a series of adventures involving a "new" Tom Swift—that is, Tom Swift, Jr., the eighteen-year-old son of Tom Swift and grandson of Barton Swift. In a further attempt to suggest continuity between the two series, Grosset & Dunlap indicated that these new adventures were narrated by Victor Appleton II, who was not, however, the son of Victor Appleton, but his nephew! In actuality, Victor Appleton II was just another house-name of the Stratemeyer Syndicate.

The real reason for the 1954 appearance of a second Tom Swift series was the resurgence of interest in children's and young adult science fiction that had been precipitated by the 1947 publication of Robert A. Heinlein's *Rocket Ship Galileo* and its favorable reception by librarians, teachers, and, most important, young readers. Prior to 1947, although mainstream publishers had expressed little interest in juvenile science fiction, it was still very much alive, especially in comics format—witness, for instance, the Buck Rogers, Flash Gordon, and Superman comics and funnies. However, Heinlein's success—he went on to write eleven additional science fiction juveniles—opened publishers' eyes to the viability of a new market. Consequently, other science fiction juveniles began to appear, some of them written by authors who were to become well known, for example, Andre Norton, Lester del Rey, Poul Anderson, Robert Silverberg, Jack Vance, and Isaac Asimov (writing as Paul French). Included among these juveniles was a number of series devoted to science adventure or science fiction— John Blaine's Rick Brant (1947), Paul French's Lucky Starr (1952), Carey Rockwell's Tom Corbett (1952), and in 1954 the Stratemeyer Syndicate entry, the new adventures of a new Tom Swift. The latter, although neither the first nor the last of these series to appear, prospered the longest, the final volume, *Tom Swift and the Galaxy Ghosts,* coming out in 1971—perhaps convincing evidence of the attractiveness of the elements the Stratemeyer Syndicate first used in vintage Tom Swift and then updated for the 1950s: a young genius-inventor, wondrous engineering exploits, mystery-adventure, and a series fiction format.

Having his father's "same deep-set eyes" and blond hair, eighteen-year-old Tom Swift, Jr., closely resembles his father except that he is "slightly taller and more slender" (*Tom Swift and His Flying Lab* 1). Like his father, Tom, Jr., too is an inventor who "from earliest childhood," readers are told, "had shown all his father's flair for invention" (*Flying Lab* 5). Further, the son at 18 is already a more committed, skilled, and imaginative inventor than his father had been at the same age. Despite being caught up in many adventures, Tom, Jr., seems always capable of improvising, even turning out inventions when he is supposed to be resting. For instance, in *Tom Swift and the Phantom Satellite,* while puttering at his work-bench to take his mind off more immediate problems, he puts together a scrambling device he can use to monitor his enemies' radiotelephone system. U.S. government agencies are pleased to acknowledge the youth's reputation as "one of the best informed young inventors of the entire country" (*Flying Lab* 5). In short, the eighteen-year-old son's accomplishments already rival those of his father who, by the way, directs most of his energies to overseeing Swift Enterprises, the large, prosperous company he founded with the aid of his lifelong friend, Ned Newton. It would seem, then, that as each generation of Swift males emerged it surpassed in creative genius the immediately preceding one.

The results of Tom, Jr.,'s inventive genius are impressive and diverse as evidenced by a sampling of the titles in the series: a rocket ship, an atomic earth blaster, an ultrasonic cycloplane, a space solartron, a three-dimensional tele-phone, a diving seacopter, a triphibian atomicar, and a repelatron. Definitely more exotic and typical science fiction than those of the first series, these inventions are usually meant to operate in outer space: either to abet space travel and exploration for commercial purposes or to shield the United States from invasion or attack by hostile agencies both on and off Earth. This emphasis on national defense and outer space probably reflects not just post-World War II advances in rocket weaponry and various attempts to utilize nuclear power, but also Cold War fears and anxieties. Moreover, the number and variety of Tom, Jr.,'s inventions and engineering applications attest that the second series, like vintage Tom Swift, celebrates the American flair for invention and enterprise, in particular the preeminence of the individual inventor. For Tom, Jr., despite the financial support of his father's company, is still essentially an individual inventor in the mold of Thomas Edison or Alexander Graham Bell, just as his father had been. Finally, the array of inventions as detailed in the individual volumes bespeaks the publisher's hunch that young Americans in the post-World War II period, like youth before and after World War I, manifested a "gee whiz" attitude toward technology in general and gadgets in particular.

Like his father before him, Tom, Jr., has only a few relatives, friends, and associates, all of whom are white Americans. Tom, Sr., as the series goes on, becomes more and more a stock character whose task it is to serve as liaison with governmental bodies and, along with Mrs. Swift, confer parental approbation on their son's activities. Tom, Jr., has a sister, Sandy—like her brother a skilled pilot—whose best friend, Phyllis, is the daughter of Ned Newton. Phyllis and Tom, Jr., date but throughout the series remain just friends, the editors this time apparently unwilling to risk losing readers by allowing the young couple to "get serious," let alone marry. Bud Barclay, test pilot for Swift Enterprises and participant in many of Tom, Jr.,'s adventures, is the youth's closest friend. Completing the cast of major characters is Chow Winkler, a Texan much older than Tom, Jr., who is a cook either at the Swift family home or during Tom, Jr,'s expeditions. Winkler's talk and behavior, moreover, are the occasion for most of the humor that is sprinkled throughout the stories but, in general, is ineffective in lightening the overall serious tone of the new adventures.

Very much like vintage Tom Swift, the second series presents the Swift family as beset by "enemies" who are uncannily adept at piercing even the most elaborate security devices the Swifts are capable of and thereby manage to interfere with the youth's plans or damage his products. These enemies alternate between being personal rivals of the Swifts or agents of Brungaria, a country somewhere in Eastern or Central Europe that is very hostile both to the Swift family and the United States. Consequently, Tom, Jr.,'s schemes to outwit his enemies are motivated by both personal and patriotic reasons. Incidentally, the rivalry between Swift Enterprises and Brungaria is, in all likelihood, one more reflection of Cold War tensions. Like vintage Tom Swift, the second series also aimed both to satisfy young readers' fantasies of solid accomplishment and demonstrable competence and to function as a practical guide for effectively surviving the transition from childhood to adulthood. In short, the second Tom Swift series is typical series fiction that, although containing relatively colorless writing, large chunks of often stilted dialogue, "cardboard" characterization, and predictable variations of the adventure/mystery formula, facilitates reader identification and eases the transition from childhood to young adulthood.

Several differences between the two series do stand out. First, the second series emphasizes multiple incidents to such an extent that it seems that every several pages Tom becomes embroiled in another adventure. Second, the 1954 series appears consciously designed to be educational inasmuch as many of the volumes contain up-to-date information about topics the editors believed interesting or useful to American youth. For example, details about subaquatic life fill the pages of *Tom Swift and His Subocean Geotron*, while the description of the Australian outback country is the focus of *Tom Swift and His Sonic Boom Trap*. Third, and finally, the second series contains large blocks of scientific information that were intended as rationalization for as many of Tom, Jr.,'s inventions as possible, or so implied Andrew E. Svenson, a partner in the Stratemeyer Syndicate at the time when the series was being published, who remarked that the latter was "based on scientific fact and probability." On the other hand, he claimed, vintage Tom Swift was "in the main adventure stories mixed with pseudo-science" (Dizer 45). There is no reason to gainsay Svenson's sincerity in describing the syndicate's intentions. Nevertheless, whatever plausibility the editors hoped to gain by including a degree of rationalization was unfortunately eroded by the difficulty many readers experience believing that one individual can generate so many inventions or can do so by foreshortening the invention process of discovery, modeling, testing, and production.

* * *

Ten years after the demise of the second Tom Swift series, the Stratemeyer Syndicate chose once more to test the viability of youth-oriented science adventure stories within a series fiction format. It is understandable that the syndicate would try again, given its two previous successes. For its third attempt, however, the syndicate essayed a somewhat different mix of particulars that, it hoped, would attract young readers of the 1980s. These readers, the syndicate had good reason to suspect, would differ significantly from previous generations inasmuch as the former were having their tastes and expectations molded by the growing popularity of science fiction in film and television as well as in print. Accordingly, the third series is both similar to and different from its predecessors.

The third series—entitled simply "Tom Swift" followed immediately by a subtitle—totaled just eleven volumes, which were published from 1981 to 1984. Hence, this series ran for the fewest years and numbered the least titles. Moreover, the Stratemeyer Syndicate changed publishers, switching from Grosset & Dunlap to Simon & Schuster, and the housename reverted to Victor Appleton, the name used for the first series. The hero is a Tom Swift who is eighteen, clear-eyed, and blond, although taller and stockier than his father who, readers are to presume, is the protagonist-hero of the second series. Because Swift Enterprises (now headquartered in Shopton, Arizona, rather than Shopton, New York, and boasting factories out in space) continues to thrive, Tom, Sr., is advantageously placed to finance his son's adventures, while at the same utilizing his inventions. Prominent, as before, are young Tom's resourcefulness and ability to improvise under pressure; new, however, is an emphasis on his physical courage.

Even more than its predecessors, the third series is definitely teen oriented. Tom's parents and family, and adults in general (except for the youth's arch rival, David Luna), play relatively minor parts in the plots. More important, Tom's two closest friends and associates are not only his age but nonstereotypical. Benjamin Franklin Walking Eagle is a Native American and an extremely competent computer programmer, and Anita Thorwald, formerly a rival pilot of Tom's, is now his colleague. The characterization of Anita, in particular, reflects the syndicate's attempt to satisfy the expectations of a new generation of readers. An especially attractive redhead, she has had a miniature computer placed within her right leg while it was being rebuilt after an accident. An unanticipated result is that she has become ESP enhanced and sensitive to nearby excitement and disturbance, especially of an emotional nature. This ability assists Anita in solving mathematical or engineering problems, as well as in teasing Tom who, not immune to the young woman's physical charms, is not always capable of cloaking his feelings toward her.

Like its predecessors, the third Tom Swift series is science fiction; unlike them it is set not on Earth but either in a colony out in space, New America, or somewhere in the galaxy—and even outside it since Tom has invented a space drive that permits jumping through hyperspace! In general, the 1980s series does not spend much time describing Tom's actually inventing something, indicating that he can toss off multiple inventions within a relatively brief time span, or including details of the invention process. Perhaps the third series' deemphasis of Tom, "the individual inventor," and corresponding emphasis of his associates' activities and contributions is the syndicate's way of acknowledging that the era of the individual inventor is over, replaced by the corporate or government research team. Yet receiving special attention is one of Tom's own inventions in particular, an advanced robot that he names Aristotle because he is impressed with the creature's reasoning skills. As a matter of fact, so taken with the creature is the young inventor that Aristotle becomes a member of Tom's circle of intimate friends and associates. The occasional source of humor because of its habitual self-deprecation, Aristotle seems modeled in part upon R2-D2 and C-3PO of *Star Wars* fame—one more indication of the syndicate's determination to appeal to contemporary taste.

The third series also focuses on the adventures occasioned by Tom's inventions. As before, it features a heavy reliance on dialogue and modest amounts of technological exposition. As in vintage Tom Swift, there are relatively few incidents; and the anonymous writers attempt to flesh out these in far greater detail than was customary in the second series. The third series too devotes a considerable part of its plots to Tom's fending off the devious plans of a rival—this time David Luna, a brilliant, smooth-talking, and unscrupulous millionaire who prefers to operate outside the law whenever possible and believes everyone has his or her price. Not necessarily hostile to the United States or Earth, Luna is enamored with power, seeks it constantly, and does not like to lose out to anyone, especially Tom Swift. Of interest is that Luna, unlike previous rivals, is not always successful in his attempts to steal from Swift Enterprises. Consequently, in the third series the Swift family does not come off looking like bunglers who seem incapable of protecting their professional secrets. Tom does have other rivals, but none with the tenacity or fascination of Luna; one of his rivals, Anita, it should be remembered, becomes his close friend. In short, whoever was responsible for writing the third series definitely enhanced not only the credibility of what hitherto had been stock plot devices but the series' overall believability and suspense as well.

One very noticeable difference is that the plots of the eleven volumes making up the third series are sequential; hence, the series is one long narrative. One unexpected and pleasant consequence is that the relationship among Tom, Anita, Benjamin and Aristotle slowly deepens, thereby producing a richness absent in previous characterization of Tom and his friends. Perhaps the most striking difference between the first two series and the 1980s one is that the latter's level of writing is definitely of a higher quality: it is less stiff, more colloquial, and at times even imaginative:

Tom blinked the sweat from his eyes. He felt too drained to reach up and brush the moisture away with his hand. This was as close to the Sun as anyone had ever come. Tongues of flames caressed the hull of the *Exedra*. Intense gravity pulled him deep into the cushions on his couch. And the heat built . . . and built . . . and built.

Finally Tom passed out.

Visions of steamy waterfalls danced in his head. He moaned and tried to roll over. Pain seared his body, bringing him back to a state of awareness. The air felt as if he'd been dropped into a hot sponge. (*Gateway to Doom* 131)

In brief, of the first three series, the 1980s one, considered as narrative writing, is the most imaginative in conception and execution.

* * *

In its fall 1990 catalogue, Simon & Schuster announced that the 1990s, like the 1980s, are to have their own Tom Swift.

Meet Tom Swift a high-tech inventor and adventurer for the '90s. Generations have grown up reading Tom Swift stories. . . . Like his father, Tom is a brilliant young inventor, but these days his toys are decidedly more high-tech. Robots, flying skyboards and a personal portable stereo that can actually listen in on any sound within a half-mile radius, open locks, reverse magnetic fields and shoot lasers are just some of the cool inventions that come out of Tom's own lab at Swift Enterprises, where anything he imagines can be made to work.

True to its word, early the next year the publisher released two volumes of a new

Tom Swift series—*The Black Dragon* and *The Negative Zone* —and promised at least four additional titles. Given the overall success the previous Tom Swift series achieved capitalizing on a series fiction format, it is no surprise that the fourth series is also series fiction, as implied in the concluding words of the publisher's advertising blurb.

Young adult readers will identify with Tom's cool confidence and sense of adventure and will want to keep up with all his latest inventions in each and every new title!

What is genuinely surprising is that the protagonist of the just released series is Tom Swift, Jr., that is, the son of the hero of the vintage series! Having acquired from the Stratemeyer Syndicate the rights to the name "Tom Swift" as well as to publishing new Swift stories, Simon & Schuster must believe it can do essentially what it wants. Or so it would seem, for by choosing Tom Swift, Jr., as the protagonist of the new series, the publisher has abandoned any serious attempt to maintain chronological and genealogical consistency among the four series. Accordingly, the Stratemeyer Syndicate history of the Swifts from 1910 to around 2010 has been compressed into a sparsely detailed family chronicle that, commencing sometime in the recent past, has Tom Swift, the hero of the vintage series, still alive in the 1990s! In other words this new Swift chronicle not only ignores virtually all the adventures of the second series but turns the clock back, obliterating the fourth generation of the Swift family, the focus of the 1980s series.

Unsettling and provocative as these changes in the Stratemeyer Syndicate account of the Swift family may be, some of the Simon & Schuster changes are positive. For instance, Tom is an eighteen-year-old high school student in Jefferson High in Central Hills, California, where Swift Enterprises is now located. A science whiz, he is actively being recruited by Harvard and MIT. One of his friends is Rick Cantwell, star quarterback at Jefferson High and steady date of Sandy Swift, Tom's sister; another friend, Dan Coster, has his own rock band. Thoroughly acclimated to California, Tom likes skateboarding and surfing and is so familar with rock music that he uses a song by Duran Duran, "Hungry Like the Wolf," to screen visitors to his private lab. These changes and others—for example, giving Sandy Swift a somewhat larger part in the stories—may make the stories relatively more attractive to today's readers.

Like his father, young Tom is an inventor. As in the first and third series, only a few of the teenager's inventions are the focus of the plots; moreover, these inventions the anonymous writer or writers (the pseudonym Victor Appleton once more appears on the title page) do seek to rationalize. Again readily discernible is a "gee whiz" attitude toward technology and its "wondrous" results. Not surprisingly, Tom's adventures reflect contemporary research, for example, superconductivity and the nature of black holes. In *The Negative Zone,* for instance, Tom creates in his lab a black hole, is sucked into it, and finds himself in a negative zone or alternate world where a Tom Swift is a criminal, notorious for committing his brilliant mind to the planning and execution of many illegal activities! What other changes the new series may make or, more important, how closely it will adhere, as the prepublication advertising promises, to the formulas and format that have worked previously cannot, obviously, be determined. What is clear, however, is that Simon & Schuster is making a bona fide attempt to blend science fiction elements and attitudes and topics appropriate to a teen audience. Yet in the face of the array of teen-oriented science fiction currently available in various media, the prosperity of a fourth Tom Swift series is definitely problematic, especially since the series, to date, seems to lack distinctiveness with the exception of its use of the name Tom Swift. Even that feature may not suffice to guarantee success, for whatever attraction the name retains involves adult readers who recall their youthful acquaintance with Tom Swift stories and not young readers who are unfamiliar with the latter.

* * *

Eighty-some years ago the first volumes of vintage Tom Swift began to appear. Today these adventures, once so enthralling, have drastically paled; the science is not "hard" enough for contemporary expectations; and the style wins no awards for grace or sensitivity to the ways people really converse. By effectively appealing to the audience's fascination with technological innovation and satisfying that audience's vaguely articulated but real aspirations toward competence and achievement, however, the stories became one of the most successful series ever published. In so doing, vintage Tom Swift also contributed to the growth of science fiction as well as to the growth of an audience for it. Although not as popular and influential as vintage Tom Swift, the second series did assist during the 1950s in the emergence of a science fiction deliberately intended for children and young adults. The third series, in spite of its relatively effective style and carefully designed appeal to the tastes of teenagers in the 1980s, fell victim, it would seem, to its competition in film, on television, and in print. Now a fourth Tom Swift series has appeared. Whether it will prosper depends chiefly upon its publisher's success in both adapting series fiction format to the 1990s and competing with other teen-oriented media specializing in science fiction.

BIBLIOGRAPHY

Billman, Carol. *The Secret of the Stratemeyer Syndicate; Nancy Drew, The Hardy Boys and the Million Dollar Fiction Factory.* New York: Unger, 1986.

Bleiler, E. F. "From the Newark Steam Man to Tom Swift." *Extrapolation* 30.2 (Summer 1989): 101-16.

Dizer, John. *Tom Swift & Company: "Boys' Books" by Stratemeyer and Others.* Jefferson & London: McFarland, 1982.

Lanes, Selma. *Down the Rabbit Hole: Adventures and Misadventures in the Realm of Children's Literature.* New York: Antheneum, 1971 .

Molson, Francis J. "Three Generations of Tom Swift." *Children's Literature Association*

Quarterly 10 (1985): 60-63.

_____. "Tom Swift." *A Survey of Science Fiction Literature*. Ed. Frank N. Magill. Englewood Cliffs, NJ: Salem, 1979.

Moskowitz, Sam. "Teen-Agers: Tom Swift and the Syndicate." *Strange Horizons: The Spectrum of Science Fiction*. New York: Scribner's, 1976.

Tom Swift Series (Vintage)

Tom Swift and His Motor Cycle or, Fun and Adventures on the Road. 1910.
Tom Swift and His Motor Boat or, The Rivals of Lake Carlopa. 1910.
Tom Swift and His Airship or, The Stirring Cruise of the Red Cloud. 1910.
Tom Swift and His Submarine Boat or, Under the Ocean for Sunken Treasure. 1910.
Tom Swift and His Electric Runabout or, The Speediest Car on the Road. 1910.
Tom Swift and His Wireless Message or, The Castaways of Earthquake Island. 1911.
Tom Swift Among the Diamond Makers or, The Secret of Phantom Mountain. 1911.
Tom Swift in the Caves of Ice or, The Wreck of the Airship. 1911.
Tom Swift and His Sky Racer or, The Quickest Flight on Record. 1911.
Tom Swift and His Electric Rifle or, Daring Adventures in Elephant Land. 1911.
Tom Swift in the City of Gold or, Marvelous Adventures Underground. 1912.
Tom Swift and His Air Glider or, Seeking the Platinum Treasure. 1912.
Tom Swift in Captivity or, A Daring Escape by Airship. 1912.
Tom Swift and His Wizard Camera or, Thrilling Adventures While Taking Moving Pictures. 1912.
Tom Swift and His Great Searchlight or, On the Border for Uncle Sam. 1912.
Tom Swift and His Giant Cannon or, The Longest Shots on Record. 1913.
Tom Swift and His Photo Telephone or, The Picture That Saved a Fortune. 1914.
Tom Swift and His Aerial Warship or, The Naval Terror of the Seas. 1915.
Tom Swift and His Big Tunnel or, The Hidden City of the Andes. 1916.
Tom Swift in the Land of Wonders or, The Search for the Idol of Gold. 1917.
Tom Swift and His War Tank or, Doing His Bit for Uncle Sam. 1918.
Tom Swift and His Air Scout or, Uncle Sam's Mastery of the Sky.   1919.
Tom Swift and His Undersea Search or, The Treasure on the Floor of the Atlantic. 1920.
Tom Swift Among the Fire Fighters or, Battling with Flames from the Air. 1921.
Tom Swift and His Electric Locomotive or, Two Miles a Minute on the Rails. 1922.
Tom Swift and His Flying Boat or, The Castaways of the Giant Iceberg. 1923.
Tom Swift and His Great Oil Gusher or, The Treasure of Goby Farm. 1924.
Tom Swift and His Chest of Secrets or, Tracing the Stolen Inventories. 1925.
Tom Swift and His Airplane Express or, From Ocean to Ocean by Daylight. 1926.
Tom Swift Circling the Globe or, The Daring Cruise of the Air Monarch. 1927.
Tom Swift and His Talking Pictures or, The Greatest Invention on Record. 1928.
Tom Swift and His House on Wheels or, A Trip to the Mountain of Mystery. 1929.
Tom Swift and His Big Dirigible or, Adventures Over the Forest of Fire. 1930.
Tom Swift and His Sky Train or, Overland Through the Clouds. 1931.
Tom Swift and His Giant Magnet or, Bringing Up the Lost Submarine. 1932.
Tom Swift and His Television Detector or, Trailing the Secret Plotters. 1933.
Tom Swift and His Ocean Airport or, Foiling the Haargolanders. 1934.

Tom Swift and His Planet Stone or, Discovering the Secret of Another World. 1935.
Tom Swift and His Giant Telescope. 1939.
Tom Swift and His Magnetic Silencer. 1941.

Except for the last two volumes, which were released by Whitman Publishing (Racine, WI), all the volumes of vintage Tom Swift were published by Grosset & Dunlap (New York).

Tom Swift, Jr. (Second Series)

Tom Swift and His Flying Lab. 1954.
Tom Swift and His Jetmarine. 1954.
Tom Swift and His Rocketship. 1954.
Tom Swift and His Giant Robot. 1954.
Tom Swift and His Atomic Earth Blaster. 1954.
Tom Swift and His Outpost in Space. 1955.
Tom Swift and His Diving Seacopter. 1965.
Tom Swift in the Caves of Nuclear Fire. 1956.
Tom Swift on the Phantom Satellite. 1956.
Tom Swift and His Ultrasonic Cycloplane. 1957.
Tom Swift and His Deep-Sea Hydrodome. 1958.
Tom Swift in the Race to the Moon. 1958.
Tom Swift and His Space Solartron. 1958.
Tom Swift and His Electronic Retroscope. 1959.
Tom Swift and His Spectromarine Selector. 1960.
Tom Swift and the Cosmic Astronauts. 1960.
Tom Swift and the Visitor from Planet X. 1961.
Tom Swift and the Electronic Hydrolung. 1961.
Tom Swift and His Triphibian Atomicar. 1962.
Tom Swift and His Megascope Space Prober. 1962.
Tom Swift and the Asteroid Pirates. 1963.
Tom Swift and His Repalatron Skyway. 1963.
Tom Swift and His Aquatomic Tracker. 1964.
Tom Swift and His 3-D Telelector. 1965.
Tom Swift and His Polar-Ray Dynasphere. 1965.
Tom Swift and His Sonic Boom Trap. 1965.
Tom Swift and His Subocean Geotron. 1968.
Tom Swift and the Mystery Comet. 1966.
Tom Swift and the Captive Planetoid. 1967.
Tom Swift and His G-Force Inverter. 1968.
Tom Swift and His Dyna-4 Capsule. 1969.
Tom Swift and His Cosmotron Express. 1970.
Tom Swift and the Galaxy Ghosts. 1971.

All volumes were published by Grosset & Dunlap (New York).

Tom Swift (Third Series)

City in the Stars. 1981.
Terror on the Moons of Jupiter. 1981.
Alien Probe. 1981.
War in Outer Space. 1981.
Astral Fortress. 1981.
Rescue Mission. 1981.
Ark Two. 1982.
Crater of Mystery. 1983.
Gateway to Doom. 1983.
The Invisible Force. 1983.
Planet of Nightmares. 1984.

All volumes were published by Simon & Schuster (New York).

Tom Swift (Fourth Series)

The Black Dragon. 1991.
The Negative Zone. 1991.

Both volumes were published by Simon & Schuster (New York).

2

Heinlein's Juveniles: Growing Up in Outer Space

C. W. Sullivan III

Although he is much better known for the adult short stories and novels, which began with "Life-Line" (1939) and ended with *To Sail Beyond the Sunset* (1987), and is perhaps best known for his controversial *Stranger in a Strange Land* (1961), Robert A. Heinlein would, in all probability, continue to be highly regarded as a science fiction author if he had written only the twelve books published by Scribner's between 1947 and 1958 and commonly labeled "Heinlein's juveniles." Heinlein's juveniles include *Rocket Ship Galileo* (1947), *Space Cadet* (1948), *Red Planet* (1949), *Farmer in the Sky* (1950), *Between Planets* (1951), *The Rolling Stones* (1952), *Starman Jones*, (1953), *The Star Beast* (1954), *Tunnel in the Sky* (1955), *Time for the Stars* (1956), *Citizen of the Galaxy* (1957), and *Have Space Suit—Will Travel* (1958).[1] Jack Williamson has called these books "a pioneer effort, quickly imitated" (15), and I have argued elsewhere that Heinlein's juveniles, almost a half-century after the publication of the first one, "are still 'contemporary,' and are still among the best science fiction in the YA range" (Sullivan, "Heinlein's Juveniles" 64).[2] Heinlein's juveniles set a standard for young adult science fiction by which subsequent works may be judged and by which a surprising number will be found wanting (Franklin 73; Williamson 15; Wollheim 101).

Heinlein's juveniles are certainly a part of his total science fiction output, sharing as they do many characters, settings, events, and themes with his adult novels and short stories.[3] Moreover, the juveniles are a part of Heinlein's Future History outline and have, thereby, their definite place or places in the future he envisioned. As a result, the juveniles have been examined, to some extent, as part of Heinlein's complete oeuvre by such critics as H. Bruce Franklin, Alexei Panshin, and David N. Samuelson. It is as important, however, to look at Heinlein's juveniles outside the context of his other work and to examine them for what it is that they offer the young reader—as science, as fiction, and as science fiction.

* * *

In *Heinlein in Dimension,*Panshin comments that "if there is anything amazing about [Heinlein's] writing it has been his ability to write for, say, ten pages, as he does on space suits in *Have Space Suit—Will Travel,* without losing or even seriously slowing his story" (89). What is true of the last novel in the series is true, for the most part, of all of them. In each book, Heinlein serves up great portions of scientific information that he manages to make germaine to the story. In *Rocket Ship Galileo,* the descriptions of space suits, rocket trajectories, and the like are quite brief, usually less than a page, but each explains something about the scientific and technological aspects of actually getting to the Moon. Heinlein's explanation of weightlessness is particularly significant:

They did not bounce up to the ceiling. The rocket did not spin wildly. None of the comic strip things happened to them. They simply ceased to weigh anything as the thrust died away. (109-10)

This very short passage is a harbinger of things to come in the juvenile series.

First of all, Heinlein is explaining what would actually happen as people in a rocket ship became weightless. He is, as he will do throughout the series, providing accurate scientific and technological information for his young readers. In *Space Cadet,* he spends a whole novel describing the education a person might have to complete to be commissioned in the Interplanetary Patrol and includes, among many explanations, a discussion of the workings of a ship's hydroponics system. *Red Planet* describes the seasons on a planet significantly farther from the sun than Earth is. *Farmer in the Sky* is a novel about homesteading that details terraforming in a most extreme situation. *The Rolling Stones, Starman Jones, Time for the Stars,* and *Citizen of the Galaxy* all have lengthy discussions about how ships travel and navigate in space—all grounded on the theoretical physics involved in speculations concerning faster-than-light travel. And *Have Space Suit—Will Travel,* of course, contains the ten-page discussion of space suits to which Panshin referred.

In addition to providing the correct information, Heinlein often ridicules those who are ignorant of what he feels anyone should know. In *Farmer in the Sky,* Bill Lermer is waiting for the shuttle that will take him to the *Mayflower,* the interplanetary ship that will take him, and the other colonists, to Ganymede. A woman beside him asks her husband which ship parked there on the ground is the *Mayflower.*

Her husband tried to explain to her, but she still was puzzled. I nearly burst, trying to keep from laughing. Here she was, all set to go to Ganymede and yet she was so dumb that she didn't even know that the ship she was going in had been built in space and couldn't land anywhere. (36)

Bill may seem a bit too critical of the woman, but as Heinlein later shows, such ignorance separates the successful "pioneers" from the unsuccessful ones, the "elect" from the nonelect (Slusser, pass.). In *Between Planets*, Don Harvey encounters a woman distressed by the sight of the Venerian dragon who calls himself Sir Isaac Newton. This attitude toward aliens is most explicitly rejected in *The Star Beast*, wherein Heinlein lampoons such intolerance in the person of Dr. T. Omar Esklund of the Keep Earth Human League and others similarly closed minded about aliens. Aliens, as Heinlein had already begun to illustrate in *Red Planet*, are not to be feared automatically. The inability to accept the new or the strange is a major characteristic of "those who fail" in Heinlein's novels.

Finally, Heinlein's comment about "comic strip" weightlessness in *Rocket Ship Galileo* is the first of his several attempts to distance himself from the kind of science fiction with which he does not want his writing confused. In *The Rolling Stones,* Roger Stone, an engineer, is currently making a great deal of money by writing a media series entitled *The Scourge of the Spaceways*, which chronicles "the gory but virtuous career of Captain John Sterling" (186) and his duels with the Galactic Overlord; the writing is soon taken over by Roger's mother who, with the help of Roger's four-year-old son, Lowell, makes the series even more successful. All of this is in direct contrast to the rather mundane activities of the Stone family as they travel from the Moon to Mars and, eventually, the Asteroid Belt. *The Scourge of the Spaceways* and the Galactic Overlord show up again in the banter of "Ace" Quiggle, the lout who is Kip Russell's local nemesis in *Have Space Suit—Will Travel*. And another writer of "comic strip" science fiction, Beaulah Murgatroyd, in *The Star Beast*, is the author of the stereovision Pidgie-Widgie series.

Pidgie-Widgie is a puppet about a foot high. He goes zooming through space, rescuing people and blasting pirates and having a good ole time . . . the kids love him. And at the end of each installment Mrs. Murgatroyd comes on and they have a bowl of Hunkies together and talk. (182-83)

As Heinlein's various comments on writing science fiction illustrate, he takes the craft very seriously, has little tolerance for those who do not do their research, and does not want anyone to be able to compare his novels with "comic strip" work.[4]

The science in Heinlein's juveniles is an integral part of the story; the knowledge the main characters acquire is necessary to their success. Bill Lermer, however determined, will not be able to "prove a farm" in *Farmer in the Sky* unless he learns the details of terraforming his property. In *Starman Jones*, Max Jones's "eidetic" memory would do him no good without the knowledge of how to apply the figures he has memorized. And Thorby could save neither himself nor his ship in *Citizen of the Galaxy* without the gunnery training he has aboard the *Sisu*.

Heinlein's point is that knowledge is useful and that the person with the most knowledge or the right knowledge (for the right time and place) is going to be successful. At the end of *Have Space Suit—Will Travel*, Kip suggests that he has been very lucky and is told that "'good luck' follows careful preparation; 'bad luck' comes from sloppiness" (250). Heinlein's main characters prepare (and are prepared) carefully, and they succeed; the detailed scientific and technological discussions in the books are not only educational but also provide examples of the kind of "real" knowledge that leads to success.

* * *

Heinlein is not writing textbooks on science or success, however; he is writing fiction, and it is his ability to tell a good story that has made these books so enduring.[5] The Heinlein critics, like most literary critics, pass quickly over the story so that they can comment on plot, theme, character development, or other aspects that they feel make a work significant. As C.S. Lewis has said:

Those forms of literature in which Story exists merely as a means to something else—for example, the novel of manners where the story is there for the sake of the characters, or the criticism of social conditions—have had full justice done to them; but those forms in which everything else is there for the sake of the story have been given little serious attention. (3)

Certainly Heinlein is telling a story that does have a theme and in which characters develop, but first and foremost, he is telling a story; and critics generally agree, however little they comment on it, that he tells his story well (Wollheim 99).

A primary reason for Heinlein's success is that he neither writes down to his readers (Franklin 74) nor "insults the reader's intelligence" (Samuelson 131; Williamson 16) by watering down his material. In fact, Heinlein has said that

I have held to that rule [i.e., not writing down] and my books for boys differ only slightly from my books for adults—the books for boys are somewhat harder to read because younger readers relish tough ideas they have to chew and don't mind big words—and the boys' books are slightly limited by taboos and conventions imposed by their elders. (Fuller 109)

In fact, adults who go back to the juveniles often find them to be "as absorbing as ever" (Williamson 16). These adult readers, as C.S. Lewis might argue, are not reading for plot now, they know what happens to the hero in the end; they are reading for the story and for the rewards that rereading a book of some depth and texture will bring.

In the most general terms, each Heinlein juvenile (and perhaps the series as a whole) is a bildungsroman. In each book, a young protagonist grows up—if not always in years, certainly in experience and maturity. Each one must make critical decisions based on his own experience and on advice from those he respects, decisions that often go against the advice or orders of an authority figure. According to H. Bruce Franklin, with the exception of *Rocket Ship Galileo,*

the boys' books consist of extended tests of endurance, loyalty, courage, intelligence, integrity, and fortitude. They dramatize a personal ethic and pervasive social Darwinism, displaying how and why "fit" types survive while the "unfit"—the skulkers, the weaklings, the whiners, the lazy, the self-centered, the vicious—are eliminated. (76-77)

This is, of course, the perfect plot for the young reader—if not for any reader—who, himself or herself, is trying to make decisions and survive in what may seem an eminently hostile world.[6]

Each specific book has its own plot, of course, and each of them carries its protagonist through similar occasions of trial and (self) discovery, each made different by the environment in which it takes place and the science and technology that shape the way in which the protagonist is tested and meets that test. In *Tunnel in the Sky*, for example, the ultimate mode of travel, the Ramsbotham Gate, which just opens a doorway between places, allows students to take their survival test on an uninhabited planet light years from Earth. When the gate breaks down due to a supernova, however, there is no way to rescue the stranded students (as there would be if their test was taking place on Earth), and the students, with considerably less technology at their disposal than the reader has at his or hers, must survive. The science fiction technology makes possible a Robinson Crusoe story, and the stranded students' lack of technology is in sharp contrast to the expectations of the average science fiction reader. Thus, Heinlein uses the creative possibilities within science fiction to present a story of survival in a situation of advanced training but limited technology.

The Mars setting of *Red Planet*, the academic environment of most of *Space Cadet*, the Venus setting of *Between Planets*, and the rest of the similarly developed different settings with their indigenous technologies allow Heinlein to present several protagonists achieving maturity in similarly structured ways—but in separate contexts. Taken as a whole, however, the series itself has been interpreted as humanity's bildungsroman, an epic story in which humans (Terran variety, anyway) come of age. As several critics have pointed out, the series generally chronicles the movement of humanity outward from Earth to the Moon, in *Rocket Ship Galileo*, to the planets within the solar system, in the novels from *Red Planet* to *The Rolling Stones*, and out into the galaxy and beyond, in the novels from *Starman Jones* to *Have Space Suit—Will Travel* (Franklin 74; Williamson 15-16).[7] At the end of the last novel, Kip Russell completes the pattern by traveling the farthest, all the way to the Lesser Magellanic Cloud, and returning home to Earth. This species bildungsroman or "faith in the future of humanity" (Wollheim 101), like the faith in the well-prepared individual, makes for an appealing story, especially for young readers for whom the future means all of the possibilities in Heinlein's books.

Finally, Heinlein's stories have many levels. The reader who wants action and adventure will surely find it in most of the juveniles; from the conflict with the Nazis in *Red Planet* to the threat of the Wormfaces in *Have Space Suit—Will Travel*, Heinlein places his characters in situations in which they must take action, action based on what they have learned throughout the book. In addition to action and adventure, Heinlein presents a banquet of scientific, social, and political theory. *Time for the Stars* and *Have Space Suit—Will Travel* contain speculations on the nature of relativity; *Space Cadet* and *Citizen of the Galaxy* depict matriarchal societies; and *Red Planet* and *Between Planets* discuss the nature of revolution. Moreover, Heinlein is something of a mystic (Knight 84; Panshin 172-75; Samuelson 105). The ghost of a dead astrogator calms Max Jones during a particularly tense scene in *Starman Jones*, and the noncorporeal third stage of Martian development discussed briefly in *Red Planet* will become an essential part of *Stranger in a Strange Land* (1961). For the best readers, Heinlein drops in bits of information—literary and historical references, Latin phrases, bits of famous quotations, and the like—that only a few will recognize and understand, a technique that brings those best readers inside the novel with Heinlein himself to share a moment that most of the readers will miss and makes the novels much richer stories for those readers.[*]

* * *

There are more particular reasons for Heinlein's success with young readers (and, to some extent, with older readers as well), and examples of them can be seen within each and, for the most part, all of the novels. I have isolated six topics,

1. growing up in the atomic age,
2. the importance of education, formal and informal,
3. contemporaries, good, bad, and other,
4. adults as advisors and impediments,
5. powerful aliens, good and bad, and
6. the elevation of the ideal,

which, I believe, account for the success of this specific series. While these topics can be important in any piece of fiction, they are especially important and compelling to a young reader dealing with all of them (or their contemporary equivalents) on an immediate basis; moreover, Heinlein creates the conflicts between his protagonists and adults or other authority figures (conflicts that are a staple of fiction for young readers) in such a way that they are a part of the science as well as a part of the fiction.

Growing up in the atomic age, the first of these topics, derives from Heinlein's original title for *Rocket Ship Galileo*; he called it *Young Atomic Engineers*, and he had planned a whole series with such titles as *The Young Atomic Engineers on Mars*, or *Secret of the Moon Corridors*, *The Young Atomic Engineers in the*

Asteroids, or *The Mystery of the Broken Planet*, *The Young Atomic Engineers in Business*, or *The Solar System Mining Corporation*, and there were to be more (Virginia Heinlein 43). The style and content of these titles were obviously based on the titles in such series as Tom Swift and the Hardy Boys, but the "atomic" orientation was fairly new. Heinlein's overriding concept was that of a "period of extreme change. . . . and unchecked technical progress" (Virginia Heinlein 41-42), and he planned his series accordingly.

Heinlein, however, was doing more than just cashing in on the literary possibilities inherent in a period of extreme technological change. He was also writing books for boys that, I believe, he felt would make them comfortable with and in the atomic age. That is, he was attempting to write stories about young protagonists dealing successfully with technological change and with the new products, processes, and events that such change would bring. These successful young protagonists would help the reader develop a positive attitude toward the future that Heinlein saw approaching so rapidly, and although he knew that he was not preparing them for a specific future, he also knew that he was helping to prepare them for a certain kind of future. He was later to say in "Science Fiction: Its Nature, Faults and Virtues":

I claim one positive triumph for science fiction, totally beyond the scope of so-called main-stream fiction. It has prepared the youth of our time for the coming age of space. Interplanetary travel is no shock to youngsters, no matter how unsettling it may be to calcified adults. Our children have been playing at being space cadets and at controlling rocket ships for quite some time now. Where did they get this healthy orientation? From science fiction and nowhere else. Science fiction can perform similar service to the race in many other fields. (60)

Anyone who has compared the average forty-year-old's willingness to use a computer with that of the average twelve-year-old can see the truth in Heinlein's statement.

The juveniles are full of young people comfortable with a technology that often seems "wondrous" to the reader. In *Rocket Ship Galileo*, three boys about to graduate from high school help atomic scientist Donald Cargraves build a rocket and fly it to the Moon. The boys are scientifically oriented from the beginning and have conducted their own rocket experiments; they have the education and the skill, and Cargraves gives them an opportunity and the proper supervision. Heinlein does not minimize the danger of such technology; when they reach the Moon, they discover that the same kind of power that took them there has also taken some refugee Nazis there, and those Nazis are planning an atomic attack on Earth. Atomic power is atomic power, Heinlein is saying; the use of it separates the wise from the foolish, the good from the bad.

In the other books in the series, technology is similarly showcased and made a part of daily life. *Space Cadet* is about school—the education one needs for the new age. *Red Planet* and *Farmer in the Sky* are about technological adjustments to living off Earth. *Between Planets* explores the possibility of interplanetary war. The Stone family takes an extended vacation within the Solar System in *The Rolling Stones*; their station wagon is a 150-foot-long spaceship, but their problems and pleasures are similar to those of any family on such a trip. *Starman Jones*, *Tunnel in the Sky*, and *Time for the Stars* take their protagonists into deep space, and *The Star Beast* brings aliens to Earth. The four-part *Citizen of the Galaxy* presents four different societies of the future. *Have Space Suit—Will Travel* finishes the series by showing us that Earth (for all of its science, technology, exploration, and conquest) is a rather small, young, and by comparison primitive planet in the universe after all—but it does have potential (perhaps a metaphor for the reader as well as the main characters).

The second topic, the importance of education, is central in Heinlein's juveniles as it is in virtually all of his fiction. The adult fiction, however, features protagonists who have already completed most of their formal education and are now in the position of applying it or of adding to it; in the juveniles, Heinlein is writing about protagonists of high-school age, and their formal educations are not only included but often commented on during the course of the novels. The education received in the course of each juvenile enables the protagonist to mature and make independent decisions that result in his survival and, often, the survival of those around him. As an adult, he will be one of Heinlein's capable individuals, a character so obvious that many critics have commented on him (Knight 81; Panshin 129-30, 169-77; Samuelson 107-9; Sarti 109; Williamson 16,18).

In some of the books, the education is formal. Much of the action of *Space Cadet* takes place at the military academy of the future, a school that has an orbiting campus, the *P. R. S. James Randolph*, as well as a land-based campus— prophetically set in Colorado, now the site of the Air Force Academy, which graduated its first class eleven years *after* Heinlein wrote his novel. No other novel contains such a detailed account of education in the future, but in many— especially *The Rolling Stones* and *Time for the Stars* —the young protagonists aboard ship are required to attend regular classes. Various characters in *Tunnel in the Sky* refer back to the educations that prepared them for the survival test and recall the advice given by their teachers. The first section of *Citizen of the Galaxy* describes Baslim's education of Thorby, the slave boy he has bought, and includes Baslim's comments on the importance of knowledge and the importance of knowing how to think and learn—comments that are almost certainly what Heinlein himself would have said.

In *Space Cadet*, the formal educational setting opens the universe to Matt Dodson and his classmates; in *Red Planet*, the school Jim Marlowe attends is run by an autocratic headmaster against whom Jim rebels to begin his rite of passage. At various points in the series, Heinlein suggests that the American education system may not be doing as good a job as it might. In several novels, the older characters comment on the advanced math the young protagonists have learned in school; but those courses were not being offered in the schools of the 1950s, and most of them are still only offered in colleges today. Heinlein's most serious criticisms of education come in *Have Space Suit—Will Travel.* Kip Russell's father discovers that his son is taking "social study, commercial arithmetic, applied English (the class has picked 'slogan writing' which was fun), handicraft . . ., and gym. . . . I was doing well in school and knew it" (8). Kip's father calls his course of study, "Twaddle! Beetle tracking! Occupational therapy for morons!" (11), switches him to "algebra, Spanish, general science, English grammar and composition," and then augments the school's meagre offerings with Latin, advanced algebra, solid geometry, trigonometry, analytical geometry, chemistry, physics, electronics, and more (12-13). Kip's local nemesis, "Ace" Quiggle, had not finished high school, "a distinction since Mr. Hanley believed in promoting everybody 'to keep age groups together'" (19). The satire is obvious—even to a juvenile reader.

The third topic, other youth, provides Heinlein with an additional way to characterize his successful protagonist; that is, he surrounds his main character with other characters who are friends and may be as capable, with enemies (or at least contrasting figures) who are not capable, and with others who have potential but do not use it. Each of the three boys in *Rocket Ship Galileo* has his special ability; Matt Dodson, the protagonist in *Space Cadet* has capable fellow cadets, one of whom takes over as acting captain during the last stage of the book (a role Heinlein might well have reserved for Matt). In *The Star Beast*, John Thomas Stuart and his pet, Lummox, are defended in court by Betty Sorenson, a young woman of John's age who will be, by the end of the novel, his fiancee. And in all of the other novels, the main character has a friend or friends who act along side him, for some of the time at least.

There are also young people in these novels who are there as contrasts to the main character or characters. Girard Burke, who makes light of the Patrol's values early in *Space Cadet*, later drops out of the academy and, in the last segment of the novel, has to be rescued by Matt and his fellow cadets. Simes in *Starman Jones* and Peebie in *Citizen of the Galaxy* are jealous of the abilities of Max Jones and Thorby Baslim, respectively, and attempt to cause trouble for them—Simes and Peebie, like Burke, are the self-centered and lazy whiners referred to earlier. A more interesting contrast is presented by Bill Arensa in *Space Cadet*. Arensa is a bright student who has been at the academy an unusually long time when Matt arrives. Eventually he leaves the academy because he does not want the responsibility of being a peacekeeper, a responsibility that might require him to drop bombs onto Earth from orbiting stations. Heinlein is suggesting that intellectual ability without commitment is not enough, and the points of contention and contrast are very much a part of the science fiction context Heinlein develops.

The fourth topic, adults as advisors and impediments, is also a common one in juvenile literature. The young protagonist must find out which adults are worth listening to and which are not, which will help and which will hinder. In this series, Heinlein creates adult advisors who help the protagonist learn the things he needs to know to survive and achieve maturity. Heinlein sets the pattern in *Rocket*

Ship Galileo when he has Art's uncle, Donald Cargraves, serve as advisor to the three boys; and although an actual uncle only appears once more in the series, Tom and Pat Bartlett's uncle Steve in *Time for the Stars*, avuncular figures are in virtually all of the other books—Johann Schultz in *Farmer in the Sky*, Sam Anderson in *Starman Jones*, Deacon Matson in *Tunnel in the Sky*, and Baslim the Cripple in *Citizen of the Galaxy*. In all of these cases, the uncle figures possess the knowledge and experience the protagonist can tap into when he needs to make his own decisions.

Other adults are there to provide the negative aspects of the rite of passage that the protagonist must successfully complete. Headmaster Howe, in *Red Planet*, is an obvious example. He is not interested in the boys' education, just in running a tight ship and figuring out how to get his piece of the corporate action (not too difficult when you have the same last name as the chairman of the Company). Howe's kidnapping of Willis, Jim Marlowe's Martian pet, is the catalyst to Jim's open rebellion—taking Willis back, crossing Mars to get home, and providing the colonists with the information they need to organize the rebellion that will free them from the Company. Various other adults in the series—sometimes family members like Max's stepmother and her new husband in *Starman Jones*, Rod Walker's parents in *Tunnel in the Sky*, or Thorby's uncle Jack in *Citizen of the Galaxy*—attempt to control the protagonist who then must figure out not only what to do and how to do it but also why he should act.

Powerful aliens, the fifth topic, were in the process of becoming only a stereotypical aspect of science fiction when Heinlein began his series of juveniles. The stereotype, of course, portrayed the alien as a ruthless invader from another planet and was a major reason for science fiction's success in the pulps and the movies. Heinlein, however, knew that an immense universe could contain all sizes, shapes, and sorts of aliens—friendly, unfriendly, and indifferent. Beginning with Willis, the Martian roundhead in *Red Planet*, Heinlein created a series of attractive and friendly aliens that were to be a hallmark of his juvenile fiction and, perhaps, the direct forbears of Steven Speilberg's E.T. Some of those aliens, like Willis or Lummox in *The Star Beast*, are central characters in their respective novels; others, like the Hesperian spider puppy in *Starman Jones* or the Martian flat cats in *The Rolling Stones*, are less central to the action.

The unfriendly aliens fall into two categories. The waterseekers that attack other Martians and humans in *Red Planet*, the centaurs that kidnap Max and Ellie in *Starman Jones*, the various animals that threaten the survival of the students in *Tunnel in the Sky*, and the sea creatures that kill a number of the crew members in *Time for the Stars* have no specific dislike for humans; they would react that way toward any intruder. The only aliens out for conquest that threaten the existence of the human race and Earth are the Wormfaces of *Have Space Suit— Will Travel*. Part of the reason for the lack of stereotypical alien invaders in Heinlein's juveniles is that Heinlein rejected the stereotype, but another reason, shown by example throughout the series and made explicit by Deacon Matson in *Tunnel in the Sky*, is that, as Matson says, "Man is the one animal that can't be tamed" (11). If man has the ability to be the most successful and enduring creature, it must also have the ability to be the most dangerous—to others of its own species as well as to whatever other species are out there.

However, there are powerful aliens out there. The Martians in *Red Planet* can make their enemies literally disappear (in *Stranger in a Strange Land* the process will be called discorporation). The people of the Moon destroyed their world, according to Dr. Cargraves in *Rocket Ship Galileo*; and according to findings in *Space Cadet*, the Asteroid Belt is the remains of a planet that was totally destroyed by its own warring people. Lummox's people will vaporize Earth in *The Star Beast* if they are not allowed to take her home, and the Three Galaxies Court in *Have Space Suit—Will Travel* can destroy a planet by "rotating" it into another dimension without its sun and threaten to do so to Earth. Man may have the potential to be the most dangerous creature in the universe—and even the Three Galaxies Confederation recognizes that threat—but until that potential is fulfilled, there are still powerful forces of which to be aware and beware.

The final topic, the elevation of the ideal, is the most abstract, but basically, Heinlein is articulating a belief that there are values and that those values are worth defending and preserving. Throughout the juveniles there is recurring emphasis on personal freedom and on making decisions on an individual basis. Matt Dodson's choice to go into the Patrol in *Space Cadet* may seem like opting for regimentation, but rather than teaching its members to obey without thinking, the Patrol Academy actually attempts to develop an officer capable of making decisions in situations for which there may be no precedent, of thinking for himself. Thus, Dahlquist, who violated his superiors' orders and thereby foiled the Revolt of the Colonels, is a hero in Patrol history; he gave his life for the ideal. And Matt Dodson, should he be required to do so to prevent a war, would have to be able to drop a bomb on his "native" Iowa.

Throughout the series, Heinlein presents the reader with concrete examples of values that are worth fighting for. The *Red Planet* colonists' revolt against the Company is described in terms of the American Revolution, but in fact, the science fiction context of that revolt, that is, the Martian setting, makes the rebellion necessary for their literal survival. In *Between Planets*, the American Revolution overtones are still there, but the literal survival is dropped and the philosophical justification is somewhat more fully developed. And in *Rocket Ship Galileo*, of course, the Americans are still fighting the Nazis and racing to beat the Russians. In some of the novels, the ideal is worth dying for. The unnamed major in *Between Planets* who dies on the fence, as Don Harvey escapes, shouts "Venus and Freedom" before he falls back (125). Sam Anderson, in *Starman Jones*, sacrifices himself battling the centaurs to buy time for Max and Ellie to escape (Max is the only hope to navigate the ship back to known space). Grant Cowper dies leading the defense of the settlement in *Tunnel in the Sky*, and to underline the importance of that sacrifice, Heinlein has Rod Walker convince the others to stay and keep the land that "Grant paid for" rather than move to a safer location (205). And Baslim, the spy in *Citizen of the Galaxy*, pays for his desire to wipe out interplanetary slavery with his life. The concept of ideals worth dying for is not lost on young readers looking for or trying to articulate their own ideals and sense of worth.

* * *

There are certainly many other topics to be examined in these novels, but they are finally about growing up and becoming independent. Matt Dodson realizes that he has achieved a different perspective from that of his family after a visit with them in the middle of *Space Cadet*, Bill Lermer's decision to stay on Ganymede in *Between Planets* is partly motivated by his not wanting to be associated with the people who have already signed up to go back to Earth, people whom Bill has thought of as losers throughout the novel. Max Jones discovers that he cannot just jump ship and settle on a frontier world but must go back and face the consequences for forging the papers that got him aboard ship early on in *Starman Jones*. Tom Bartlett has to come to terms with the fact that he actually hates his brother, Pat, before he can come to terms with himself in *Time for the Stars*. And late in *Citizen of the Galaxy*, Thorby realizes that he must stay on as head of Rudbek Enterprises, which he feels is another kind of slavery, if he is to carry out his, and Baslim's, desire to fight interplanetary slavery.

The reader who sees these, and other, characters change in the course of Heinlein's juveniles may himself or herself change as well. Heinlein presents a great deal of material not discussed in detail here that might effect that change. There is much in these books in the way of social criticism, speculation (physical, scientific, philosophical, technological, and psychological, among others), mysticism, and a great deal more to catch the reader's attention and make him or her think about familiar topics from a new perspective. But the books succeed as science fiction juveniles because they are good science fiction, that is, science and fiction, and because of the six topics I have discussed, topics that are of special interest to the young reader and that Heinlein has made an integral part of his science as well as his fiction. In some books for young readers, the context is really only a background or backdrop against which the problem of the novel is enacted; in Heinlein's juveniles, the science fiction context is an organic part of the story. Because of that, this series is still "a fine primer for the new reader" (Williamson 31), still in print, and as I have said before, "still contemporary after all these years" (Sullivan, "Heinlein's Juveniles" 66).

NOTES

1. Two other novels, *Starship Troopers* (1959) and *Podkayne of Mars* (1962), might have been in this series—had not Scribner's refused to publish *Starship Troopers* —and are often mentioned along with the others. There are thematic reasons for including them, but the present examination intends to focus on the Scribner's series, which, even though it certainly encouraged its readers to seek out other Heinlein books, had a definite following

of its own that began, as the other two did not, in the public and public school libraries.

2. I am not overlooking Heinlein's male orientation or seeming elitism when I suggest that his juveniles are still contemporary. On the contrary, there are women in positions of power and responsibility throughout the series, and in a number of the books, the "girls" prove smarter than the "boys." Betty is clearly thinking more effectively than John Thomas in *The Star Beast,* Jackie is a better survivor than Rod in *Tunnel in the Sky,* Ellie is far superior to Max at three-dimensional chess in *Starman Jones,* and at least two alien societies—the Little People of Venus in *Space Cadet* and the Hroshii of *The Star Beast*—are matriarchal. Much of the male orientation and lack of sex and sexuality in the novels was forced on Heinlein (see note 6). On the charge of elitism, Heinlein is clearly guilty. He believes that there is or should be an elite of intelligent, well-educated, independent, and well-prepared people; but this elite group is open to anyone who can qualify—regardless of race, creed, color, sex, or any other arbitrary demarcation among people (or aliens). I am not sure that this is an elitism we could not live with.

3. The possibility that the inhabitants of the Moon destroyed themselves, suggested by Donald Cargraves in *Rocket Ship Galileo,* first appeared from Heinlein in a short story, "Blowups Happen" (1940). In *Space Cadet,* Matt Dodson and several other new cadets see a display in honor of Lieutenant Ezra Dahlquist who died preventing a coup d'état; Dahlquist's story is told in full in "The Long Watch" (1949). The Martians of *Red Planet,* especially in their third stage of development and their water-sharing ceremonies, prefigure the Martians in *Stranger in a Strange Land* (1961). The character of Hazel Meade, the references to the lunar revolution, and the concept that people might live longer in the lower gravity of the moon found in *The Rolling Stones* are all developed in much more detail in Heinlein's *The Moon is a Harsh Mistress* (1966). There are many other examples.

4. See especially Heinlein's comments in "Science Fiction: Its Nature, Faults and Virtues" in Basil Davenport's *The Science Fiction Novel,* (17-63), "On the Writing of Speculative Fiction" in Damon Knight's *Turning Points,* (199-204), and *Grumbles from the Grave,* a posthumous publication of some of Heinlein's correspondence and speeches, edited by Virginia Heinlein.

5. There is a difference between the terms *story* and *plot* which may need some clarification. By *plot,* I assume the standard concrete definition of plot as a narrative sequence of actions and incidents. *Story,* on the other hand, is more abstract. By *story,* I mean a whole that is more than the sum of its literary handbook parts (i.e., a whole that includes the author, the text, and the reader), so that when we say, "That was a good story," we are speaking not only of the the text but also the experience of reading the text. The evaluation, "That was a good story," comes from an emotional response as well as an intellectual/analytical response to the text.

6. A major aspect of growing up, an individual's awareness of sex and sexuality, is noticeably absent from these books. Most critics have felt that the absence of sex and sexuality was due to censorship at the publisher's office and/or from the librarians who made up the initial major market for the series (Knight 89; Sarti 108; Williamson 26-27); and the correspondence published in Virginia Heinlein's *Grumbles from the Grave* bears this assumption out. For those who have forgotten or never knew 1950s morality, it is

especially informative to read the material on Martian procreation that Heinlein was forced to remove from *Red Planet* (Virginia Heinlein 252-56).

7. While it is true that *The Star Beast* takes place on Earth, Heinlein's central alien character does come from a very distant star and believes that she is the captor and John Thomas Stuart is the pet (or the latest in a series of pets), thereby turning the usual science fiction perspective on its head as effectively as Ray Bradbury does in the chapter "Ylla" in *The Martian Chronicles*.

8. I first articulated the idea that Heinlein drops in "casual references that look like items from a trivia game" for the best readers in "Heinlein's Juveniles: Still Contemporary After All These Years." I have been taken somewhat to task by Fred Erisman, who argues that Heinlein "anticipates and illustrates, in short, the principles of cultural literacy" (51). Erisman accuses me of selling Heinlein short and missing "his determination to sensitize young readers to the cultural, social, and intellectual range necessary to function in a complex and changing world" (51). In looking at the trees, however, Erisman misses the forest, that whole emphasis on education in the juveniles—from the formal classrooms in *Space Cadet* to the Beggar's Plaza in *Citizen of the Galaxy* —which is included to "sensitize young readers" to the importance of knowledge. The specific items Erisman so painstakingly catalogs reinforce—again, for the best readers; even Erisman admits that Heinlein's books will not "create cultural literacy" (51)—what Heinlein asserts throughout the novels: Those who can learn the most, who know the most, and who can apply what they know are an elite group, a group defined by Heinlein and a group to which the best readers may aspire or with which the best readers may identify after having been brought inside the novel by the author.

BIBLIOGRAPHY

Erisman, Fred. "Robert Heinlein, the Scribner Juveniles, and Cultural Literacy." *Extrapolation* 32 (1991): 44-53.

Franklin, H. Bruce. *Robert A. Heinlein: America as Science Fiction*. New York: Oxford, 1980.

Fuller, Muriel, ed. *More Junior Authors*. New York: Wilson, 1963. 109-110.

Heinlein, Robert A. "On the Writing of Speculative Fiction." *Turning Points*. Ed. Damon Knight. New York: Harper, 1977. 199-204.

_____. "Science Fiction: Its Nature, Faults and Virtues." *The Science Fiction Novel*. Ed. Basil Davenport. Chicago: Advent, 1959. 17-63.

Heinlein, Virginia, ed. *Grumbles from the Grave*. New York: Ballantine, 1989.

Knight, Damon. *In Search of Wonder*. Chicago: Advent, 1967.

Lewis. C.S. "On Stories." *Of Other Worlds*. Ed. Walter Hooper. New York: Harcourt, 1966. 3-21.

Panshin, Alexei. *Heinlein in Dimension*. Chicago: Advent, 1968.

Samuelson, David N. "The Frontier Worlds of Robert A. Heinlein." *Voices of the Future*. Ed. Thomas D. Clareson. Bowling Green, OH: Bowling Green UP, 1976. 104-52.

Sarti, Ronald. "Variations on a Theme: Human Sexuality in the Work of Robert A.

Heinlein." *Robert A. Heinlein.* Ed. Joseph D. Olander and Martin Harry Greenberg. New York: Taplinger, 1978. 107-36.

Slusser, George Edgar. *The Classic Years of Robert A. Heinlein.* San Bernardino, CA: Borgo, 1977.

Sullivan, C.W. III. "Growing Old With Robert A. Heinlein." *Death and the Serpent.* Ed. Carl B. Yoke and Donald M. Hassler. , Westport, CT: Greenwood, 1985. 115-24.

_____. "Heinlein's Juveniles: Still Contemporary After All These Years." *Children's Literature Association Quarterly* 10 (1985): 64-66.

Williamson, Jack. "Youth Against Space: Heinlein's Juveniles Revisited." *Robert A. Heinlein.* Ed. Joseph D. Olander and Martin Harry Greenberg. New York: Taplinger, 1978. 15-31.

Wollheim, Donald. *The Universe Makers.* Harper: New York, 1971.

Heinlein's Juveniles

Heinlein, Robert A. *Rocket Ship Galileo.* 1947. New York: Ballantine, 1977.

_____. *Space Cadet.* 1948. New York: Ballantine, 1978.

_____. *Red Planet.* 1949. New York: Ballantine, 1977.

_____. *Farmer in the Sky.* 1950. New York: Ballantine, 1975.

_____. *Between Planets.* 1951. New York: Ballantine, 1978.

_____. *The Rolling Stones.* New York: Ace, 1952.

_____. *Starman Jones.* 1953. New York: Ballantine, 1975.

_____. *The Star Beast.* New York: Ace, 1954.

_____. *Tunnel in the Sky.* New York: Ace, 1955.

_____. *Time for the Stars.* 1956. New York: Ballantine, 1978.

_____. *Citizen of the Galaxy.* New York: Ace, 1957.

_____. *Have Space Suit—Will Travel.* New York: Ace, 1958.

3

The Formulaic and Rites of Transformation in Andre Norton's Magic Series

Roger C. Schlobin

Like many popular children's and juveniles' books, Andre Norton's are formulaic. Recurrent patterns—like those used in the Hardy Boys, Nancy Drew, and Tom Swift series—provide particular comfort to readers, one to which they return again and again. This phenomenon is not restricted to younger people. Comfort has vaulted the predictable puns of Piers Anthony's Xanth series onto the best-seller lists and rewarded Manly Wade Wellman's lockstep Silver John Chronicles with many readers. In fact, there is a strong case for fantasy literature and particularly its heroic form as formulaic prose: Evil is abroad in the land, a hero and fellowship arise with the prerequisite wizard, a psychomachia occurs, and good is restored. So Andre Norton's high library circulation and sales, along with the translations of her works into numerous languages and her numerous fans, indicate that her formidable, six-decade-long canon that began in 1934 with the boys' adventure *The Prince Commands* continues to draw an avid audience for its predictability as well as its craft. Further, as one of the pioneers of strong and credible female characters, her fiction has appeal to both genders (Schlobin, *Andre Norton: A Primary* xxx; Yoke, "Slaying the Dragon" pass.).

Much of Norton's juvenile fiction and the Magic series in particular— *Steel Magic* (1965), *Octagon Magic* (1967), *Fur Magic* (1968), *Dragon Magic* (1972), *Lavender-Green Magic* (1974), and *Red Hart Magic* (1976)—concentrate on the dynamics of coming-of-age, self-realization, and rites of transformation as her young people discover themselves and their strengths. The formula is 1) a child, teenager, or a fellowship of either is displaced into a new and alien environment from the ordinary world (Schlobin, *Andre Norton: A Primary* xxx-xxxii; Yoke, *Roger Zelazny* 13); 2) the protagonists are anxious, unhappy, and confused. They are troubled by awkward events and frequently perceive their displacements as abandonments (Schlobin, *Andre Norton: A Primary* xxx-xxxi);

3) through some set of events, a portal or means to a fantasy world is discovered; 4) the other world (usually one based on history or mythology) is entered and a task of heroic magnitude, a struggle against evil to which both worlds are liable, is presented; and 5) by meeting the challenges, the characters are transformed into better people than they were at the onset (Schlobin, *Andre Norton: A Primary* xxvii; Yoke, *Roger Zelazny* 13; Wendland 9). In this process, they are often aided by guides, learning, and art, and their triumphs are part of one of the oldest and most appealing of literary quests: "the success and elevation of the innocent" (Schlobin, *Andre Norton: A Primary* xxviii).

Two factors are the primary causes of the standard openings: 1) awkward and problematic separation from a warm home and 2) troublesome parents or guardians and/or difficulties in the new environment. These combine to produce both alienation and loneliness among Norton's youngsters (Schlobin, *Andre Norton: A Primary* xxx-xxxii; Yoke, *Roger Zelazny* 13). Cory Adler, in *Fur Magic*, tries to avoid natural order by clinging to the mechanized jeep when he is daunted by the wilderness challenges of the West, his absent father, his new family, his xenophobia (13) and equinaphobia, and his own feelings of inadequacy and cowardice (36). Holly, of *Lavender-Green Magic*, is distrustful of the rustic, homespun world compared to her city home, and Crock, her brother, is sure that the other children look down on them because their grandparents live and successfully scavenge in a junkyard for special treasures that people have ignorantly and insensitively discarded. *Red Hart Magic's* Chris Fitton and Nan Mallory both feel abandoned by their respective families and are initially at odds with each other (36). Both children's parents have remarried, and here—as with the children's fathers in *Fur Magic* and *Lavender-Green Magic* who are, respectively, stationed and missing-in-action in Vietnam—Norton provides real-world problems for her characters and readers. Also separated from her family, *Octagon Magic's* Lorrie Mallard has even had her own sense of history taken from her; she discovers that, in Canada, "she had learned the wrong kind." In America, it's "Social Studies" (14). Thus, Lorrie, like many other Norton characters, must cross "from a rejected past—an empathically dead past—to an undefined but developing future" (Wendland 11).

In addition to this, Lorrie now must live with her Aunt Margaret who is slow to recognize her need for solitude and creativity (37). The insensitive guardian who does not have true parental empathy is a common theme in Norton and is one of the links between the normal discomfort of the characters' simply moving to new environments and the unusual unpleasantries of living in new places. Another major occurrence of this is Aunt Elizabeth, in *Red Hart Magic*, who asks questions but never waits for answers (10-11, 25). Thus, Norton uses the familiar to lead her readers to the unfamiliar.

This alienation from the adult nurturer is compounded by the behavior of the children's peers, depriving the protagonists of any support (other than the occasional sibling who is still initially contentious). In *Octagon Magic*, Lorrie is taunted by "mean, hateful boys" (who later become friends as her understanding grows) with a typical, childish doggerel: "Canuck, Canuck, walks like a duck!" (13). Other illustrations of negative peer interaction from the Magic series are Nan's bouts with her peers' shoplifting and dares in *Red Hart Magic* (77, 81), the African-American children's excessive consciousness of their race and their imagined bigotry in *Lavender-Green Magic* (44-46) and *Dragon Magic* (10-11), and Kim's concern with his adopted status in *Dragon Magic* (25). These specific difficulties do not usually call for heroic action, but Norton cleverly uses these normative concerns to foreshadow greater discomforts to come, for example, Holly's carsickness early in *Lavender Green Magic* (2) foreshadows larger dificulites later. However, whether they are majestic or ordinary, the stresses always have great and quick impacts at intimate levels: Holly, for example, immediately feels that her world has gone to pieces and she is among strangers (2-3).

Amid their personal agonies, the characters are sustained and aided by, but never fully dependent upon (cf. Yoke, "Slaying the Dragon" 7), wise and often supernaturally gifted guides. Here Norton displays the deep reverence for art, learning, and wisdom that is one of the trademarks of her entire canon. Miss Charlotta Ashemeade, the mentor in *Octagon Magic,* states this Norton edict: "to forget or set aside any art is an unhappy thing" (55).

While there is certainly no explicit animosity toward formal schooling in Norton's canon, she generally favors the one-to-one sharing between mentor and acolyte. The mentors are encouraging, rigorous, and non-directive, stimulating the children's self-reliance and self-discovery, perhaps the only true form of learning as all that is acquired belongs to the children and is not derived from external, dictatorial forces. In *Octagon Magic,* the child's guide is the long-lived Miss Ashemeade, whose life parallels the history of the octagon-shaped house and whose needlepoint, sewing, and golden needles have supernatural qualities (57). The children of *Steel Magic* are initially greeted and instructed in the ways of Avalon by Huon of the Horn and later are supported by Merlin. Cory shares shape and knowledge with the far more survivalwise beaver, Yellow Shell, whose body he shares in *Fur Magic.* His return to the ancient time of American Indian mythology and encounters with the Nez Perce's Changer and other animal shamans (i.e., the Thunderbird) provide him with profound insights into the nature of reality and the benefits of trying. So, too, the children of *Lavender-Green Magic* learn from the folk art and crafts of their grandparents and from the wicca of the good witch, Miss Tamar.

The only other mode of learning that receives special favor is independent study in libraries, which almost achieve the status of sacred places. Lorrie in *Octagon Magic* loves the library (31, 33), and characters in the other volumes of the Magic series find them to be both sanctuaries from unpleasant onslaughts and fonts of information. Here Norton-the-author's character is mirrored in her fiction. She too loves books and research with their gifts of information and insight about the past (Schlobin, *Andre Norton: A Primary* xvi-xxii). As she describes it in "On Writing Fantasy": "But the first requirement for writing heroic or sword and sorcery fantasy must be a deep interest in and a love for history itself. Not the history of dates, of sweeps and empires—but the kind of history which deals with daily life, the beliefs, and the aspirations of people long since dust" (8).

Norton's faith in art, nature, and mentoring is in direct contrast to her disgust for technology (Schlobin, "Andre Norton: Humanity" pass.). Toward the end of *Octagon Magic,* when it becomes apparent that Miss Ashemeade's house will be bulldozed to make way for a highway, a now-wiser Aunt Margaret makes this quite clear: "in the name of progress more than one crime is committed nowadays. I wonder just who will rejoice when the last blade of grass is buried by concrete, when the last tree is brought down by a bulldozer, when the last wild thing is shot, or poisoned, or trapped" (106). Were there any doubt of Norton's stance here, she makes it emphatically clear: "Yes, I am anti-machine. The more research I do, the more I am convinced that when western civilization turned to machines so heartily with the industrial revolution, they threw away some parts of life which are now missing and which lack of leads to much of our present frustration" (quoted by Brooks 22, and Schlobin, *Andre Norton: A Primary* xxvi).

As mentioned and in contrast, wisdom is unequivocally linked to nature and natural processes. Turning away from nature and tradition and depending upon technology, as Cory does when he clings to the jeep in *Fur Magic,* is a crime against humanity's essential bonds to its past and its natural home, and no good comes of it. Miss Tamar, the benevolent witch of *Lavender-Green Magic,* shares the law of the necessary bonds and laws between humanity and nature: "That thou lovest all things in nature. That thou shalt suffer no person to be harmed by thy hands or in thy mind. That thou walkest humbly in the ways of men and the ways of the gods. Contentment thou shalt at last learn through suffering, and from long patient years, and from nobility of mind and service. For the wise never grow old" (70). Thus, the combination of knowledge, experience, and understanding of the past and nature yields wisdom and harmony. Of course, wisdom and harmony (Schlobin, *Andre Norton: A Primary* xxxii) are the ends of Norton's children's quests for truth and the reasons her fiction has verisimilitude. What is most important to understand here is that the mentors' non-directive approaches mandate that the children learn for themselves through their adventures. Frequently, the children's malleability and willingness to learn make them far better students than their elders, and sometimes, as with Chris and Nan in *Red Hart Magic* and the four boys in *Dragon Magic,* they prosper with little or no adult intervention and are successful when and where adults cannot be (as in a number of popular contemporary films like *War Games, Home Alone,* and *Young Sherlock Holmes*).

Either before reaching a mentor or with the help of one, Norton's female (Yoke, "Slaying the Dragon" 5) and male children always use sentient portals to gain access to the challenges of the fantasy realm. These gates open when the proper people arrive in the proper states (usually disrupted ones) at the proper times to confront conflicts of universal significance. To add further magnitude to these conflicts, Norton frequently provides settings of epic proportions. One of the best of these occurs at the beginning of *Merlin's Mirror* :

Time had been swallowed, was gone, and still the beacon kept to its task, while outside [Merlin's] cave nations had risen and decayed, men themselves had changed and changed again. Everything the makers of the beacon had known was erased during those years, destroyed by the very action of nature. Seas swept in upon the land, then retired, the force of their waves taking whole cities and countries. Mountains reared up, so that the shattered remains of once-proud ports were lifted into the thin air of great heights. Deserts crept in over green fields. A moon fell from the sky and another took its place. (5)

Norton's use of these gates into magical places to mark the beginnings of the rites of transformation is yet another common characteristic of her canon (cf. *Witch World*; Schlobin, "Andre Norton: Humanity" 29-30) and is an example of a frequently used technique in fantasy literature, "rationalized fantasy" (Schlobin, *The Literature of Fantasy* xxvii-xxx). The gates help readers suspend disbelief, as they too journey with the characters into fantasy realms, and also provide credibility and stature for the young characters, who are the only ones special enough to be accepted by the gates. Also, on a simpler level, the gateways to and the lure of the secret and unknown world have long had special appeal to both young and old, as with C. S. Lewis's Narnia Chronicles' wardrobe.

However, before giving the characters' imaginations and courage too much credit, it should be noted that the gates sometimes give the children no choice about entering. The magical puzzles in *Dragon Magic* are compulsive in their lure (31), and *Fur Magic's* Cory must enter the Changer's past to remedy his own ignorant tampering with a medicine bag (30-31, 43-44; cf. Yoke, "Slaying the Dragon" 6).

In *Octagon Magic,* magic portals figure prominently as both the microcosmic doll house and the macrocosmic octagon house that surrounds it open special ways for Lorrie to follow (61). The large house only opens certain rooms for Lorrie, and as she follows Sabrina, the black cat she rescued from the abusive and rambunctious boys, she is guided to the small doll house. Its magic doll-filled drawers and openings selectively lead her to adventures in the past. Moreover, the experiences the doll house creates are more real, more alive, than those of Lorrie's actual day-to-day existence (62). Much the same occurs in *Red Hart Magic*: Chris Fitton and Nan Mallory discover that an old and intricate peep show—modeled on an Elizabethan British inn—and a dream pillow (32) lead them to shared dreams (51 ff.) of the past that are far more meaningful and yield more insight than their waking lives. *Lavender-Green Magic's* gate is a maze (57, 118-19); prophetic dreams guide its protagonists through its dark and bright sides to its corresponding witches, Tamar and Hagar, and Colonial America. *Steel Magic's* four gates open to the Arthurian realm (38-39), and *Dragon Magic's* four, interrelated tales use the compulsion of a four-part dragon puzzle to draw each boy back into his ancestral past: Sig Dortmund to Scandinavia, Artie Jones to Arthurian Britain, George "Ras" Brown to Africa, and the adopted Kim Stevens to China. In all cases, the gates either force or foster the drives toward transformation and growth common among Norton's characters (Schlobin, *Andre Norton: A Primary* xxxi) .

The worlds beyond these gates are linked to normal existence despite their superficial incongruities. They are without confusion and have and revere clear lines of good and evil, right and wrong. These values are obvious to the clear-eyed and are truer than those of the normal world, which is typical of fantasy literature's more rigorous ethic systems. These realms provide the characters with far more freedom than they might have and/or with releases from too much control. As Chris observes in *Red Hart Magic*, "Kids were like animals at the old zoo. They were all in cages. Maybe you couldn't see the cages really, but they were there" (29). Thus, the other worlds provide far more autonomy and responsibility. Often, the characters have to discover and adjust to these new challenges themselves. *Fur Magic's* Cory, for example, has difficulty learning to accept the animals' world and truths (61-124), which, although they are alien to him, actually are intuitive wisdom once he learns to overcome his inhibitions and phobias.

As mentioned earlier, the normal worlds' prosperity is tied to the fantasy realms'. Thus, in *Steel Magic*, Avalon is the bulwark against the "dark" (44), and the wars and pestilence of Earth are the results of Avalon's weakening. Throughout the Magic series, these double burdens are mighty challenges, and the young characters are assailed in mind and body by both external threats and their own self-doubts and weaknesses (Yoke, "Slaying the Dragon" 13). Predictably, in *Fur Magic*, it is the evil of the Changer versus Cory's and the animals' desire to postpone the Changer's creation of humanity (158) because, with its becoming, it will dominate the animals and destroy their sentience. In *Red Hart Magic*, the children are central in saving both people and property amid the persecution of the Papists in England. The three children of *Steel Magic* must use the magically transformed steel utensils in their picnic basket to recover the three treasures of Britain—Merlin's ring, Arthur's Excalibur, and Huon's horn—and to save, not only Arthur's Avalon, but their own world as well. *Lavender-Green Magic's* characters' adventures in time lift the Dimsdale family curse in Sussex, Massachusetts (12).

The rewards for Norton's characters are invaluable and stress the didactic nature of productive change (cf. *Octagon Magic* 176). *Red Hart Magic's* children discover friendship in their common dreams (71), and later this friendship transfers to their real world (179). Chris first discovers courage and Nan independence in their dreams, and the two children bring these virtues to fruition and effectiveness later in their mundane lives. Chris is falsely accused first in his dream, and the same situation occurs later at school; the first experience prepares him to deal successfully with the second (166-72). The necessity of the return from the fantasy world is always stressed, for to do otherwise would be "running away" (*Red Hart Magic* 175).

The essential quality of Norton's characters' successes is change (*Octagon Magic* 176) and self-actualization. These occur through the instructive values of experience, learning, wisdom, and open-mindedness. These transrealm successes and epiphanies are of both cosmic and personal natures and occur through the children's creation of a bridge between worlds and each one's inhabitants. The sentient, tool-making animals of *Fur Magic* transform Cory's view of his own world (173-74), as do the encounters with the dragons for the boys in *Dragon Magic* (183-92). Eric, Greg, and Sara in *Steel Magic* each overcome personal weaknesses in Avalon (impatience, aquaphobia, and arachnophobia, respectively) and are much more functional when they return. So too, *Fur Magic's* Cory loses his fear of horses when he is a beaver in the prehuman world of the sentient animals (173). Lorrie is cured of her prejudice about boys by becoming the dolls in the doll house's drawers and helps the other children overcome their own bigotry (108) by participating in the Civil War past that the magic doll house recreates. She also learns how to interact with the other children in her real world. This process is outlined by Robert Scholes in *Structural Fabulation*. He observes that readers return changed by the fantasy experience (26); so, too, Lorrie and all the Magic series' characters return with different perspectives and attitudes after each of their travels.

Were this all the characters gained, Norton's fiction could be accused of being egotistic and self-serving, that her children operate only for themselves and their own gain despite whatever empathy and sympathy her readers feel. However, the revelations are not just subjective. Often, they are returns to or discoveries of the traditional values of family, self, and friends (without prejudice). Sometimes both immediate and/or extended families are found. Beyond this, Norton's characters return to their normal worlds as powerful forces (Schlobin, *Andre Norton: A Primary* xxxi-xxxii) that create harmony among all who surround them. In fact, if there is a common theme throughout all of Norton's canon, it is harmony through arduous effort (Schlobin, *Andre Norton: A Primary* xxxi-xxxii). This is not just the integration of people either. Her fiction's dynamic interactions among a myriad of conflicting forces—natural law and technology, good and evil, pettiness and largess, selfishness and generosity, alienation and union, action and passivity, prejudice and tolerance (Schlobin, *Andre Norton: A Primary* xxviii-xxix; Yoke, *Roger Zelazny* 21; Wendland 21-22), ignorance and wisdom—set amid history and mythology reach from the past through the present to a generative, promising future that is a celebration for her readers and characters.

Although all these dynamic interactions may justify the literary merit of Norton's formula, it still does not explain her ongoing popularity among the young and the old. That answer comes from her gifts to her characters and readers, and much of her appeal results from the identification of reader with character, a point well made by Albert Wendland (2, 23). Primary among these is empowerment. Clearly, the fictive escape from the negatives of alienation and estrangement that many feel is a characteristic that has ennobled much fiction in general. Add to this the message that the young, the "odd-ones-out," also are offered special tasks that are theirs and theirs alone, and Norton offers a positive alternative to the powerlessness that young people feel in the face of the authority figure, who they are sure does not understand them. Wendland articulates this desirous state well: "It's . . . when a reader, awash with longings and expectations, might want to trade in the past, to break from the confinement of childhood and parental authority to move out of the prison of the defined past and the defined self (defined by parents and environment) to enter a larger world of freedom and adventure, to test and thus to find a self through the exploration of a new landscape beyond the old confines." Further, the "longing of adolescence . . . is not so much a desire to know what's out there but more the desire not to know, to maintain the sense of wonder and yet to find oneself capable of encountering it" (8-9). This freedom is enhanced by the insistent message that, regardless of what the adult and peer others might say or believe, Norton's characters have special powers and prerogatives that take them beyond their critics and detractors, that they can operate with both understanding and confidence (Bettelheim 47-48, 61). However, this is not an elitist stance. Rather, it becomes one of the primary impetuses for the theme of harmony as her protagonists return to their detractors to make friends and create positive situations, relationships, and "new homes" (Wendland 10, 12). Thus, the characters' transformations, achieved through personal traits and arduous trials, become a boon to all and emphasize the ancient truths of wisdom, art, and learning.

However, beneath all this highmindedness (didactic messages, which certainly appeal to parents selecting books for their children) is an even simpler appeal. Through their hard work, efforts, and transformations, Norton's characters gain (and share with her readers) popularity with their peers and with adults. So, the rewards are two-fold: yes, there are adventures and transformations, but there are also acceptances and recognitions, perhaps the best of all adolescent worlds.

BIBLIOGRAPHY

Bettelheim, Bruno. *The Uses of Enchantment: The Meaning and Importance of Fairy Tales*. New York: Vinatge/Random House, 1977.

Brooks, Rick. "Andre Norton: Loss of Faith." *The Dipple Chronicle* 1 (Oct.-Dec. 1971): 12-30. Rpt. in *The Many Worlds of Andre Norton*. Ed. Roger Elwood. Radnor, PA: Chilton, 1974. 178-200.

Norton, Andre. *Merlin's Mirror,* New York: DAW, 1975.

_____. "On Writing Fantasy." *The Dipple Chronicle* 1 (Oct.-Dec. 1971): 8-11, 30; rpt. in *The Many Worlds of Andre Norton*. Ed. Roger Elwood. Radnor, PA: Chilton, 1974. 61-69.

_____. *The Prince Commands. Being the Sundry Adventures of Michael Kane, sometimes* [sic] *Crown Prince & Pretender to the Throne of Morvania*. New York: D. Appleton-Century, 1934.

_____. *Witch World*. New York: Ace, 1963.

Schlobin, Roger C. *Andre Norton: A Primary and Secondary Bibliography*. Boston: G. K. Hall, 1980.

_____. "Andre Norton: Humanity Amid the Hardware." *The Feminine Eye:*

Science Fiction and the Women Who Write It. Ed. Tom Staicar. New York: Ungar, 1982. 25-31, 134-36.

_____. *The Literature of Fantasy: A Comprehensive, Annotated Bibliography of Modern Fantasy Fiction.* New York: Garland, 1979.

Scholes, Robert. *Structural Fabulation: An Essay on the Fiction of the Future.* University of Notre Dame Ward-Phillips Lectures in English Language and Literature. Vol. 7. Notre Dame, IN: U of Notre Dame P, 1975.

Wendland, Albert. "Reader-Response Theory and Andre Norton." Twelfth International Conference on the Fantastic in the Arts. Dania, FL, 23 Mar.1991.

Yoke, Carl B. *Roger Zelazny and Andre Norton: Proponents of Individualism.* Columbus: The State Library of Ohio,1979.

_____."Slaying the Dragon Within: Andre Norton's Female Heroes." Twelfth International Conference on the Fantastic in the Arts. Dania, FL, 23 Mar. 1991.

The Magic Series

_____. *Steel Magic.* Cleveland: World, 1965.

_____. *Octagon Magic.* Cleveland: World, 1967.

_____. *Fur Magic.* Cleveland: World, 1968.

_____. *Dragon Magic.* New York: Crowell, 1972. New York: Ace, 1973. Citations here are to the Ace edition.

_____. *Lavender-Green Magic.* New York: Crowell, 1974.

_____. *Red Hart Magic.* New York: Crowell, 1976.

4

Asimov: Man Thinking

Elizabeth Anne Hull

One of the best-known science fiction writers in the world, Isaac Asimov has become a household name. He is solidly identified with the genre, although the majority of his 400 plus books have been non-fiction, covering a vast array of subjects, from Shakespeare to the Bible, as well as countless branches of science.

He began reading science fiction as a teenager and made his first sales at eighteen. The science fiction he had read was largely adventure or "space opera," which was basically what was being published in the few existing magazines till 1937, the year when Isaac was seventeen and also the year John W. Campbell, Jr., took over *Astounding* and began to change the face of magazine science fiction in America. Naturally enough, when Asimov began to write, his stories were largely adventurous, too. His first sales were to *Amazing*, and over the first few years of his writing career he was also contributing regularly to *Planet Stories*, *Astonishing Stories*, and various other non-Campbellian magazines.

When science fiction book markets began to open up in the early 1950s, his literary agent, Frederik Pohl, asked Asimov to create a manuscript to offer the first major publisher to establish a science fiction line, Doubleday & Co. Asimov was ready with a short novel (*Grow Old Along With Me*) rejected by the market it was intended for, *Startling Stories*. Originally judged too short for book publication, the expanded version published by Doubleday in 1950 became *Pebble in the Sky*.

Because he shunned vulgar language and the depiction of explicit personal scenes in his writing, nearly all of Asimov's work—both fiction and nonfiction— is suitable for young readers, that is, for any readers old enough to grasp the meanings of the words and the concepts. In fact, he makes it a point not to condescend in vocabulary and ideas throughout his work, though his knack for a "plain style" is much underrated. Besides clear, grammatical prose, he has a genius for fresh similes and analogies to make difficult or unfamiliar concepts accessible to a naive reader as well as interesting to a sophisticated reader.

Few critics, however, have discussed at any length that part of Asimov's fiction that is meant especially for young readers. Most Asimov critics have simply ignored the juveniles or glossed over them rapidly. Joseph F. Patrouch, Jr., finds them good at visualizing alien landscapes and thus creating a sense of wonder but finds their highest value as "first rate mystery stories" (158-59). Hazel Pierce also finds them interesting chiefly as detective stories (Olander and Greenberg 37-39). William Touponce suggests that the most interesting thing about the Lucky Starr books is "the encroachment of error into science fiction narrative, which bases itself on connections with the real world as known by science" (97). James Gunn gives more consideration to the Lucky Starr novels (the Norby books had not yet been published), yet concludes by comparing Asimov's juveniles to those of Robert A. Heinlein: "One might speculate that Heinlein juveniles lead young readers to read more science fiction; those by Asimov to read more science" (168). As late as 1991, Donald M. Hassler fails to mention the Norby series, except in his bibliography, and glosses quickly over the Lucky Starr books. The most extensive and sympathetic discussion of the Lucky Starr series is by Jean Fiedler and Jim Mele, who still dismiss them rather lightly, concluding that *Lucky Starr and the Big Sun of Mercury* is the weakest of the six books: "The only thing of interest in this book is the introduction of robots and the Three Laws of Robotics" (84). None of these critics adequately accounts for the continued popularity of the Asimov juveniles, which I believe rests, as does that of all enduring literature, on their thematic content.

Asimov actually wrote (or collaborated on) *two* series intended for younger readers, the Lucky Starr books of the 1950s and the Norby books beginning in the 1980s. By the mid-1950s Asimov was a professor at Boston University and his writing for some time had been primarily for *Astounding* and, more recently, for Horace Gold at *Galaxy*. Neither Campbell nor Gold had much interest in straight adventure stories. Much has been made of Campbell's influence on Asimov's career, but the first Lucky Starr book was dedicated to Walter I. Bradbury, his editor at Doubleday, "without whom this book would *really* never have been written" (the second in the series was dedicated to Pohl, "That contradiction in terms—A lovable agent"). Perhaps one reason Asimov wanted to do the Lucky Starr books was nostalgia for the kind of stories he had read as a teenager and had been writing at about the same age. In any case, he agreed to do the series for young readers—under the pseudonym Paul French—with the idea of dramatizing the stories for the then relatively new medium of television (Fiedler and Mele 81). Although this ambition was never realized, it is easy to see that visual aspects of the novels are quite vividly portrayed.

Throughout his fiction, Asimov's general tone is celebratory of the potential for human ability to deal with the universe and solve problems rationally, yet cautionary that such coping does not come easily, especially since human beings are so often their own worst enemies. This in part is why Asimov regards his own work as "social" science fiction; despite its foundation in the "hard" sciences and adventures with robots in space, it relies not merely on gadgets to resolve difficulties but tries to provide plausible motivation for everyone, even the vilest antagonist, on the premise that no one thinks of *himself* or *herself* as a villain. In fact, the motivations of his antagonists are usually more fully developed than those of his protagonists, who are often just well-meaning people in search of interesting adventures, someone for the reader to identify with as a would-be hero.

Besides the idea that problems *are* solvable through negotiation and the use of reason, some of the major themes that run throughout Asimov's work are that friendship is vitally important, that snobbery and prejudice are universal human weaknesses, and that first impressions are frequently wrong. The adversary is nearly always a combination of environmental danger and human values in conflict.

Asimov's reputation in science fiction comes largely from two areas, the concept of psychohistory from his Foundation stories, and his Three Laws of Robotics (composed at age twenty-one under Campbell's influence). Of the latter, Asimov said, they "proved to be the most famous, the most frequently quoted, and the most influential sentences I ever wrote" (*Robot Visions* 8):

1. A robot may not injure a human being, or, through inaction, allow a human being to come to harm.
2. A robot must obey the orders given it by human beings except where such orders would conflict with the First Law.
3. A robot must protect its own existence as long as such protection does not conflict with the First or Second Law.

These laws provide much of the plot interest both in the Lucky Starr and in the Norby books.

The first of the Lucky Starr series, *David Starr: Space Ranger* (1952), introduces the protagonist and his sidekick, John Bigman Jones, a scrappy, five-foot-two, red-headed Martian farmboy who is sensitive about his lack of stature, demanding to be addressed only by his middle name. Both David and Bigman are young men, but Starr is very well educated and wise beyond his years—the youngest member of the interplanetary Council of Science, the unofficial rulers of the human race, both on Earth and elsewhere—while Bigman is just the sort of relatively uneducated good guy who has trouble controlling his temper, a characteristic that many young rebel-readers would find appealing to identify with. Their friendship is built on loyalty, trust, and respect for one another's strengths. Hector Conway, Chief Counselor of Science, and Dr. Augustus Henree, both old school friends of David's father and admirers of his mother, are also introduced as mentors and surrogate "uncles" for the orphaned David.

Trying to solve the mystery of the poisoned food supply on Mars, David (who doesn't become "Lucky" till the second book) discovers the previously unsuspected native Martians, creatures of pure intelligence who, ironically, are *not* a threat to humans. As a token of their goodwill, David receives from them the gift of a mask that allows him to become the almost mythical Space Ranger. Using the mask and his own intelligence, he finally solves the mystery of the tainted food supply that had brought him to Mars.

The sabotage is the work of a man with an inferiority complex, but not Bigman. David explains, "There are more ways of being small than in size. Bigman compensates for his size by belligerence and loud assertion of his own opinions. The men here respect him because of this. Benson, however, living here on Mars among men of action finds himself despised as a 'college farmer,' ignored as a weakling, and looked down upon by men whom he considers much his inferiors" (180-81). The first book ends with the pledge of friendship between David and Bigman: "'Together then,' said David, 'wherever we go'" (186).

When the Lucky Starr novels were republished fifteen years later, Asimov wrote introductions to each to inform his readers of discoveries in scientific knowledge and theory which affected his stories; of the second book in the series, *Lucky Starr and the Pirates of the Asteroids* (1953), he said, "If I had to write the novel today, I would hardly have to change a word" (vi).

Wedged in between the events of the adventure story Asimov teaches bits of astronomy in context to make it palatable:

A three-dimensional map of the Solar System would have the appearance of a rather flat plate. In the center would be the Sun, the dominant member of the System. It is *really* dominant, since it contains 99.8% of all the matter in the Solar System. In other words, it weighs five hundred times as much as everything else in the Solar System put together.

Around the Sun circle the planets. All of them revolve in nearly the same plane, and this plane is called the Ecliptic.

In traveling from planet to planet space-ships usually follow the Ecliptic. (155)

Also wedged into the stories are social, moral, and political values that are still relevant; some even seem ahead of their time. For example, long before the "war on drugs," Lucky will accept an alcoholic beverage offered in a social situation, but Asimov makes a point of mentioning that Lucky will leave his drink untouched, and Asimov frequently makes the villain a smoker.

In *Pirates* Lucky shows his wisdom when he advises Uncle Hector and Uncle Gus, "Our best bet is not to start a war, but to prevent one" (152). The Sirians (not an alien species, but space settlers who have grown so apart from their roots that they no longer identify with the rest of humanity) are established as the opponents of the inhabitants of the Solar System. Although the Sirian agent (the cigar-smoking Hansen) is captured and prevented from further mischief, the Sirian threat remains at the end of the book. Especially in the context of the Cold War at the time of original publication in the middle fifties (still an issue at republication in the late seventies), the analogy of a continuing threat to world peace could make the battle relevant to young readers. Even in post-Cold War times, the idea will probably continue to apply to disputes between nations.

In *Lucky Starr and the Oceans of Venus* (1954), Asimov introduces the concept of mind control via the native life-forms, seemingly harmless V-frogs—the ideal pet for humans homesick for Earth. In this book Asimov also shows that Bigman's diminutive size can be not just a handicap to be overcome, but actually a positive virtue, when Bigman courageously volunteers to crawl into a duct space too small to fit a full-sized man in order to make repairs and save the colony.

However, the real opponent is not a Sirian, but a human Solarian, Turner (a smoker), who has constructed a machine to control the V-frogs. Lucky does not regard him as an unredeemable villain, however, and it is ironically Turner's love for his wife that gives him away. Despite Turner's being a traitor and a murderer several times over who definitely has dictatorial ambitions, Lucky says, "more important . . . is the fact that he created a work of genius" (185). Lucky imagines the use to which the invention might be put: "It may offer us an entirely new method of attack on mental diseases, a new way of combatting criminal impulses. It may even, conceivably, be used to prevent wars in the future or to defeat the enemies of Earth quickly and bloodlessly if a war is forced upon us. Just as the machine was dangerous in the hands of one ambition-riddled man, it can be very useful and beneficial in the hands of the Council" (185-86).

Lucky expresses optimism that Turner can be rehabilitated (partly through the incentive of being reunited with his wife) and the reconstructed machine may be used to "investigate Turner's own mind, help cure it of his abnormal desire for power, and save for the service of humanity a first-class brain. . . . it is easy to 'protect society' by executing a criminal, but that will not bring back his victims. If one can cure him instead and use him to make life better and brighter for that society, how much more has been accomplished!" (186).

In *Lucky Starr and the Big Sun of Mercury* (1956), the conflict seems to be again with the Sirians, involving robots. The dangers of surviving in a hostile environment so close to the Sun faced by Lucky and Bigman and the small human colony are complicated by a robot of Sirian manufacture in which the Three Laws have been tampered with. Lucky and one of the astronomers discuss the Sirian development of more sophisticated robots and the reasons Earth has let the Sirians get ahead of them in this technology. Dr. Peverale says, "It would upset our economy; and we place the comfort and security of today above the safety of tomorrow. We use our scientific advance to make ourselves weaker" (64). Again with the Cold War as a frame of reference, the analogy to the Soviet accomplishment of *Sputnik* seems apparent. Another message, an antitechnophobe one, is clear: robots are tools, that can be used properly or improperly. These insights may be relevant to other rivals in the world as time passes, but the principle remains persuasive.

Ultimately, however, the real villains once again turn out to be not Sirians, but Solarian humans, the scientists on Mercury, using the Sirians as a beard. (One of them, Cook, is another smoker.) Their motivation is to protect their scientific project, but their end clearly does not justify the means. Regarding the need for honest opposition, Lucky concludes: "The Council of Science needs its critics, just as Congress and the government do. If ever the Council began to consider itself above criticism, then the time might come when it would establish a dictatorship over the Earth, and certainly I wouldn't want that to happen" (190-91). Asimov's political philosophy regarding disinformation techniques of powerful institutions is also quite clear.

Asimov further explored the idea of giving people an opportunity to reform in *Lucky Starr and the Moons of Jupiter* (1957). Lucky is in search of Sirian spies and wants to use the V-frogs to probe the minds of the miners on a Jovian moon. Norrich, a blind man, explains the attitude of one of the men:

You've got to understand about Summers. He's had an unfortunate life: broken home, no real parents. He got into the wrong crowds. He's been in prison, yes, for being involved in some minor rackets. If he'd stayed on Earth, his life would have been one long waste.... He's made a new life here. He came out as a common laborer and he educated himself. . . . He's respectable, admired, well liked. He's found out what it is to have honor and position and he dreads nothing more than the thought of going back to Earth and his old life. (74)

In fact, Norrich explains, Summers generously arranged for a replacement for Norrich's Seeing Eye dog when his old dog was killed in a force-field short circuit. As it turns out, the adventure of the story centers on solving a puzzle, using the Three Laws to deduce that the dog is a Sirian-made robot. Lucky warns Bigman of the dangers of preconceptions to discovering the truth: "I was so convinced that I was looking for some human that my mind refused to see that point" (191).

In the final book of the series, *Lucky Starr and the Rings of Saturn* (1958), Lucky and Bigman again must cope with the adversary, the Sirians, who have tried to establish an outpost on one of the moons of Saturn and force a confrontation with the Earth-dominated inhabitants of the Solar System. With the launching of *Sputnik* fresh in the minds of his original readers, Asimov has Lucky acknowledge the challenge of Sirian superiority in their robotics:

We'll just have to learn to build our own, Bigman. These robots are a human achievement. The humans that did the achieving are Sirians, yes, but they are human beings, too, and all other humans can share pride in the achievement. If we fear the results of their achievement, let's match it ourselves or more than match it. But there's no use denying them the worth of their accomplishment. (86)

Yet Asimov does not let his readers forget the lessons learned during World War II about those who think they are the master race. One of the Sirians recognizes Lucky's superiority over the average Earthman and invites Lucky to become one of them because his abilities and accomplishments are wasted on Earth. Lucky argues that Sirians are descended from Earthmen. The Sirian, however, insists

So they are, but not from all Earthmen only from some, from the best, from those with the initiative and strength to reach the stars as colonists. . . . We have weeded out the unfit from among ourselves so that we are now a pure race of the strong, the fit, and the healthy, while Earth remains a conglomerate of the diseased and deformed. (106-7)

The Sirians do not see themselves as villains; they regard Earth as a "terrible menace, a bomb of sub-humanity, ready to explode and contaminate the clean Galaxy" (106). The Sirians can hardly regard Bigman as a human because he's short and (they think) inferior as a warrior. Lucky insists, "Fitness comes in all shapes and forms. The great men of Earth have come from the tall and the short, from all manner of head shapes, skin colors, and languages. Variety is our salvation and the salvation of all mankind" (106). This very much sounds like a summary of American melting-pot values.

These values are further discussed when a Sirian challenges Lucky to defend some of Earth's unsatisfactory rulers. Lucky admits that we have had any number of vicious ones, "but we are a miscellaneous lot on Earth we vary. No ruler can stay in power very long if he doesn't represent a compromise among us. Compromising rulers may not be dynamic, but neither are they tyrannical" (138-39). Reluctantly the Sirian decides that Lucky might not make a very good Sirian after all. The final book of the series ends with a standoff avoiding war and achieving the goal of ejecting the Sirian threat from the Solar System. The enemy is not destroyed, but defused for the time being.

Isaac Asimov also wrote two nonseries science fiction novels for beginning readers. *The Best New Thing* (1971) fits well into Gunn's idea that Asimov might lead young readers into reading more science rather than reading more science fiction. The protagonist is a little girl, Rada, born on Earth but raised in space. Rada must be taught what to expect from Earth before she returns to it. Of course, the reader learns about space by contrast. The story is very simple and straightforward, ending as Rada and her brother, Jonathan, roll down a hill, experiencing Earth's natural gravity for the first time.

The Heavenly Host (1975), though specifically aimed at very young readers, ages seven to ten, is far more complex both conceptually and thematically. The protagonist of *The Heavenly Host* is Jonathan Derodin (*not* the little brother of *The Best New Thing*), born on Ceti Four. At age twelve Jonathan has never seen Earth. He is traveling with his mother to Earth to spend Christmas with his father, a mining engineer, when his mother, a planetary inspector, receives emergency orders to report to a fledgling colony on the planet Anderson Two.

There they find strange beings called Wheels, something between mineral and animal life, which feed directly on the energy of the sunlight (like the aliens in *The Gods Themselves*). Jonathan discovers that they communicate by flashing colors. Councilman Caradoc, one of the leaders of the settlers, believes in shooting first and asking questions later. He tries to coerce Inspector Derodin to rule that there is no intelligent native life form on the planet, so it can be fully exploited as a human settlement with millions of people.

Communicating telepathically with a young Wheel, Yellger, Jonathan learns that this year the Wheels will celebrate Wing-Day on Christmas, and all the young

Wheels will fly together. In return, Jonathan explains as much as he can about Christmas. The alien perspective of Pink, Yellger's mother, is particularly effective in creating sympathetic aliens and highly reminiscent of the alien perspectives in the second part of *The Gods Themselves*. The implicit theme of tolerance is clear.

In vain, Jonathan tries to persuade his mother that the Wheels are indeed intelligent, but she is pressured by Caradoc to sign the documents authorizing the colonization of Anderson Two. Just as she is about to yield, the young Wheels fly overhead and form a Star of Bethlehem. (The Wheels are illustrated to look like a cross between an angel and a dove.) The book ends in the spirit of Christmas: "In the universe, peace, good will toward all intelligent beings" (80).

The Asimovs: Man and Woman Thinking (and Feeling) Together

In later fiction for young readers, written with his wife, Dr. Janet Jeppson (Asimov), similar themes are expanded and made more complex. Sometimes the lessons are still explicit, as when a character opines that "absolute certainty is not compatible with high intelligence" (*Norby and the Lost Princess* 88); other times the reader is expected to observe and make inferences (for example, that female chauvinism is just as silly as male chauvinism), and moral precepts are dramatized (for example, the principle that people can "reform" as they mature is made evident by showing people actually doing so).

The Norby books continue much of Asimov's moral, political, and social themes, but Asimov brought the benefit of thirty-some more years of writing experience and his wife, Janet Jeppson, brought her perspective as a woman and as a psychoanalyst. The result is interesting both stylistically and philosophically. Asked about how much each contributed to the collaboration, Asimov and Jeppson agreed that Norby was her original idea, but he did far more actual writing and revising in the first three books than in the later ones, for which he became a sort of supereditor for her completed manuscripts.

The first of the series, *Norby, the Mixed-Up Robot* (1983), introduces the main characters. The protagonist is fourteen-year-old Space Cadet Jeff Wells. Jeff is a lanky teenager who has trouble with his studies but great ambitions to serve the Federation Space Command. Like Lucky Starr, Jeff is an orphan, but unlike Lucky, he suffers throughout the series from the lack of a father to guide him, a problem shared by many young people in the 1980s and 1990s.

Instead of a flat, predictable character like Bigman to accompany him, Jeff acquires Norby, a robot built by a nonhuman species, the Others. After Norby crashed in the Solar System, he was repaired (by a now dead spacer, Moses McGillicuddy) with parts of human manufacture, making him truly mixed up. Ironically, this complexity allows the robot to behave more "humanly," that is, less predictably, than Bigman did.

Young readers are sure to delight in the way Norby and Jeff outwit the shopkeeper who would obviously try to swindle Jeff because of his youth if he could get away with such tactics. Norby retains some of the Three Laws, especially the first and second; he is made so he cannot lie or cause harm to organic life. However, he doesn't obey anyone but Jeff, and then only because of their special relationship of mutual respect and affection. He has feelings that can be hurt, and he develops genuine loyalty and friendship for Jeff, not just a programmed devotion. He also has special talents, like antigravity, which came from the technology of the Others and over which he does not have perfect control, having been imperfectly repaired.

The reciprocity of all relationships is emphasized when Jeff and Norby celebrate the solstice and affirm their oneness with the universe, a ritual frequently repeated throughout the series. Norby says, "What's more, the universe is at one with me." Jeff responds, "I think it's more fitting for you to be at one with the universe." However, Norby wisely insists, "I think it would be nice to consider the universe's feelings, too, Jeff. I think the universe would be pleased to be at one with me," Jeff concedes, "Well . . . maybe" (57). Norby surprises Jeff by talking of beauty and explains: "The trouble with you protein creatures is that you think you invented beauty. . . . I can appreciate anything you can appreciate, and I can do anything you can do. I'm strong and I'm super-brave, and I'm a good companion in adventure. Let's have adventures, and I'll show you. Then you'll be glad you have me" (42).

One of their adventures takes them through hyperspace via another talent Norby really can't control perfectly. They travel to Jamya, a planet circling a far distant star, and meet a race of small, civilized (all female) dragons who share the gift of telepathy with Norby and Jeff. In due time it is revealed that the dragons have been bioengineered by the mysterious Others, who left a type of robot called Mentors to assist the dragons; these Mentors had originally created Norby and sent him across space searching for the Others.

Jeff's (ten years older) brother, Farley Gordon Wells, known familiarly as Fargo, tall, dark, handsome and irresistible to women, is his only surviving family. During the story the brothers meet Albany Jones, policewoman and daughter of the mayor of New York City (which has become politically independent from the United States); Albany later will become Fargo's fiancee.

Another major character in Jeff's life is Admiral Yobo, head of the Space Command, a gourmand and native of Mars (of African heritage) who thinks the only civilized tongue is Martian Swahili. It is Jeff's difficulty in learning Swahili that inspires Yobo to give Jeff just enough funds to buy an economical used teaching robot. When Yobo learns of some of Norby's gifts, he agrees that Jeff has struck a good bargain.

Two other significant characters are introduced in the first book. The principal antagonist in the story is Ing the Ingrate, who is power-mad and wants to destroy the Space Command and become emperor of the Solar System. In Central Park, Norby and Jeff also meet Miss Higgins, an umbrella-brandishing birdwatcher in the tradition of Mary Poppins, who helps keep the park safe for people.

When the revolution of Ing is over, Admiral Yobo says, "The men of the Manhattan police force have done nobly." Albany explicitly reminds him that half the police force are women, and he acknowledges, "So are half of the soldiers in my Space Command" (93).

Norby, the Mixed Up Robot was packaged with *Norby's Other Secret* when the two original novels were reissued by Ace in 1986 (under the title *The Norby Chronicles*), and in some ways they do seem to be a single long story. This second book begins with Admiral Yobo's warning Jeff that the Inventor's Union may be coming to kidnap Norby to take him apart and discover the secret of his miniaturized antigravity capacities. Actually, Yobo feels considerable ambivalence, since he wants to find out Norby's secrets himself. He says, "If we can find out how he works, everyone will want a Norby instead of the stupid, dutiful machines the Federation allows" (17). Norby shows up with a lion whose origins cannot be accounted for, but before this mystery can be solved, Jeff and Norby flee through hyperspace and find themselves once again in Jamya.

The dragons tell Jeff about the Mentors, robots given to the Jamyns by the Others. The Jamyns recognize that Norby is different from the robots they know, and Jeff explains that they are not owner and possession, but partners. They discover something that looks like a hassock that the dragons have regarded as a tail rest but turns out to hold a green fuzzy All-Purpose Pet named Oola, capable of taking on the shape of her owner's favorite type of animal.

They have several adventures through time (time travel turns out to be Norby's other secret, explaining the lion brought from the gladiatorial pits of Christian martyrs) and have conflicts with the master of Jamyn robots, Mentor First, all of which are resolved when the Mentor robot's sanity is restored by its being reunited with its pet, Oola, and Norby acts as a conduit to the energy of hyperspace to recharge Mentor First. Yobo continues to covet Norby for his own scientific research till he gets a first-hand demonstration of Norby's unreliable talents for time travel and finally concludes that Norby is too dangerous to meddle with. Fargo, having charmed the Grand Dragon, returns from Jamya with another hassock egg that will produce Oola Two, Jeff's very own All-Purpose Pet.

Norby and the Lost Princess (1985) begins with Jeff and Fargo practicing for a singing contest, while Admiral Yobo worries about some humans who may have been abducted from Earth during the Ice Age. He has inferred that the Others must have come to Earth at least once to obtain the genetic material from which they bioengineered Oola, who seems to be related to cave bears or saber-toothed tigers, though her species is now strictly vegetarian.

Leaving the young dragon Zargl (heir apparent to the throne of Jamya) to babysit with Oola, Jeff, Fargo, Albany, and Yobo set off in the Wells' family spaceship, the *Hopeful*, now powered by Norby's hyperdrive, to find the planet Izz, where the lost humans have been taken. There they meet Queen Tizz and her consort King Fizzwell and discover the planet is undemocratically ruled by a hereditary monarchy and is thoroughly female chauvinist, a satiric mirror of Earth at its worst. The royal couple enlists the aid of Jeff, Fargo, Albany, Yobo, and

Norby to search for their spoiled ten-year-old daughter, Princess Rinda, who has been stranded on the planet Melodia.

The rescue party takes Einkan, chief scientist of Izz, with them to hunt for the lost princess. Einkan is suspicious of the Earthlings' motives, imagining they have come to conquer. Yobo assures him, "We would not dream of taking your world, . . . We wouldn't want to upset the economy of your world. That would be against our ethical principles" (45). Einkan, however, cannot rise above petty motivations. He acts obstructively through most of their efforts to recover the princess, who is being held captive by some repulsive creatures the Terrans call Slithers. The Slithers, sensitive to music, have absorbed Rinda into a tree and are holding all the humans captive.

After suffering captivity and humiliation, Rinda expresses to Jeff her desire to become a better person: "I've been selfish and willful all my life, and now I want to try to be more like you" (103). The theme of learning to be a better person through adversity is echoed in Einkan, the scientist largely responsible for all the trouble, who also claims to have reformed: "I've fallen in love and have changed—I am now thoroughly honest and reliable. . . . I am going to be a genuine, hard-working scientist" (120).

In the course of their travels through time and space, Jeff and Norby discover a female robot named Pera (short for Perceiver, "I watch and record and wait" [80]), which Jeff leaves with Rinda, admonishing her to treat Pera as an equal, since Pera thinks for herself. The story ends with Rinda's assurances to Jeff that she will treat Pera well and that she has learned from Jeff's example of courage and selflessness. She adds that she hopes he will wait for her to grow up before he marries.

Jeff and Norby meet additional alien creatures in *Norby and the Invaders* (1985), which was packaged with *Norby and the Lost Princess* by Ace in 1987 under the title *Norby: Robot for Hire*. The implicit theme of this book is that aliens may be good or bad and that one should reserve judgment till the facts are clear. Till adequate evidence is apparent, it is best to assume neither malice or benevolence.

As the story opens, Jeff, Norby, and Oola transport directly through hyperspace to Jamya in response to a call for help from Norby's "father," Mentor First. There they find both the dragons and their mentor robots incapacitated by Invaders who have even taken away the dragons' mini-antigrav collars and kidnapped the Grand Dragon. Jeff and company are in turn captured and transported to the home planet of the tentacled, oceanic Invaders, where Norby is encapsulated and separated from Jeff and Oola. To calm his fears, Jeff recites a version of his solstice litany:

I am a Terran creature, part of the life that has evolved on Earth. I am far away from home, but I am still part of the Universe, part of its life. Everything is part of the Universe, no matter how strange or dangerous it may seem at some time. I will try to let go of my fear so that I can decide what to do. (22)

He discovers that the Grand Dragon has been caged like a zoo animal for the Hlenos and is guarded by a meditative sentient plant, called Dookaza, who turns out to be somewhat lonely. When the Hleno come to inspect the Grand Dragon, they make sounds that she interprets as mockery. "Jeff wanted the poor dragon to retain her self-respect, but privately he hoped they *were* laughing. Any species of intelligent creature, however unreasonable and dangerous, is bound to seem less frightening if it displays a sense of humor. Laughter can be cruel, of course, but surely for the most part it implies tolerance" (52). As in all of the Norby books, there is plenty of adventure and action, during which Jeff and Norby meet one of the natives, a child named Uhfy, face dangers, and survive by their wits.

As they are negotiating their freedom, Jeff learns that the Nuhlenonians had taken an ancient vow against the use of technology. Jeff tells them that technology is "that which gives you spare time for thought and culture, without which intelligent life is not worth living. It is not technology itself that is harmful, but the unwise use of it" (117).

Still, the Hleno are unwilling to release the hostage robots until Oola gives them one of her eggs, which hatches into a water creature, the perfect pet for Uhfy, and the Jamyn dragons bestow the gift of telepathy on the Nuhlenony. They leave the aliens with the task of restoring enough technology to repair their life support systems and then detour on their return through New York's Central Park in the late twentieth century, observing how dirty it is. The indirect lesson for the twentieth-century reader is underscored: Even a badly damaged infrastructure *can* be restored.

Based on an actual eighteenth century event, the next book in the series, *Norby and the Queen's Necklace* (1986), is largely a detective-mystery pure-action story on its surface level, with bits of history for spice, and Jeff finally gets to meet one of the mysterious Others. Yet even here, strong elements of Asimovian philosophy are implanted in the action. Jeff observes, "Scientists say that magic is a name we use for something we don't understand" (14), a sentiment echoed later in the story by none other than Benjamin Franklin.

The necklace of the title is a copy of a relic at the heart of the French revolution, made for Marie Antoinette, which turns out to be a time travel device. Through their adventures, the protagonist group learns how changing events in the past can affect the future, a cautionary message to be sure, but also an implicitly optimistic one in that the reader can infer that even small actions by ordinary people do and will matter. This causality of human actions implies a strong moral responsibility toward improvement of the present world.

As in other stories in this series, "throwaway" lines contrast our present with the past and the future. For example, Jeff meets with scornful derision in late eighteenth century France when he threatens the wrath of America if he is not treated better—"That new country you claim as your own is very small and weak, and in no condition to take offense at anything a great power like France might want to do to foreign spies" (20)—and in our future of Earth (in Jeff's "present") women perform jobs that are largely dominated by men in the late twentieth century; for example the Holovision director is a female.

The novel encompasses cautious optimism once again in a recurring cautionary theme in all of the Asimovs' work, the importance of the search for truth: "When everyone believes a lie, it might as well be the truth" (41), balanced by Jeff's youthful optimism when prospects look darkest: "I'm never going to give up. I'm going to act as though there's hope, because if I don't then I may miss some opportunity for finding a solution" (125).

In *Norby Finds a Villain* (1987), the sixth in the series, Rinda returns with her robot Pera, and they and Jeff become involved with Ing the Ingrate again (disguised as the clown Threezy), who inadvertently creates an alternate time line by trying to destroy the universe he cannot control. They meet yet another intelligent (female) computer called Yib (You Immense Brain), controller of the ship of an Other, whom Jeff calls Rembrandt, because the Other is also a renowned artist. Far in the future of the alternate time line, they encounter villains worse than Ing, invaders from an alternate universe who call themselves the Masters. Norby refuses to give them that title and dubs them Biguglies.

By now Jeff is fifteen and Rinda is eleven, and they are both beginning to grow up and face reality and their own mortality. Stranded in the alternate universe with little hope of rescue and feeling powerless to save themselves, Rinda tells Jeff, "I wish I were home with my parents, who are difficult but not impossible and they love me" (69). A little later she tells Jeff:

I may be just a spoiled little princess, but I'm intelligent and I can face dying. I think. Would it be all right if we took a nap on the same bed? . . . I wish we could be lovers. Couldn't we, even now? (76)

Rebuffed by Jeff, Rinda concedes, "We're too tired and besides, Mother would boil you in plurf" (76-77). Jeppson reports that this passage brought complaints from some librarians who reviewed the book prior to publication, but she stood her ground, based on her knowledge of child psychology and the development of human sexuality. The passage is certainly no more explicit than the sexuality of *The Gods Themselves* , but it seems to be a breakthrough in a book directly aimed at a juvenile readership.

Jeff and Rinda discover that there are two kinds of alien Biguglies, the M.C.s (standing *not* for male chauvinists, but for the Master Cult) and a more peaceful tribe, represented by the female Blif, who regard themselves as underground pirates. Rembrandt reveals that he and Blif share a similar social history, "including a period of tyranny that was eventually overthrown by an underground that called themselves pirates. Tyranny is always possible when an intelligent species becomes too populous and too powerful before it becomes wise." He advises, "improvement is always possible. . . . Never become self-satisfied. . . . Nothing is invulnerable. There's always change." When Jeff expresses doubts about humanity's ability to cope with change, Rembrandt tells him, "Don't cope. Move with change and enjoy the ride" (96).

In the alternate universe the brain injuries that cause Ing to be antisocial are cured, partly by intelligent trees called Twintas and partly by the affection of Oola, who turns herself into his ideal pet. With his restored self-esteem, Ing decides to resume his identity as the clown Threezy, giving pleasure to others. With the assistance of the Twintas, Blif and her species are persuaded to help Jeff's group to return to their own universe. As payment for their help, Norby and Threezy entertain the Twintas, making them laugh. As they laugh, the trees gain power, so they are even stronger after helping the group return than they were before. Though implicit, the message of altruism as its own reward is clear.

As the title suggests, *Norby Down to Earth* (1989), the seventh book in the series, takes place mostly in New York, and its theme focuses on ecological conservation. The book is dedicated "To Planet Earth—First and, so far, only home. May we humans take better care of her."

The bird-watcher Hedy Higgins returns and is found to be the long-lost sweetheart of Albany Jones's father, Mayor Leo Jones, and the love story of the middle-aged pair is a backdrop for the action. Hedy also turns out to be the granddaughter of Moses MacGillicuddy, the inventor-spacer who discovered and repaired Norby. Hedy has a brother with a mild learning disability, Horace, and their mother is a former star of the screen, Merlina Mynn, who dislikes all robots, due to jealousy of her father's interest in them. Merlina turns out to be the one who is menacing Central Park in her personal taxi, Lizzie, another robot brain altered by MacGillicuddy. (A romance between Lizzie and Mentor First is also hinted at.)

The instrument of terrorism, which seems to be a sort of gun, is finally revealed to be an aid to artistic expression, which, in the right hands, can be a powerful tool for good. Merlina is finally convinced that her father did love her when she sees holograms made by Norby and Jeff when they time traveled and learned that MacGillicuddy's motivation for going into space was to support his beloved daughter.

Rembrandt returns to comment on the value of art. He says, "You humans live for a short time compared to us, yet all biological lives are ultimately brief in a huge universe." Jeff asks, "Do you think that even the briefest life can contribute something to the development of the universe?" Rembrandt replies: "That is why I am an artist" (89).

Norby and Yobo's Great Adventure (1989) tackles some of the contemporary issues of the day, such as feminist independence and children's need for parenting, as well as further exploring the place of art in human culture. Yobo enlists Jeff and Norby to help him travel into the past to take holophotographs of an elephant while it is still alive and bearing the tusks that will be carved into an ivory family heirloom of the Yobo family. Before they leave for the past, they visit Mars to pick up the artifact and are served high tea by Yobo's snobby older sister, Eevee (Elizabeth Victoria). Yobo advises Jeff to address her as Mrs. Yobo "since she married a distant cousin of ours and didn't have to change her last name, not that women do these days anyway" (9). The prime minister of the Federation, Wenoa Grachev, is described by Eevee as "simply a mongrel . . . mostly old-time Russian, mixed with Welsh and Spanish and of course that Native American grandmother after whom she's named" (11). Wenoa and Boris Yobo were at one time sweethearts, but she married a man of Scandinavian ancestry and produced a pale blond daughter, Natasha Bergaard, who is sent to play with Eevee's grandson, Martin (named for Martin Luther King) Chen. Eevee's claims of and desire for pure African heritage are set against a background of Mars as a true melting pot of all of Earth's peoples. Boris Yobo is clearly uncomfortable around his sister and former girlfriend and is glad to flee to hyperspace with the ivory artifact, which Wenoa also claims as her family's heritage.

In hyperspace they meet Rembrandt again and *his* sister, whom Yobo names for the goddess Euterpe, "she who gladdens" (30). Euterpe, a fine musician, asks Jeff and Yobo to record some of Earth's music from the past for her. Homing in on the vibrations of the relic, they land in what they at first take to be prehistoric Africa, but which turns out to be northern Europe. They encounter still another powerful female, the chief of a tribe, who carves the original ivory. A series of time paradoxes and other adventures reveals the truth about Wenoa's and Eevee's claims to the family heirloom: It is carved from a fragment of tusk of a woolly mammoth, not an elephant, and both families are descended from a common ancestor, which belies Eevee's belief in her "pure" African heritage. Jeff is wounded, and Yobo acts as his champion in battle; Jeff looks on Yobo as the closest thing he has had to a father since he was orphaned at age ten.

Upon their return to the Others' spaceship, Norby attempts to sing (off-key) for Euterpe, which she can hardly bear to hear. They discuss music as another form of artistic communication and Euterpe says, "Perhaps each of us contributes a piece of the understanding.... Perhaps each life is part of the music of reality that we all share" (90-91). Yobo is totally smitten with Euterpe and speculates about the possibility that he and she could one day mate and produce a child: "For all we know these Others can juggle DNA around to make it possible for two completely different species to—" (91). As it turns out when they return to Mars, the union of the two human Martian families is confirmed by a marriage license, and both branches are entitled to the ivory carving. The children, Natasha and Martin, return from playing in the garden to announce their intention of marrying when they grow up. Jeff concludes, "It's good to know that if you go back far enough, we're all related. . . . All humanity is one" (99).

Norby and the Oldest Dragon (1990) treats the problems of both the young and the old. The story opens with an invitation to Jamya to celebrate the Grand Dragon's birthday. Admiral Yobo cannot attend due to a previous engagement, and Jeff does not want to go with Fargo and Albany because he feels that the only reason he and Norby were invited was that they are needed to travel through hyperspace. He frets because he is being treated like a kid, but Norby points out that despite his being nearly six feet tall, Jeff often acts like a kid. For example, he forgot to get a present for the Grand Dragon's party, and he spitefully ignores Norby's packing suggestions.

Arriving in Jamya, Norby goes off to help Mentor First set up a holovision broadcast station, and the group finds that the Grand Dragon's fondest wish is to have her grandmother, the Dowager Grand Dragon, attend her party. The Dowager, however, has gone into seclusion, meditating for the last fifty years, and has no wish to return to civilization before she dies. Norby and Jeff seek her out and are trying to persuade her to return with them when Jamya is enveloped by a cloud, an organic intelligence with great powers and the ability to destroy all life on Jamya. This cloud has been drawn to Jamya by the holovision broadcasts, a seemingly innocent technology—again the implicit message of caution about "progress."

Finally convinced that she is needed, the Dowager and Jeff try to cope with the cloud. Fargo tries to help, but he is captured by the cloud. After much negotiation, the cloud, now named Monos, agrees to accept the Dowager in exchange for Fargo. Monos will now know death when the dragon dies, even though Monos will live till the end of the universe. Monos even has the hope that by then it will have learned how to survive the end of the universe and perhaps take other life forms with it into the new universe.

Although all of the humans and dragons think Monos's goal is naive, they, too, have hope that with all the time till the end of this universe to work in, Monos may discover a way none of them can now imagine. The Dowager says of Monos: "he's not so bad, after all. Just a youngster who needs an older person around for a while. . . . It doesn't matter if individuals are mortal as long as knowledge is passed on" (101). Throughout, the Norby series embraces the values implicit in Isaac Asimov's earlier juveniles, indeed in all his science fiction.

Jeppson also has written a nonseries science fiction novel for youngsters, *The Package in Hyperspace* (1988). In it she uses the Three Laws of Robotics as well as the concepts of hyperspace and miniantigrav as developed in the Norby series. The story centers on two orphans, Ginnela Wayd, the twelve-year-old protagonist, and her nine-year-old brother, Petevus, who get stranded in hyperspace when their pet alien loffo runs away as they are set to evacuate their spaceship after a collision with an "unmanned" alien craft. The loffo (Lof) is pink and reliant on sulfur for survival but otherwise very much like the all-purpose pet of the Norby series. The children gradually grow as they take care of themselves and of their pet, making mistakes, but helping each other overcome their limitations.

As they strive to find a way back to normal space, Pete and Ginn take turns being discouraged and cheering up one another. They finally learn to communicate with the alien ship through its computer and a toy package that responds to music, the universal communication.

Certainly Asimov had considerable impact on Jeppson's writing career. In the Norby stories, their talents and visions merge to produce stories that embody many of Isaac's lifelong concerns for rational thought and tolerance as instruments to promote the social improvement of humanity. Janet developed these themes and added much hope for human salvation through beauty (particularly art and music), humor, friendship, and love. Although it is outside the scope of this chapter, the next study of Isaac's work might do well to study *her* influence on *his* later adult fiction.

On the morning of 6 April 1992, Isaac Asimov died of heart failure and other complications. Illness *did* slow him down toward the end, but he continued some writing almost up to the last minute, and several works are still to be published. He left behind a legacy of nearly 500 books, the overwhelming majority of which were nonfiction. Long after his writing on popular science is out-of-date, however, his fiction—both for adults and for juveniles—will continue to be read for the visions he offered of the human condition.

BIBLIOGRAPHY

Asimov, Isaac. *The Best New Thing.* Illustr. Symeon Shimin. New York: World Publishing, 1971.

_____. *The Heavenly Host.* Illustr. Bernard Colonna. New York: Walker, 1975.

_____. *Pebble in the Sky.* New York: Doubleday, 1950.

_____. *Robot Visions.* New York: Penguin (Roc), 1990.

Asimov, Janet. *The Package in Hyperspace.* New York: Walker, 1988.

Fiedler, Jean and Jim Mele. *Isaac Asimov.* New York: Frederick Ungar, 1982.

Gunn, James. *Issac Asimov and the Foundations of Science.* New York: Oxford UP, 1982.

Hassler, Donald M. *Issac Asimov.* San Bernardino: Borgo, 1991.

Patrouch, Joseph F., Jr. *The Science Fiction of Isaac Asimov.* Garden City, NY: Doubleday, 1974.

Pierce, Hazel. "Elementary My Dear. . ." *Isaac Asimov's Science Fiction Mysteries.* Ed. Martin Harry Greenberg and Joseph D. Olander. New York: Taplinger, 1988.

Touponce, William F. *Isaac Asimov.* TUSAS 578. Boston: Twayne, 1991 .

The Lucky Starr Series

Asimov, Isaac. *David Starr: Space Ranger.* New York: Doubleday, 1952. New York: Gregg, 1978.

_____. *Lucky Starr and the Pirates of the Asteroids.* New York: Doubleday, 1953. New York: Gregg, 1978.

_____. *Lucky Starr and the Oceans of Venus.* New York: Doubleday, 1954. New York: Gregg, 1978.

_____. *Lucky Starr and the Big Sun of Mercury.* New York: Doubleday, 1956. New York: Gregg, 1978;

_____. *Lucky Starr and the Moons of Jupiter.* New York: Doubleday, 1957. New York: Gregg, 1978.

_____. *Lucky Starr and the Rings of Saturn.* New York: Doubleday, 1958. New York: Gregg, 1978.

The Norby Series

Asimov, Janet, and Isaac Asimov. *Norby the Mixed-Up Robot*. New York: Walker, 1983.
_____. *Norby's Other Secret*. New York: Walker, 1984.
_____. *Norby and the Invaders*. New York: Walker, 1985.
_____. *Norby and the Lost Princess*. New York: Walker, 1985.
_____. *Norby and the Queen's Necklace*. New York: Walker, 1986.
_____. *Norby Finds a Villain*. New York: Walker, 1987.
_____. *Norby Down to Earth*. New York: Walker, 1989.
_____. *Norby and Yobo's Great Adventure*. New York: Walker, 1989.
_____. *Norby and the Oldest Dragon*. New York: Walker, 1990

5

The "Terrible Journey" Past "Dragons in the Waters" to a "House Like a Lotus": Faces of Love in the Fiction of Madeleine L'Engle

M. Sarah Smedman

A prolific and award-winning author of more than forty books, the contemporary writer Madeleine L'Engle, although perhaps best known for her children's books, the Newbery Medal-winning *A Wrinkle in Time* (1963), with its sequels, and the Newbery Honor novel *A Ring of Endless Light* (1980), conceives of all her writings as of a piece. For that reason, she plans to leave her manuscripts to a library interested not only in her fantastic fiction but also in her realistic fiction, not only in her literature for children but in her poetry, fiction, and journals for adults, as well.[1] Certainly, her conception of the wholeness of her work is supported by the repeated recurrence of basic themes, themes so intertwined that any attempt to separate one from the other is like separating an egg yolk from the white, tricky and reductive. However, the unifying, enveloping theme, the eggshell so to speak, comprises answers to the questions L'Engle probes in work after work: What is love? What is its nature? How does one love? In a world whose social values are influenced—if not determined— by the mass media and Madison Avenue, which glibly portray love as a "warm, fuzzy feeling," as sentimental, cheap, instant, and as easily accessible and palatable as most fast foods, L'Engle's fiction answers those questions with a reaffirmation of the traditional Christian doctrine of love as an unselfish act of the will requiring difficult and lasting commitment. However, L'Engle's understanding of that doctrine is radical enough often to be original, even iconoclastic.

A constant preoccupation in L'Engle's writings is with the nature of human love because, as Father Duarte says in her adult novel *The Love Letters* :

It is not so extraordinary . . . that we seek to understand divine love in terms of human love. It is our only means of understanding it because we are human. It is never God but only we who make a travesty of human love. (141)

L'Engle's exploration of the nature, manifestations, and effects of human love pervades all her fiction (as well as her journals and poetry) from *The Small Rain* (1945) to *An Acceptable Time* (1989). Her best-known work, her first book for children and her first science fantasy, *A Wrinkle in Time* (1962), is a milestone in fiction for young readers not only because of its nontraditional female hero but also for its blend of science and mythology, fantasy and realism, philosophy and radical theology. The book can, nonetheless, be most richly comprehended in the context not only of the trilogy that it initiates but of the author's complete works. At the core of *A Wrinkle in Time* are thematic motifs that resonate backward to the author's earlier realistic novels for older readers and forward to all her subsequent poetry and fiction: motifs of the nature of good and evil and the arduous combat they inspire; of the human freedom essential for the knowledgeable choice between good and evil; of the responsibility entailed by such freedom; of the moral fiber required to commit to one's choices—all strands woven together in the exigency of collaboration of head and heart to fathom the meaning of love and to live lovingly. Aspects of relevant themes embodied in *A Wrinkle in Time* are implied, reiterated, embellished, and extended throughout the L'Engle canon, even as its characters or their descendants reappear and mingle with characters and their relatives from other of her works.

Painfully tesseracting to Camasotz, Meg Murray moves toward maturity, first, by realizing that her father cannot always resolve her every problem and, then, by freely choosing responsible action to save others as well as herself. Meg discovers that the most heinous of evils is pure intelligence, IT, a brain severed from human emotion and compassion that, because it mistakes equality for sameness, renders individuality impossible. Using the gifts given her by the supernatural Mrs. Ws, Meg discovers the courage to act on her own, as well as that something within herself that IT lacks. Through love, Meg can overpower IT, as Charles Wallace, whose *hubris* feeds upon his intelligence, cannot. Although Meg is unable to find within herself the grace to love IT, she can love her brother, and that love enables her to wrestle Charles Wallace from IT's grasp. Keeping her wits about her, wrapping her father and Charles Wallace in forgiveness and love, Meg brings everyone home, successfully completing her quest.

Themes sounded in *A Wrinkle in Time* are extended in the later books. In the second book of the trilogy, *A Wind in the Door* (1973), a less credible book than *Wrinkle* because it leans more toward allegory than toward novel, Meg must include the stereotypical pedantic principal, Mr. Jenkins, within the province of her love, and good ultimately prevails only through the sacrificial "death" of the cherubim, Proginoskes. In the third book, *A Swiftly Tilting Planet* (1978), more universal in time and place than its predecessors, the most difficult choices are made by Mrs. O'Keefe, the mother of Meg Murray's by-now husband, Calvin. A crabbed woman who had long repressed her feelings as protection against suffering the loss of anyone she might love, Mrs. O'Keefe finally enters her painful past to discover the link that insures the triumph of benevolence over tyranny in the course of history.

Subsequent L'Engle works replay these themes with variation. In general, they depict love as concomitant to difficult choices, neither easy nor consolatory, and possible only when head and heart work together. *The Love Letters* and *Dragons in the Waters* develop the disillusionment Meg experienced at her father's inability to make everything right through express articulation of, as L'Engle would say, the dangers of making idols of one's points of reference. *Dragons in the Waters* and *The Other Side of the Sun* make explicit the danger and debilitation consequent upon retreating from suffering into withdrawl from life. *A House Like a Lotus* focuses on forgiveness nurtured by empathy and compassion.

In all of L'Engle's stories, as in *A Wrinkle in Time,* characters take long journeys. The geographic journeys parallel the characters' voyages of self-discovery, of the growth in maturity that results from their looking straightfor-wardly at evil and death and seeing therein love. In fiction after fiction L'Engle posits that the object of life's quest—Love—is to be found only on "the other side of the sun" and that the narrow way leads past "dragons in the waters," through—not around—searing pain and terror. Those innocents who are unaware of the reality and power of evil and those fainthearted who flinch before the awesome-ness of love will experience neither its beauty nor its joy: "The truth of love can sometimes be irrational, absurd, and yet it is what makes us grow to maturity, opens us to joy" (*The Summer of the Great-Grandmother* 181).

The attempt of L'Engle's characters to comprehend love seems to derive from the seventy-four-year-old author's firm but ambivalent commitments to marriage, the family, and friendship and from her life-long search for faith in a provident God who cares for individuals. When after a period of atheism Madeleine L'Engle embraced Christianity, she explained: "Conversion for me was not a Damascus Road experience. I slowly moved into an intellectual acceptance of what my intuition had always known" (qouted in Forbes, "Allegorical Fantasy" 15). Nonetheless, L'Engle has never stopped asking hard cosmic questions about the reconciliation of evil with love, of death with a beneficent eternal God. L'Engle's resilient faith has not vanquished a concomitant doubt.

Although themes of love sound and resound throughout L'Engle's lengthy canon, each work focuses on a distinct though not a disparate aspect of her subject; frequently one novel minutely maps a province entered in a previous work or examines the same territory from a different perspective. Music provides an appropriate figure for the way in which L'Engle's works interplay. The author, like many of her characters, is an accomplished musician who often expresses her love of Bach, whose "world" she has described as

crystal-clear, and yet it is not bathed in the white light of intellectual certainty. It has more to do with the underwater world, the world in which I meet the characters and people of my stories, the world in which I understand the language of the C minor Fugue. (*The Summer of the Great-Grandmother* 70)

The fugue, a polyphonic form in which a theme is stated sequentially, then imitated and developed contrapuntally, is an apt metaphor for the intricate, often improbable, plots and the complex connections among the larger-than-life characters that compose L'Engle's stories. The fugue is an equally appropriate metaphor for the ways in which novel builds upon novel.

To see how L'Engle states and develops themes of love in her work, let us examine selected fictions representative of the various types she has written. Although L'Engle disapproves of classification of her stories and it is impossible to categorize her fiction definitively, some novels are more clearly for children than for adults; some works for children are more clearly fantastic than realistic; some for adults, more clearly historical romance than realism. Here, after laying a thematic foundation through discussion of two early works, *The Small Rain* (1945) and *Camilla* (1951), first published for adults and in 1965 republished for the more lately discovered young adult market, I will focus on two novels and a fantasy-romance for young readers—*The Moon by Night, A House Like a Lotus,* and *Dragons in the Waters* —and a contemporary and an historical novel for adults—*The Love Letters* and *The Other Side of the Sun* —in the order of their publication over a forty-year period, the sequence that best demonstrates their fuguelike interaction and reaction. Because *A Wrinkle in Time* and *A Ring of Endless Light* have been discussed in other contexts elsewhere, I will only make relevant allusions to those works, whose heroes triumph because, respectively, Meg Murry discovers the power of love over the evil wreaked by unmitigated rationality, and Vicki Austin discovers the necessity of simultaneously accepting the inevitable horror of death and denying its darkness permission to destroy one's love for life.[2]

Generally, L'Engle's treatment of human love is more subtle in her earlier works, the tone more exploratory and tentative; that tone becomes progressively more definitive and didactic. *The Small Rain* is a perceptive, delicate, engrossing story with few of the pedantic conversations of subsequent novels in which characters analyze their experiences and responses. Katherine Forrester, the novel's sensitive, talented protagonist, has to contend not only with the typical adolescent crises of insecurity, loneliness, and self-discovery, but also with the problems contingent upon the children of famous artists. Katherine suffers keenly the pain inflicted through her relationships—those with parents and stepparents, teachers, schoolmates, friends, and lovers. Terrified by the confrontation of her own mortality occasioned by the death of a classmate in a tragic sleepwalking accident, infatuated with her piano teacher, Justin Vigneras, and angry over her parents' insistence that she return with them from Paris to New York, Katherine turns for solace to Charlot, her aunt Manya's ward who has been like a brother to her. After too much wine and the hypnotizing play and pretense of a carnival, Katherine is temporarily confused by Charlot's declaration of love for her and makes love with him. She realizes, however, that physical attraction and comfort alone are not love but lead to self-destruction. She also realizes that when she loosened her hold on resentment, "something that had been stretched to its utmost limit inside her snapped, and something warm spread all through her; . . . she realized that this warm feeling was love" (89). Katherine learns, too, the truth of Justin's words: "As long as things happen to you, you'll be all right," he said.

You're strong enough to take them . . . you'll learn and be all right. Remember that, no matter how dreadful things may seem sometimes. (249)

At the end of the novel Katherine is conscious that while, at eighteen, she still has much to learn about love, she will affirm life, choosing to embrace its vicissitudes rather than hiding from them. She returns to Paris to study again with Justin Vigneras, whom, we learn in *The Severed Wasp,* a novel published thirty-seven years after *The Small Rain,* she does marry.

   Camilla, like *A Wrinkle in Time,* focuses on the need for the mind and heart to work together to plumb the depths of love. Either, by itself, will mistake an illusion for the reality. Camilla learns this through her own experience, conversations with other characters, and eavesdropping on her parents. Although the story is Camilla's, manipulating so complex a theme through the point of view of a teenager becomes difficult, consequently other characters speak the major thematic lines. Camilla's role is to listen with the ears of the heart and to assimilate the lessons to be learned from what others have discerned. Significantly, Camilla's name derives from the Etruscan, designating a noble youth assisting at religious rites.

   The subplot centers on the marital difficulties between Camilla's parents, who epitomize, respectively, intellect and emotions. The craving of her mother, Rose, for affection grows from love made "desperate" by the gulf between her husband's brilliant intellect and her own pedestrian mind, her constant awareness of the fleetingness of time, and her need for constant reassurance that she is loved (214). Her husband, not demonstrative by nature, finds it easier to show affection "when it isn't clamored for" (139). Because it is her mother's lover who explains the root of her parents' discord, Camilla's "mind recorded and then discarded his words":

What Rose needs is warmth and tenderness and affection. Rose must be emotionally protected. . . . Whereas your father . . . is basically a cold man. (87)

Though Camilla's parents love each other, the novel leaves some doubt about whether they can sufficiently reconcile their differences to save their marriage. Caught in her love for both parents, Camilla's heart gradually "began to know what her mind had been telling it every day, that everything was changed, that nothing could ever be the same again" (172). Her awareness implies that she will be both wiser and stronger than her parents.

   The major plot develops Camilla's friendship with Luisa and her love for Luisa's brother, Frank. The fact that their parents, too, are getting a divorce and fighting for the loyalty of their children provides an immediate bond among the three. Ultimately, parental decisions separate Frank and Camilla. He goes to Cincinnati with his father; she is to be sent to boarding school.

Both the novel's plot and subplot illustrate that possessive love is destructive, a point emphasized by Camilla's friend David, dying from a war injury. Like Camilla's, his mother loves obsessively: "Wants to protect me. Can't get it through her head the last thing I want is protection" (270). It is David, too, who articulates Camilla's feeling that her first love will be permanent, although she may never again see its object:

It's when someone you've loved tries to make the beautiful thing there's been between you into nothing, tries to deny it, that you lose it. You and Frank always possess what you've had together even if you never meet again. (272)

Angry at her mother's trivialization of her feelings because she is young, Camilla at last realizes that Frank does not say good-bye because he believes his inability to put his feelings into words would diminish his love for her. She knows then that her first love "pulsed and throbbed with living light" like "a single bright star" in the black sky (278), that metaphor being one of L'Engle's most enduring for a love that can be depended upon for its constancy.

The tension in this novel is capsulized by Camilla's astute, if not brilliant, mother: "Sometimes," she tells her daughter, "I think the world would run a lot better if it weren't for love . . . but if it weren't for love I couldn't live. Your father could" (238). What Camilla finally understands is that love is more than embraces and kisses and that while she can live, however sorely, without the gestures, she cannot live without love.

In *The Moon by Night* (1963), the second title in the Austin family series, fourteen-year-old Vicki grapples primarily with two problems endemic to adolescence, her relationship with the opposite sex and her relationship with God. Vicki's adolescent experience with boys parallels her attempt to accomodate her childhood faith to the realities of the world. L'Engle is one of the few contemporary writers for youth who treat in realistic fiction, as well as through symbolic fantasy, the quest for God. For many of her readers, coming to terms with God is as integral a part of growing up as interacting with the opposite sex, both aspects of the human quest to love and be loved. Because the author eschews platitudes, her works are honest, if unconventional and iconoclastic. Readers who acknowledge doubts about God as well as about human beings and recognize that both are centered in the same self avidly read L'Engle's novels as giving back images of their own minds and hearts.

As Vicki Austin, with her family, makes a camping trip across North America, she establishes relationships with her first two boyfriends, very different young men: The self-centered, materialistic, and morose Zachary Grey excites her; the practical, protective, nature-loving Andy Ford makes her feel comfortable. Vicki's turbulent relationship with Zachary, whose name in Hebrew means "God is renowned," and her easy relationship with Andy, whose name derives from the Greek equivalent of *manly*, span from "Z to A" (254), symbolic extremes. Zachary has a diseased heart, is erratic and self-seeking, unlovable. Andy is healthy, reliable, considerate, easy to love. Vicki's family likes Andy, but none of them approves of Zachary. However, Vicki intuitively perceives his hatefulness to be the facade for loneliness and insecurity, symbolized by his physical illness. She is stimulated by the challenge not only of discovering what is good beneath Zach's prickly surface but also of learning to love the unlovable (and by so doing enabling Zachary to live up to his name). The story of Vicki and Zachary is a "Beauty and the Beast" story, one that moves Vicki's ability to love up a step from Meg's in *A Wrinkle in Time*. Meg, incapable of loving the unlovable IT, can yet overpower the disembodied brain by loving her little brother. Vicki, on some level, does love Zachary, but her love alone cannot transform him. He must love himself, too, and will his own transformation.

Zachary broods about the violence and evil in the world and denigrates Vicki's naive faith in God, which occasions her first religious crisis. The catalytic incident in *The Moon by Night* occurs when Zachary takes Vicki to see the play *The Diary of Anne Frank*. Like Vicki, Anne Frank had believed in "the goodness of human beings . . . and that God would preserve her going out and coming in. But he didn't. She died in a concentration camp. Before she had time to live" (159). Confronted by the heinous injustice of the Nazis' massacre of innocents, Vicki doesn't "want God if things like that are His way" (168). In the kind of didactic conversation that becomes prevalent in subsequent L'Engle novels, Uncle Douglas explains to Vicki that *the* mystery *is* that a loving God does *not* vitiate the evil men choose to do. Humans must take care not to cast God in their image. Although Uncle Douglas has decided that "a kind and loving God could never be proved," he believes

there isn't any point to life without him. Without him we're just a skin disease on the face of the earth, and I feel too strongly about the human spirit to be able to settle for that. (170)

Uncle Douglas, whose faith experience mirrors that of the author as expressed in her journals, implies that the human spirit must love in the face of paradox. What he tells Vicki is the same truth that Justin Vigneras speaks to Katherine Forrester: that growing up is never completed and

goes right on being rough for ever. . . . What happens as you keep on growing [to be interpreted as learning to love] is that all of a sudden you realize that it's more exciting and beautiful than scary and awful. (*The Moon by Night* 163)

Not much more subtle in symbolism than in dialogue, *The Moon by Night* employs several obvious symbols, that nonetheless resonate and that form a pattern repeated through L'Engle's works, namely, the moon, stars, and rocks. The title *The Moon by Night* derives from Psalm 121, various verses of which run through the book as a refrain, unifying several of its distinct themes. "The sun shall not smite thee by day," promises the psalm, "Nor the moon by night." And by the end of the novel the light of the moon, that archetypal symbol of the transitoriness of life, which had so often disturbed Vicki on her journey, bathes her in peace. The protagonist's cross-country trip not only integrates the incidents of the plot but coincides with her interior quest. For Vicki, as well as for numerous L'Engle characters and the author herself, the stars, majestic and mysterious, are testaments to the order and beauty of the universe. Because they bespeak the presence of God in the world, they inspire awe and joy. Vicki has always contemplated the stars with greater serenity than she has the moon. Rocks, the symbol of solidity and integrity, also pervade the novel. In a climactic scene, Vicki stays with Zachary when he is trapped by a rockslide until they are rescued, proving herself physically as well as spiritually his ballast. The book begins and ends with Vicki, sitting on a rock in a cove on her grandfather's island, in solitary contemplation of the sea. The Hindus believe an island to be "an area of metaphysical force where the forces of the 'immense illogic' of the ocean are distilled"; Carl Jung interpreted an island "as a refuge from the menacing assault of the 'sea' of the unconscious," or the "synthesis of consciousness and will" (Cirlot 160). Traditionally, an island signifies isolation and death. By the end of her journey, Vicki has lost much of her innocence; through intricate human relationships she has become aware of chaos in the world and the enormity of its problems and has gathered her inner forces to combat their assault. As she herself says:

The last time I'd sat on the rock . . . I'd been full of fear and confusion. . . . all the pieces of the puzzle that made up my picture had been scattered, and now they had come together and I knew who I was. I was myself. (254-55)

Knowing that she is Vicki Austin, however, is but the beginning of the girl's quest. Two subsequent novels continue the story of her growth toward understanding that death and life, suffering and joy, hate and love constitute paradoxical spokes in the wheel of life. In the second novel, *A Ring of Endless Light,* Vicki, divested of self-interest, understands that, difficult as living, loving, always in the presence of death have been, she has been asked to bear no "more than the ordinary burdens of life, the things that come to everybody sooner or later" (316).

L'Engle's adult novel *The Love Letters* (1966) is a reworking of the situation between Camilla's parents, a union between a woman desperately needing overt reassurances of love and an undemonstrative man who finds it easier to show affection when it is not demanded, this time from the point of view, not of a daughter observing her parents, but of two women caught in that situation. The first is Charlotte Napier, a young wife estranged from her husband over the death of their child. When Patrick, unable to share his grief and comfort his wife, blames her as a careless mother, Charlotte runs from home in New York to Violet, her mother-in-law in Portugal, not to seek her counsel but just to gain objectivity from seeing the woman-artist who has become her "point of reference" (168-69). Contrapuntal to Charlotte's story and structurally linked through setting and situation is that of Mariana Alcoforado, the seventeenth-century nun whose extant love letters record her affair with a soldier who then left her in order to marry another woman more befitting his social position. Bach's "Two Part Inventions" is motif and metaphor for the novel, "the theme moving back and forth . . . from the low voice to the high, answering, moving in time, in space" (220-21). *The Love Letters* is a long, leisurely, frank exploration of love between a man and a woman, the most thorough in L'Engle's canon. Lacking the restraint, simplicity, and directness requisite of a juvenile novel, this one is overindulgent and deserves the criticisms it received as "old-fashioned," "sentimental," and conventional." [3] However, the seriousness of the issues it raises and the author's passionate concern for both those issues and her characters prevent the book from being "tedious" or trite.

Charlotte Napier, like all L'Engle's protagonists, intelligent, sensitive, privileged, and lonely, is hurt as a child by those she loves and so begins when she is but a schoolgirl simultaneously asking what love is about and retreating from it. A high school teacher, appropriately a nun, tells her that the Incarnation of Jesus means that people

can only love God through loving people. . . . But we must learn detachment because far too often our love isn't sharing, it's demanding. We don't think nearly as much about giving love as we do about getting. We have to be involved in the people we love, but we have to be detached from our own selfishness. And this hurts. . . . But where did anybody get the idea that it wasn't supposed to hurt. (108)

Charlotte and Mariana, through temporary infidelity to vows both come to consider binding and enduring, learn that love is not a matter of feeling but of commitment. Fidelity to that commitment requires recognition of the personhood of the Other, which means loving people as they are; allowing them to be themselves rather than demanding that they measure up to expectations; giving rather than receiving, but not drowning the Other in one's own love; pardoning even the unpardonable. Commitment to love entails taking risks, becoming vulnerable to failure and suffering.

Both Charlotte and Mariana learn to make commitments with their whole selves to realities they understand much more clearly through their own failures. The young wife and the nun both travel through an "abyss of nothingness" in their respective retreats from suffering to a place where "you go when there are things you can't bear. You go into the abyss so deeply that you barely exist. You go into nonbeing" (255). That kind of denial of life, L'Engle believes, derives from pride and is a greater sin than any infidelity. Mariana emerges from the abyss ready to acknowledge that her lover is right: "Love and marriage have nothing to do with each other. You have duties to God that you can't avoid. I have duties to my king and my country and my family" (251). She is able to "open [her] hands and [her] heart and let [Noel] go" (323), renew her religious vows, and go on to become abbess of her community. Charlotte, in her passage through the abyss, learns that marriage, "a commitment to the impossible," can succeed only if acceptance and endurance of one's mate are stronger than passion. A "marriage that is a marriage has to accept the fusion of the violence of the union of all love's parts" (253, 254). Like Mariana, Charlotte decides that what is required of her is to turn away from herself and back to her spouse. Both the seventeenth-century nun and the contemporary wife, purged through suffering, accept as truth the conception that love is tainted as long as "I care whether or not my love is accepted. Unless I can love without asking anything in return it isn't love" (322).

The Love Letters, which incarnates traditional doctrines in the stories of diverse women centuries and cultures apart, conveys the universality of what L'Engle deems a hard truth. The reader senses that the author, like her characters, can testify to that truth only through disciplined adherence to a structure provided by solemn vows. Theme overpowers character in this novel. Though crafted skillfully, *The Love Letters* is as much dramatized tract as story, and readers not predisposed to believe as L'Engle does may find it unconvincing, though discomfitting.

The Other Side of the Sun, L'Engle's next adult fiction (1971), is a robust historical romance, the mode she first used for the Portuguese nun plot of *The Love Letters* and one appropriate for the theme of the impingement of the past upon the present, with the ineluctable obligation of living family members to carry on the good and make reparation for the wrongs of their forebears. A book about love and hate among social classes and races, *The Other Side of the Sun* is set in South Carolina at Illyria, where three collateral generations of Reniers live during the 1910 San Feliz white-supremacist uprising. Illyria is a beach home, actually owned by Honoria, the African princess bought by a slave trader to be his wife. Though he abused her, he built Illyria as a retreat for her during the Civil War. Honoria allows the Reniers, whom she serves, to live there and, to appease social requirements, to front as its owners. The name Illyria is obviously that of the country in *Twelfth Night,* Shakespeare's play that treats of Plato's threefold division of love: the silly love of the senses; the self-indulgent love of the intellect; and the genuine self-sacrificing love of the understanding, or, as L'Engle conceives it, that love that issues from collaboration of mind and heart.

Nineteen-year-old Stella Renier, the bride of the scion of an old, aristocratic Southern family, moves from London, where her father has just died, to Illyria, the beach home of her new husband's family when he goes off on a secret government mission. Alone, with neither father nor husband to protect her innocence nor guide her initiation, Stella learns about the Reniers and their roles in the American Civil War and in the still-simmering hatred between blacks and whites. The journals of Mado, her husband's grandmother, much as Mariana's letters in *The Love Letters,* serve to link the present with the past. Through Mado's journals, supplemented by stories of Honoria and the old aunts, Stella learns that the Reniers have both protected and exploited blacks. During the war their ancestral estate, Nyssa, was burned because the family not only freed their slaves but educated them as equals. Nyssa is appropriately named for the remote outpost that was the see of the fourth-century bishop Gregory, who fought against Arianism, that heresy that proclaimed Jesus was not God, only human in nature. Deeply affected by the writings of Gregory on the fusion of the human and divine in incarnate Love,[4] L'Engle creates in the Reniers' Nyssa a paradise where races live together in peace as lion and lamb lie down together in the peaceable kingdom on the other side of the sun. However, because real peace obtains only as a result of a "terrible journey" through "love's terrible other side" (238), Nyssa has to burn. It had been established by innocents who had no real knowledge of the depth and force of that evil that turns brother against brother, literally as well as figuratively for, as Stella discovers, the black, British-educated Dr. Ron James, source and target of the current racial tension, is her husband's brother, the son of Theron Renier and Belle Zenumin, a beautiful black "witch," who lives with her people down the river in the bush.

Complicated, with generations of characters and a fairy-tale plot, *The Other Side of the Sun* details Stella's growing awareness that innocence is "inexcusable" and "has no place in this evil world" (80), that those who withdraw from life into Edens of their own creation because they fear the damage they might do are more culpable than those who plunge into life (314). What love requires is that people do what they can to achieve a better world, not that they have to succeed (225, 299). What people must do is to make reparation rather than to seek revenge for wrongs done, to forgive even unforgivable evil, because in this imperfect world, hate will inevitably coexist with love. Love that is able not only to forgive but, paradoxically, to harm the Other for his or her greater good does not come cheaply, a theme emphasized by the oxymorons punctuating Mado's journals: "terrible love," "fiery darkness," victorious loss, time that stands still, life through death (212, 238, 264, 305, 317, 341, pass.).

Listen to Mado's words. Love's terrible other side. Terrible. . . . But you, Mrs. Renier? Do you have any idea of the enormity of the fiery darkness of the sun we have to go through before there can be any other side? . . . We have to go through it alone. (242)

In the bizarre penultimate episode set in the bush country, this novel's "heart of darkness," Stella challenges Belle Zenumin's voodoo and symbolically destroys her own innocent self, then feels as "though her entire body had been healed and cleansed by the fire" (330). Phoenixlike, she rises from the ashes, reborn in a new awareness that in a "strange passive way," by allowing herself to be "acted upon," she was responsible for the eruption of racial hostilities. Stella's struggle with Belle signals the beginning of her own action and strengthens her to weather the open war in which she is caught on her way back to Illyria.

The war on the beach, fueled by selfish intrigues of individual blacks and whites, has been occasioned by Stella's walks and talks on that same beach with her black brother-in-law. When enraged Klansmen, many of whom have been healed by Dr. Ron James, attack Illyria to lynch him, Aunt Olivia, whose memory is scarred by the lynching of Ron's father, shoots and kills Ron. A transformed Stella is, at the end, able to agree with Honoria that Olivia's action is noble, though L'Engle's unconventional ethics will certainly draw fire from some readers.

Honoria explains to Stella:

"Miss Olivia kill herself much more than she ever kill Ronnie. She love him that much, enough to do that and that be a lot of love. . . . Miss Olivia, she the one who took the pain this time. We got a grief we can bear, Miss Stella, because Miss Olivia loved." (337)

In this most overtly Jungian of L'Engle's stories, Stella (star), traveling back and forth down the river from ocean to jungle, faces the shadow of her innocence and accepts responsibility for the passivity that had been her way of retreating into "nonbeing"; she has earned the right to wear her wedding ring, originally a gift from Honoria to Mado. The two snakes entwined thereon are emblematic of divine healing and of "opposing forces balancing one another in such a way as to create a higher, static form" (Cirlot 37). No longer protected by illusions from the pain of life, Stella has embarked on her way "to the end of time which is the glory on the other side of the sun" (212).

In the structure of the novel, the young Stella's story is a reminiscence shared with her grandson by an old widow, returned to the Illyria to which she has hung on despite her descendants' wishes. Stella passes on the wisdom of generations to the seventh Theron Renier:

Sometimes, when you make your journey through the sun, many things are burned before you come out on the other side. We have to let things go. (34)

Indicating to her grandson that the journey continues throughout life but that each stage gives strength to go on, Stella at last is able to relinquish Illyria.

A companion volume for young readers to *The Love Letters* and *The Other Side of the Sun, Dragons in the Waters* (1976) recapitulates their themes, distilling them into a compelling adventure story. It is as if the author, thoroughly grounded in an ideological landscape she has previously mapped, can sketch it deftly, incorporating ideas more inobtrusively into her narrative. Major themes familiar from the two preceding works are learning to love through personal failure and the interdependence of generations. Intimated in the earlier novels and highlighted in *Dragons* is the theme that idealization of one's heroes, making "gods of one's points of reference," is a corruption of love.

A mythic blend of fantasy and realism, the improbable story of *Dragons in the Waters,* L'Engle would say, is true in everything except its events:

The "realistic" novels push me further away from the truth of things rather than bringing me closer. We cannot make mystery and miracle acceptable by trying to constrict them into the language of the laboratory or the television commercial. (*The Summer of the Great-Grandmother* 180)

Simon Renier's commitment to the Quiztano Indians at the end of *Dragons* is both mystery and miracle.

Thirteen-year-old Simon's quest begins when he leaves the security of his home with Aunt Leonis in the South Carolina back country to go with an adult cousin to Venezuela to return a portrait of their ancestor Quentin Phair, who had fought with Simon Bolivar. Simon, of the family Renier from *The Other Side of the Sun,* shares a series of dangerous misadventures with Polly and Charles O'Keefe, characters from *The Arm of the Starfish* (1965), *A House like a Lotus* (1984), and *An Acceptable Time* (1989) and children of Meg Murry and Calvin O'Keefe from *A Wrinkle in Time* (1962), and with Cannon Tallis, Mr. Theo, and Emily from *The Young Unicorns* (1968), the third in the Austin family series. In the "underwater world" where L'Engle meets her characters, they begin to meet each other, individuals of a vast and various world, reflecting the interconnectedness of the human race.

During his journey from South Carolina to Venezuela, Simon hears the legend of the Quiztanos, a primitive people still living on the shores of oil-rich Lake Maracaibo close to the "power behind the stars [that] has not made anything to be separate from anything else" (277). The legend is kept alive by the Umara, a princess trained from birth to hold the Tribal Memory, the Quiztano's chief treasure because "to be part of the memory of this power is for life to have meaning, no matter what happens" (154, 286). According to the legend, in the old days a youthful, golden-haired champion of the oppressed, Quentin Phair, after marrying an Umara and fathering her son, left on a long journey, promising to return. Because the promise had never been fulfilled, the Quiztanos still await "a young white savior from across the sea" (88).

Simon learns that his noble ancestor Quentin Phair, his "ideal of a man of perfect honor, who cared for the truth above all things and who spent his youth helping to free an oppressed continent" (190), was in fact "a human being who lied and lusted and was as other men" (314). The boy has to assimilate, first, that his forefather was "neither white knight nor scoundrel" but for "all his folly and over-idealism . . . a man of uncommon valor, vision, and a great deal of charm" (241) and second, that the Quiztanos, seeing in himself the likeness of his ancestor Quentin Phair, believe he is their promised savior. Terrified by the Quiztano's demands, Simon conquers the dragons of fear, cowardice, and incredible truth only after abandoning his incapacitated uncle-father Tallis to the assault of a jungle cat to save himself. The subsequent realization that he must forgive and love himself, imperfect as he is, empowers him to stay with the Quiztanos to redress the infidelity of Quentin Phair. Idealistic as Simon's heroic, self-sacrificing decision is, it is made credible by his characterization as a boy *not* of the twentieth century, one whose values separate him from the rapacious entrepreneurs who would displace the Quiztanos and desecrate the environment to plunder the wealth beneath the lake. Thus, the dragons and the wild cat represent societal as well as personal monsters; and the waters represent tribal memory, the individual, and the collective unconscious.

Allusions to exploitation of the natives by avaricious foreign corporate moguls, to revolution in third-world countries, to their desperate poverty and need for modern medicine, and to ecological concerns make *Dragons in the Waters* a contemporary novel as well as a fantasy. Simon, guided by his fierce, strong mother-mentor aunt Leonis, triumphs over all the dragons and makes the hard, but right, choice to give his life to helping the world's disadvantaged who had been betrayed by the rich and powerful. Like Meg in *A Wrinkle in Time,* the weak young Simon has been chosen to confound the wise and mighty, and he loves enough to answer that call. Though very different from Aunt Olivia's shooting of Ron at the end of *The Other Side of the Sun,* Simon's choice at the end of *Dragons* also dramatizes love divorced from an action that feels good. Yet the knowledge from deep inside himself that he had left home to come home is fulfilling.

A House Like a Lotus (1984) has evoked controversy primarily for its confrontation of contemporary issues. Less complex and more realistic than most of L'Engle's fiction for young readers, this novel weaves together the present and recent past of Polly O'Keefe so smoothly that the times become one. Sixteen-year-old Polly, christened Polyhymnia for the Muse of Song, is on a trip through Greece to Cyprus, where she will act as a "gofer" at a conference on literature and literacy for representatives of third-world countries. To embody its major theme—that the self housed in a mortal body must go through its feelings of revulsion, anger, confusion, and hurt to reach compassion—the story travels old L'Engle trails and blazes new, focusing on relationships between women: the lesbianism of Max and Urs (neighbors of the O'Keefes) and the friendship between Polly and Max.

When Max turns on Polly, she seeks refuge in Renny, Dr. Queron Renier, a healer like his forebears in *The Other Side of the Sun* and *Dragons in the Waters.* Like Katherine Forrester of *The Small Rain,* a betrayed and confused Polly has sex with the young intern. She enjoys the natural and comforting experience but knows that it followed from loneliness and the need to be reassured about her own sexuality, not from love.

Max, a painter and world traveler who has come home to Beau Allaire on Benne Seed Island to die of a rare parasitical disease, perceives Polly's vibrant but latent talents and, loving her as a daughter, draws her out through exposure to worlds of art, culture, medicine, religion, and sexuality beyond the limited environment of Benne Seed. In her innocence Polly idealizes Max, an attitude L'Engle's earlier novels have characterized as destructive and corrupt. Polly can assimilate, however painfully, what she gradually learns about Max's illness and sexual preference. However, when Max, in a drunken stupor induced to ameliorate her bodily suffering and her terror in the face of impending death, goes after Polly, the girl cannot forgive because she cannot understand. Understanding comes only after she has accomplished the same task as Stella Renier, articulated in this novel by Polly's uncle Sandy (one of her mother Meg's twin brothers from the Time tetralogy and an avuncular guide like Vicki Austin's Uncle Douglas): "You have to go all the way through your feelings before you can come out on the other side" (18).

The sea, the island, the moon, and the stars—stock-in-trade symbols for L'Engle—wash like waves throughout the novel and are given particular meaning by fresh images. The dominant metaphors, house and lotus, figure intricately in the characterization of many but are brought together in Max and Polly. The island on which they live is Benne Seed, literally the mysterious potential of the body. While Polly is just learning that the body, the "bone-house" of "Man's mounting spirit," [5] provides the physical and emotional structure through which humans love, Max's full-blown powers are about to be cut off by death. Max's ancestral house is Beau Allaire (translated, nurturer of beauty), both naming the place and symbolizing Max herself, who fosters Polly's growth through her own sin of acting without restraint. It is Max's use of the lotus image that brings together human and divine love. Finding it easier to believe in God as lotus rather than as father, she tells Polly:

Think . . . of that tiny speck [the nucleus of an atom], invisible to the naked eye, opening up like a flower, to become clouds of hydrogen dust, and then stars, and solar systems. That softly opening flower—I visualize a lotus—is a more viable image of God for me than anything else. I keep the portrait of Papa to remind me that God is *not* like him. (122)

Later, when Max reads aloud from the Upanishads, Polly copies the passage:

In this body, in this town of Spirit, there is a little house shaped like a lotus, and in that house there is a little space. There is as much in that little space within the heart as there is in the whole world outside. (182)

Through friendships with third-world leaders of the Cypress Conference, whose excruciating experiences have opened rather than embittered them, Polly unfolds to compassion, the power to suffer *with* Max, which in a flash enables her to understand and forgive. Able at last to phone Max to say "I love you," Polly reflects:

The cold place within me that had frozen and constricted my heart was gone. My heart was like a lotus, and in that little space there was room enough for . . . all the stars in all of the galaxies. For all those bubbles which were island universes. (307)

Other symbols in the novel reinforce the power to forgive nurtured by compassion, which is the common element in human and divine love.

The site of the conference, an old monastery in Osia Theola, is itself symbolic. Blessed Theola "was reported to have been given the gift of truth" (104). Like many pilgrims, Polly visits Theola's church to see the truth about Max and herself. A predominant symbol, the statue of the Laughing Christ, appears in the narrative at times crucial to Polly's friendships with Max and with the Bakian delegate Omio, a married man with whom she falls in love. When the Bakians first heard of the Son of God from missionaries, they gave his name to their ten-thousand-year-old nameless life-sized statue, that "gives the effect of pure joy." Max has a small reproduction of this "man with his head thrown back in laughter and delight" (35). A Christ who laughs celebrates, as well as suffers for, his flawed friends. Polly sees the Laughing Christ and loves it the first time she visits Beau Allaire.

As she flees from the drunken Max, the wooden figure significantly comes crashing down from its marble pedestal. Omio gives Polly his drawing of the original as a seal of their friendship when she learns he is married. That gesture makes Polly realize that she wants Max, not as an idol, but as the "vibrant, perceptive," "brilliant but flawed" human being that she is (302).

Having made peace with Omio, Max, and herself and having learned that those who love best love with restraint, Polyhymnia at the end of the novel is singing in her heart the song of fellowship that the conference participants often sing together, *Saranam,* translated in the delegates' various native languages as "refuge," "God's richest blessing," "love does not judge," and, in Shakespeare's words, "Love is not love which alters when it alteration finds" (265).

Themes that reverberate through L'Engle's writings coalesce into what may be called her theology, philosophy, and psychology of love, the fundamental premise of which is that the major task of maturation is to comprehend the nature of love, to become able to live with its paradoxes and strong enough to love everyone who inhabits the earth, particularly those with whom one lives most closely. To know love means to realize that it is much more than a matter of felicitous feeling, that it must be neither self-centered nor possessive, that it demands severe as well as intense commitment. Love inspires awe but also entails suffering, fear, and dread. The realization that there is no authentic love that is not "terrible" can come only when, through failed as well as successful essays, head and heart have learned to work in concert; logic, with imagination; judgment, with compassion. Through a hazardous journey to "the other side of the sun" human beings using all their faculties in search of love can come to know that

Love can't be pinned down by definition, and it certainly can't be proved any more than anything else important can be proved. Love is people, is a person. . . . 'Love is not an emotion. It is a policy.' (*A Circle of Quiet* 80)

So vital a policy that Madeleine L'Engle has spent more than forty years and forty books in search of its meaning for herself and for her readers of all ages.

The author has acknowledged that among her works *A Wrinkle in Time* has a special place in her heart because, during the long years when it was rejected by publisher after publisher, she refused to surrender to their recommendations that she alter characters, situations, and dialogue, to tone down themes.[6] Her commitment to her belief that the novel said what she wanted it to say in the way it could best be said has been rewarded by the Newbery Medal the book received in 1963 and by the force with which it has impacted readers ever since. Today, *A Wrinkle in Time,* more than any of her books (perhaps as much as most of the forty-odd others together) conveys to a large, avid, and impressionable readership the significant core of meaning for which L'Engle herself has searched and of which she has written so eloquently, so passionately.

NOTES

1. Madeleine L'Engle, in a three-hour session with my class at the College of St. Scholastica in Duluth, Minnesota, on 26 October 1983, gave this as the reason she plans to leave her papers to Wheaton College in Wheaton, Illinois. The knowledge that hers will be housed with the papers of C.S. Lewis and Charles Williams pleases her.

2. See Carter, M. L., "The Cosmic Gospel of Lewis and L'Engle," *Mythlore* 8 (1982): 10-12; Glass, Rona, "*A Wrinkle in Time* and *The High King*," *Children's Literature Association Quarterly* 6 (Fall 1981): 15-18; Patterson, Nancy-Lou, "Angel and Psychopomp in Madeleine L'Engle's 'Wind' Trilogy," *Children's Literature in Education* 14 (Winter 1983): 195-203; Smedman, M. Sarah, "Out of the Depth to Joy: Spirit/Soul in Juvenile Novels," *Triumphs of the Spirit in Children's Literature,* Francelia Butler and Richard Rotert, Ed., Hamden, CT: Library Professional Publications, 1986. 181-97.

3. Rev. of *The Love Letters . New Yorker* 5 November 1966. 246; Morrison, Freda, Rev. of *The Love Letters. New York Times* 30 October l966. 74; and Rev. of *The Love Letters . Best Sellers*. 15 November 1966. 311.

4. See, for example, *A Circle of Quiet* 245-46.

5. "The Caged Skylark." *Gerard Manly Hopkins*. Ed. H. W. Gardner. Baltimore: Penquin, 1954. 31-32. Hopkins's conviction is much like L'Engle's. The last lines of Hopkins's "The Caged Skylark" read:

> Man's spirit will be flesh-bound when found at best,
> But unencumbered: meadow-down is not distressed
> For a rainbow footing it nor he for his bones risen.

6. In the class referred to in Note 1, L'Engle spoke movingly and at length of her refusal to revise *A Wrinkle in Time* to accord with more than twenty publishers' judgments that the book as she had written it would neither appeal to readers nor be commercially successful. Farrar, Straus, and Giroux's decision to publish the book as she submitted it brought to a close a ten-year dry period during which she had published nothing. That, as well as the success of the book with readers of all ages, marks *A Wrinkle in Time* as a milestone in an author's life as well as in children's literature.

BIBLIOGRAPHY

Cirlot, J. W. *A Dictionary of Symbols*. Trans. Jack Sage. 2nd ed. New York: Philosophical Library, 1971.

Forbes, C. "Allegorical Fantasy: Mortal Dealings with Cosmic Questions. An Interview with Madeleine L'Engle." *Christianity Today*. 8 June 1979. 14-19.

L'Engle, Madeleine. *An Acceptable Time.* New York: Farrar, 1989.

_____. *The Arm of the Starfish.* New York: Farrar, 1965.

_____. *Camilla.* New York: Delacorte, 1965. Originally published as *Camilla Dickinson.* New York: Simon, 1951.

_____. *A Circle of Quiet.* New York: Seabury, 1979.

_____. *Dragons in the Waters.* New York: Dell, 1972.

_____. *A House Like a Lotus.* New York: Farrar, 1984.

_____. *The Love Letters.* New York: Ballantine, 1983.

_____. *The Moon by Night.* New York: Dell, 1981.

_____. *The Other Side of the Sun.* New York: Ballantine, 1983.

_____. *A Ring of Endless Light.* New York: Farrar, 1980.

_____. *The Severed Wasp.* New York: Farrar, 1982

_____. *The Small Rain.* New York: Farrar, 1985.

_____. *The Summer of the Great-Grandmother.* New York: Seabury, 1979.

_____. *A Swiftly Tilting Planet.* New York: Dell, 1980.

_____. *A Wind in the Door.* New York: Farrar, 1973.

_____. *A Wrinkle in Time.* New York: Farrar, 1962.

_____. *The Young Unicorns.* New York: Dell, 1980.

PART II

Specific Authors
and
Their Works

This second section of *Science Fiction for Young Readers* contains seven articles that look at specific authors whose works have appeared primarily in the 1970s and 1980s. With the exception of Anne McCaffrey, all of the authors considered in this section have not chosen the series format, or a modification of it, for their fiction. Although the action/adventure component may seem diminished—and in some cases, it actually is—many times there is less a reduction in the action than an increase in attention to details of setting and nuances of theme.

Howard V. Hendrix's return to a young adult science fiction novel he had not read in over twenty years is the basis for "The Things of a Child: Coming Full Circle With Alan E. Nourse's *Raiders from the Rings* ." This novel contains an almost archetypal "young heroes" plot as the main characters, two from Earth and one from the Rings, learn to overcome their mutual distrust and cultural differences to discover a way to bring peace between their respective warring societies. Although one of the oldest novels in this section, *Raiders from the Rings* , Hendrix argues, is a novel about the folly of war, the arms race, and hostage populations whose validity has remained undiminished by the passage of time.

In "Masters, Slaves, and Rebels: Dystopia as Defined and Defied by John Christopher," K. V. Bailey discusses what might well be considered the paradigmic dystopian/romantic future in which a small band of rebels, against all odds, may well be able to overthrow the tyrants—machines, other men, or aliens—oppressing humankind. In *The Guardians, The Prince in Waiting Trilogy,* and the Tripods trilogy, Christopher's black futures echo the dystopian possibilities perhaps first hinted at in H. G. Wells' *The Time Machine* and *The War of the Worlds*. Although the activities of the youthful rebels in these books might be a metaphor for any teenage rebellion, the plots stand on their own in fully realized future worlds.

The youthful protagonists Millicent Lenz presents in *"Danger Quotient,*

Fiskadoro, Riddley Walker, and the Failure of the Campbellian Monomyth" may change the world, but their efforts may only reestablish the patriarchal society that got them where they now are. *Danger Quotient* offers a variation of the standard male-hero-saves-the-world plot without examining any of the assumptions upon which its values rest, accepting all unquestioned. *Fiskadoro* ends with the possibility that all old values, all history, must be scrapped. Only *Riddley Walker* offers a fusion in which the male hero is taught to value the feminine side of consciousness and reject the violence and mutilating self-sacrifice inherent in the myth of the hero.

In "Growing Home: The Triumph of Youth in the Novels of H. M. Hoover," Thom Dunn and Karl Hiller suggest that Hoover offers young readers a unique perspective on their own sense of who they are and what they must do to fit into the world. Hoover's protagonists—often isolated or abused in physical, psychological, and/or emotional ways—do not reorder the world through their own actions as a traditional hero might but, rather, struggle for ways to accomodate themselves to the world as they find it. Rather than "go home" to a place that already exists, Hoover's young people must create or, as the title of this essay offers, "grow home."

According to Marilyn Fain Apseloff, in "The British Science Fiction of Louise Lawrence," Lawrence depicts situations in which young protagonists must act more for themselves than for the fates of their respective societies. Except for *Children of the Dust*, which depicts a post-holocaust world, Lawrence's novels deal with individuals or a small group of young people in a situation that pertains essentially, if not exclusively, to them alone. Rhys, in *Star Lord* , and Gareth, in *Moonwind* , for example, must decide as individuals whether or not to leave Earth; actions that, although momentous for the young men in question, will have relatively little impact on their surrounding societies. These choices, and others in Lawrence's novels, are about the individual's coming to an awarenes of self and self in relation to others, especially society, and then taking some action based on that awareness.

The focus is on the technology-versus- nature debate in "The Debate Continues: Technology or Nature?—A Study of Monica Hughes's Science Fiction Novels," but in Hughes's works, at least, the debate is not so simple as some critics have proposed. Hughes, J. R. Wytenbroek suggests, is not rejecting technology as much as she is rejecting the uses to which humans have put technology. Most of her novels contain a conclusion in which there is some reconciliation, or at least a hope for reconciliation, between the two seeming opposites so that a balance can be attained. That balance, not some romantic longing for the past, Wytenbroek maintains, is what informs Hughes's fiction and the struggle of the young men and women in that fiction.

The last essay in this group, Patricia Harkins's "Myth in Action: The Trials and Transformation of Menolly," focuses on Anne McCaffrey's Harper Hall series for young readers and discusses the way McCaffrey uses the far-future science fantasy setting developed in the Pern books to present a female hero who follows the traditional mythic, legendary, and folktale plot or pattern to self-realization and success. Menolly's triumph in spite of the restrictions placed upon her by family and society looks back, especially, to the novels of Heinlein and Norton; and her presence as a female protagonist within the archetypal heroic quest, reminiscent certainly of Norton's books, makes her especially contemporary.

The fiction examined by the essays in this section represents a broad spectrum of themes and styles, from the traditionally romantic to the nearly cynical, but virtually all of it is marked by high-quality writing (both technically and thematically), seriousness of vision and purpose, and the presentation of young protagonists whose trials and triumphs will speak to the young adult audience for which the books were written.

6

The Things of a Child: Coming Full-Circle with Alan E. Nourse's *Raiders from the Rings*

Howard V. Hendrix

Reading Alan E. Nourse's 1962 young adult novel *Raiders from the Rings* (*RFTR*) was for me the paradigmatic experience of what reading a science fiction novel should feel like—probably because it was the first science fiction novel I ever read. As I recall, I read Nourse's book in 1968, when the book was six years old and I was nine. In later years, I failed to recall much of the plot, but I always remembered the profound impact it had on me—an impact rivaled (but never equalled) by my later first readings of Arthur C. Clarke's *Earthlight,* Walter M. Miller, Jr.,'s *A Canticle for Liebowitz,* Isaac Asimov's "Nightfall," and Theodore Cogswell's "The Wall Around the World." In an attempt to understand why this book should have made such a deep impression on me, I recently returned to it for the first time in twenty-two years. What follows is an examination of what I found on my return.

The novel, first published in April 1962 by the David McKay Company, is another example of what I've come to think of as *The Day the Earth Stood Still* syndrome. Those who are familiar with Robert Wise's 1951 film of that title may be aware of some of the history I'm about to relate. *The Day the Earth Stood Still* (*TDTESS*), a film with a markedly globalist and pacifist message, managed to get public distribution at a time when the entertainment industry was under particularly intense scrutiny as a result of the anti-Communist witchhunts promulgated by Joseph McCarthy, Estes Kefauver, Richard Nixon, and others. In a time when globalism and pacifism could easily get one labeled a Communist and brought up before the House Un-American Activities Committee, how did a notably globalist and pacifist film ever get past the industry censors? The answer, according to Wise and others, was simple: because the film was "sci-fi" (oh, *that* junk), it was thought not to merit serious censorship consideration and was blithely passed along (Biskind).

We find something similar in the case of Nourse's *RFTR*. In a time period notable for the Bay of Pigs Invasion and the Cuban Missile Crisis, Alan Nourse wrote and David McKay published a book containing a message notably pacifist—opposed to war in general and Cold War armament buildups in particular. A recurring motif of the book is the idea that the preparation for and the waging of war is an example of human immaturity and childishness—a childishness that threatens the survival of the species. To the Spacer Ben Trefon and his Earth-born "prisoners" Tom and Joyce Barron, this idea is perhaps most succinctly stated in the words of the alien Searcher:

"We know that you dwellers in space still do not realize the determination of your Earth brothers to destroy you. We know that many Spacers have withdrawn to their last battlement, their Central asteroid, and that the remaining forces have gathered to prepare a disastrous counterattack on Earth itself. Should Asteroid Central fall, the trigger would be pulled and a planetary holocaust would result." The creature hesitated. "We cannot read the future. We can only predict on the basis of long and bitter experience. Should your war be pursued to its end, the odds are four to one that all human life in the solar system will be obliterated, that the spark will be extinguished once and for all. And that cannot be permitted to happen."

"But that's not possible!" Tom Barron cried. "You talk as if we were children."

"This is a war of children," the creature returned sharply. "Only children would slaughter each other out of ignorance and fear. Only children would fail again and again to learn the lessons of their foolishness, and stubbornly, blindly persist in their childishness. Don't speak to me about children—I know what children you are. But I also know the greatness you could achieve if you would only put away childish things." (159-60)

The phrase "put away childish things" recurs in a number of variants throughout the text, but all are, interestingly enough, strong echoes of the biblical passage 1 Corinthians 13:11—"When I was a child, I spoke as a child, I felt as a child, I thought as a child. Now that I have become a man, I have put away the things of a child." Compare the passage from Corinthians to the following passage from *RFTR* as told from the point of view of the Searchers:

[Human] potential was enormous; the things that they might one day accomplish in a community of intelligent races were staggering, but they were not yet ready for even a suspicion that they might have such potential, for they still thought and acted and behaved as children. (164)

The mention of the "community of intelligent beings" is another similarity *RFTR* bears to *TDTESS*. Both possess an "angelic structure" in which humanity is barred from entering into Edenic communion with the "grown ups," the mature races that have made it to species adulthood. In *TDTESS*, the ambassador/angel who both tells humanity what it is missing and bars its entry into the Galactic Eden is Klaatu; in *RFTR*, this ambassador/angel function is performed by the Searchers .

In order to understand the role of the Searchers, however, we must first understand the spatiomoral structure of *RFTR,* in which "planet-boundedness" is roughly equivalent to evolutionary, historical, and even moral stature. At the top of this hierarchy stand the Searchers, who

were not planet-born, and their lives were not bounded by the time limits of racial history. Geological ages for them were the same as minutes on their time scale; they alone could take the time to search out intelligence wherever it might arise, and nurse it to maturity, and draw it into contact with the great community of intelligent races that grew and flourished in the universe of life. For the Searchers it was a sacred trust that they could not and would not relinquish. (163)

The fact that they live entirely in space suggests the Searchers' ethereal nature, as does their "sacred trust." Though described as looking like gnomes or elves (154), in function they more closely resemble guardian angels overseeing human development: their purpose is "to care" (160) and they "want peace" (155). They are a mature species, and the surest sign of their maturity as a species is their compassion.

Human beings, on the other hand, are "like children who had never grown up," whose "raw and uncontrolled" intelligence lacks "maturity and compassion." Yet even among humans the spatiomoral hierarchy persists. The Spacers, though they "must carry Earth with [them] wherever [they] go" (as a Searcher ironically remarks, 156), are more peaceful and more morally advanced than their Earth-bound fellow humans. In the spatiomoral structure of *RFTR,* living in space makes one literally closer to heaven.

The Spacers raid Earth for supplies and women (the hard cosmic radiation of space alters one of the X sex chromosomes to a Y, so the Spacers can have only sons, we are told), yet even on the eve of such a raid—the most violent Spacer activity—the young raiders are told by their commander, "And remember: no more violence than necessary. Use your tangle-guns" (28). The aforementioned tangle guns (a uniquely Spacer invention), rather than killing or maiming their targets, ensnare and passively restrain them instead—"so we could defend ourselves on Earth raids without hurting people," as Spacer Ben Trefon puts it (119).

Though there is blood on both sides, the Spacer raiders generally do not engage in the same sort of barbaric practices that pirate vessels from Earth do, nor do they engage in the same highly vindictive mass destruction that the Earthmen engage in (such as the destruction of all the Spacer settlements on Mars—all the men, women, and children—in a lightning surprise attack). Though even the patience of the Spacers is tried by the Martian holocaust and they devise a last-resort plan for a counterstrike against Earth, that option is never exercised, and the conflict is solved peacefully. This is to be expected, since the reason the Spacers were exiled from Earth to begin with was that their ancestors, who had manned the orbital battleforts above Earth, had (with the Searchers' help) found the courage to refuse to comply with the orders of their Earthbound commanders to participate in a final atomic armageddon among the nations of the Earth. As Nourse describes it, when

the Earth forces delivered their blows at each other, expecting the massive backing of their garrisons in space, the men in those garrisons drew together shoulder to shoulder, and withheld the devastating attack they were expected to deliver. . . the space garrisons refused to deliver the suicidal blow. After the dust of the war had settled, those brave men in space reaped the reward of their deed as the councils on Earth turned against them in frustration and hatred. . . . Branded as traitors, they were exiled from the planet of their birth, driven back when they attempted to come home, forced to take up a lonely, wandering life in the great emptiness of space beyond the boundaries of Earth. (71)

For their act of blessed betrayal, the Spacers become scapegoats for Earth's fear and ignorance. By the time of the story, however, the scapegoat Spacers have grown powerful enough to be, in many ways, the equals of Earth—and a superpower hostage situation has developed.

This is, perhaps, the most insightful defamiliarization that Nourse works on his readers. Decades before the American and Soviet peace movements had begun to loudly proclaim that U.S. citizens were being held hostage to Soviet military decisions and Soviet citizens were being held hostage to U.S. military decisions— even before the military and political planners had worked out the larger ramifications of "mutually assured destruction" and its necessary correlative of mutual hostage populations—before all of that, Nourse had struck upon hostage taking as the essential metaphor of the Cold War world and exploited that metaphor in *RFTR*, his commentary on Cold War politics expressed through the defamiliarizing mask of science fiction.

At some level, Spacer Ben Trefon's naive view of Earthmen parallels 1950s American propaganda about the Soviet Union and its people as totalitarian troglodytes in beehivelike cities where the individual will is completely subordinated to Social or Mass Man. Spacer civilization, too, with its freewheeling endless-frontier style, Yankee can-do technological optimism, and recurring references to American Indian culture, can be read as a fairly transparent future analog for America circa 1960. Yet Nourse can't resist complicating the situation: Spacer Ben Trefon's full name is Benjamin Ivanovitch Trefonovsky, and he is a descendant of members of the original Russian space garrison that refused to participate in the Great War. Similarly, Tom and Joyce Barron, Ben's prisoners, are from the "beehive totalitarian city" called Chicago.

This complicating of issues is integral to one of Nourse's objectives in the novel. In the course of the action, Trefon and the Barrons discover that each side's assumptions, prejudices, and traditions about "the enemy" are simplistic, distorted, ill-informed, and often just plain wrong—based on "ignorance and fear," as a Searcher notes (160). The young people of the novel are hostages not only to each other and to the hate and fear and ignorance of their respective societies, but finally they are also held hostage to the threat of human extinction itself. In the course of the novel, Ben learns that Earthmen are far more human and like himself than he'd ever imagined, and the Barrons learn that the Spacers might not only *not* be monsters, but that their way of life might be "better" (nobler, more adventurous, more important—literally "higher") than the options available on Earth. As Tom Barron says of space, "I know as well as you do where the important work is waiting to be done" (210).

Before the novel's end, not only do Ben Trefon and the Barrons have to learn to trust each other, but also, as a result of the actions of these three young people, the Earth and Spacer societies must likewise learn to trust one another. Each society must come to see that the face of the enemy is its own face, too.

This act of maturation is paradoxical, however. If the spatiomoral scale I have outlined is correct, with the people of Earth as the least "mature," the Spacers a bit more mature (but still dependent on an umbilical attachment to Earth), and the Searchers the most mature of all because they were not "planet-born" to begin with, then immaturity is associated with still being caught up in Mother Earth's apron strings. Earth is, in fact, consistently associated with women, for in the novel, no women can be born in space (due to hard cosmic radiation), and the Spacers must kidnap women in order to keep their race alive (echoes of the Sabine Women episode of early Roman legend, perhaps). Mother Earth and the nurturing world of women are here associated with childhood and immaturity, while Father Sky and the harshness of life in space are associated with an ideal of a specifically masculine maturity.

It is no accident that the Searchers, the most mature form of life in the novel, seem to be exclusively male—referred to always with masculine pronouns and addressing each other as "brother." Born in (masculine) space and not on a (feminine) planet, they are signifiers of pure masculinity, without the taint of world or women—cosmic monks tending the sparks of intelligence through the long dark ages of the universe. Nor is it purely coincidental that, of the two Earthlings kidnapped into space by Ben Trefon, Tom Barron decides (near the novel's close) to become a Spacer like Ben, but his sister Joyce goes "back to her training in nursing in a Chicago hospital"—again emphasizing the association of women with nurturance and also with planet-boundedness. Even when Ben and Tom and Joyce are traveling through space in the novel, Joyce Barron's main job seems to be cooking and cleaning: We're told that while Ben and Tom watched the view screen, "Joyce prepared the morning meal" (89); or we read such dialog as Tom Barron's "Joyce, I'm starved. Get us something to eat while I break out the pressure suits" (142).

Significantly, it is Joyce who first "sees something" on the lonely asteroid where the trio has landed—and who in fact first accidentally stumbles upon the Searchers. She is horrified by them: "'Monsters,' Joyce Barron gasped. 'Horrible mutant monsters'" (147). Yet, when Ben and Tom encounter the Searchers, their response is quite different:

Abruptly the creature turned sharply toward him, and Ben saw his eyes, luminous eyes of a pale iridescent blue.

For a moment Ben thought the creature was blind, for the eyes had no pupils or whites. Then he saw little flecks of gold shimmering in the pale blue, and he knew that the creature could see him. But the horror and ugliness Joyce had described had been the product of her own mind, for this tiny creature was far from ugly. Rather there was an otherworldly beauty about him as he solemnly regarded his discoverers. He reminded Ben of something, something he had read of, or heard of, years before. But it was Tom who found the right word.

"Why, he looks like an elf!" he breathed.

Ben nodded. "Joyce was right, but there's nothing horrible about him." (154)

Tom and Ben regard the abrupt appearance of the Searcher as beautiful, while Joyce regards it as monstrous. Such a gender-based divergence of response among these young people suggests that it is not such a very great step to go from seeing the ancient Searchers as "signifiers of pure masculinity" (patriarchal power, in the cultural sense) to seeing these "blind ancient elves" as straightforward phallic representations (in the psychoanalytic sense). The fact that this horrible/beautiful, blind/sighted, ancient/elfin male creature is encountered in "A Cleft in the Rock" (the title of the discovery chapter) suggests another archetypal (and loudly Freudian) reason for why Tom and Ben might find the discovery of a Searcher in the rock-cleft "beautiful" while Joyce finds it "horrible ."

Despite the fact that it is a young adult novel in which all overt mention of romance and intimate sexuality is carefully avoided, *RFTR* nonetheless patterns its story of humanity's maturation upon the adolescent male's archetypal rite of passage, the boy's quest for adulthood. *RFTR* is a species bildungsroman, a novel about *man* kind's growing up and leaving behind Mother Earth (home, childhood, the world of women, "childish things") for Father Sky (space travel, adulthood, the world of men, assumption of the mantle of patriarchal power—symbolized in the novel by the belt of power that Ben dons after his father has been killed). Inevitably the issue of gender roles and even the confrontation with adult sexuality arises in *RFTR,* albeit hidden under various guises.

Yet, paradoxically, the surest sign of a species's maturity is its *compassion* —hardly an exclusively (or even particularly) male trait. Just as it was Joyce Barron who first encountered the Searchers, so, too, it is Joyce—the Other in what is primarily a "boy's book"—who first points out the path to stopping the Earth Spacer War:

"But what did the Searcher mean about stopping the war?" Joyce said. "He made it seem that we were the only ones who could hope to do anything."

"Don't you see?" Tom said excitedly. "Where else have Earthmen and Spacers joined hands and learned the truth about each other? Nowhere else. Yet you and I and Ben know that this war is pointless folly. There isn't a single valid reason for it, if each side knew the truth about the other. And that was what the Searchers were trying to tell us, that somehow we have to tell both sides the *truth* and make them believe it just as we do."

"It sounds good," Ben said, "but how? I don't have any power among my people, even if I could get to Asteroid Central, and that would mean running the Maze right under the nose of five hundred Earth ships. And as for you convincing your people—oh, it's hopeless. Who would believe us? How could we tell them a story like this and get anybody even to *listen?*"

"You already know the answer to that," Joyce Barron said quietly. "We can get people to listen just the way the Searchers got us to listen."

Ben frowned. "I don't follow you."

"There was a ship that came back from a reprisal raid, years ago," Joyce said. "An Earth ship, one of the 'pirates' you spoke of. They kidnapped a mauki and her five-year-old boy, and then destroyed the boy and tried to get the mauki back home. It didn't work; they fell into a trap, and a Spacer ship boarded them and recaptured the mauki. But the reason they were trapped was because the mauki was singing."

Ben looked skeptical. "How could *that* have been a trap?"

"You're used to mauki chants. You've heard them all your life, and still you stop and listen, don't you?"

"Well, I suppose I do."

"Yes. And when that woman in that ship began to sing, every crewman stopped what he was doing to listen."

They stared at her in silence. Then Ben said, "She's got it, Tom. She's got the answer. If we can find a way to put it to work in time." (172-73)

Here, as elsewhere in the novel, the sexual and the political coincide. The maukis are among Nourse's most intriguing inventions. They are women of two worlds, cultural amphibians, born and raised on Earth but kidnapped by Spacers in order to become "the wife of a Spacer.... His companion in the dreadful loneliness of a Spacer's life.... The mother of his boys.... The proud and loyal head of the Spacer family" (47), but also, as Ben explains, "Mauki isn't just a word, and a mauki isn't only a wife and mother. My father once told me that he wasn't sure but he thought the word itself was a corruption of an old Klickitat Indian word meaning 'warrior who sings.' There is something extra special about a mauki— it has to do with her singing and morale-building ... without maukis our life would be empty indeed" (91).

Ben is never able to adequately explain to the Barrons what a mauki is, but in the novel one particular mauki plays the role of the compassionate mediatrix. She is the woman who loses her five-year-old son to the pirates from Earth yet refuses to allow her rescuers to destroy the ship of the Earthmen who had held her captive:

"All right," Petro said grimly. "Battle stations." The tiny ship turned its six missile tubes to face the Earth ship. "Ready with one and two."

The mauki had been huddled in the corner of the cabin, sobbing. Now she looked up, tears still streaking her face. "What are you going to do?"

"What do you think I'm going to do?" Petro said harshly. "They're butchers. Kidnaping you is one thing. Murdering a five-year-old child is something else. Well, they haven't even got their battle lights on yet. We'll gut them."

The woman was on her feet. "No, please! Let them go back home."

"So they can murder more of our children?"

"You don't understand. They were afraid of him."

"Of a *five-year-old?*"

"Yes, they were afraid—until they heard me sing."

Petro stared at her, hesitating, while Jack and Tiny waited for the order. "Please," the woman said, "let them go home."

Petro shrugged and turned away, striking his fist viciously in his palm. "It's idiocy. We have them helpless."

"And if we killed them, we would be no better than they," the woman said quietly. "Is that what you want? If there is ever to be an end to this war, someone has to rise above it sometime."

Petro and his men stared at one another. Then Petro sighed. "All right," he said. "Close the Tubes. Head back to Central, while I try to think of something to tell the Council. And make it fast."

* * *

The Earth ship knew, of course, what the raiders could have done. Every man in the crew knew that, from the captain down, and no one could understand why they had been allowed to escape. Yet in their minds the haunting chant of the captive woman still echoed; they could still hear her song of longing and loneliness. Back on Earth they would remember those words, and talk about that song for years to come.

And that was what the mauki wanted. (4-5)

If compassion is the surest sign of intellectual maturity, then it is not a Spacer or even a Searcher who is demonstrably the most "mature" person in this novel—it is this unnamed mauki who appears only twice, once as a hostage in a prologue that takes place before the action of the novel proper, and finally toward the close of the novel when (again, interestingly, as a hostage) she becomes the vessel through which the Searchers' message—along with the story of Ben and the Barrons—comes to all humanity.

The war is halted and peace brokered as a result of the mauki's song. One might view this mauki as an "anti-Siren"—with her laments leading men not to their deaths but to new life. In the fact that *mauki* means "warrior who sings" and that maukis are called *heads* of households and have roots both in the female world of Earth and the adult male world of the Spacers, one might also be tempted to see a certain androgyny or hermaphroditic aspect to the characterization of these powerful women. The archetype that best fits the mauki here, however, is that of the compassionate mediatrix, the intercessor. Such intercessors abound in literature and mythology and range from fairy godmothers to the Blessed Virgin Mary. Like Mary, the mauki of the novel has lost a son to human fear and ignorance and yet, in an act of almost superhuman compassion, forgives those responsible for her son's death and works to save them. Just as it is through Mary that the Word is brought into the world as the Prince of Peace, so, too, is the Searchers' message brought into human consciousness through the mauki's peace-bringing song.

This necessity of the feminine for tempering and making truly human the masculine-associated intellect is one of the ways in which the novel tends to confound the patriarchal hierarchy inherent in its manhood quest narrative. On the black belt of patriarchal power that Ben inherits from his father, the capsule upon it that pulses when Searchers are near is egg shaped, curiously feminine. Late in the novel, after the encounter with the Searchers, Joyce is able to leave cooking behind and pitch in with the boys to repair Ben's spacecraft (143); and at the very end of the book, there is the suggestion that Earth's geneticists believe that someday soon a solution will be achieved and girl children, too, will be born in space—"and there won't even be that distinction between Earthmen and Spacers" (210).

At the end of *RFTR*, Spacer Ben Trefon and Earthgirl Joyce Barron do not become romantically involved, as they probably would have in a novel aimed at an adult audience. The fact that Tom and Ben and the adventurous boybonding of space travel have the final word in the novel seems at first blush to confirm that it's "just a science fiction boy's book," but I hope I have made clear that underlying this adventure story can be found a most curious amalgam of archetypes from manhood quests, American Indian mythology, and Christian theology and hagiography, as well as the most cogent discussion of the nature of war I have yet encountered in a work of fiction intended for young people. Returning to it after twenty-two years, I was in the end struck less by its flaws (spaceship computers that use punch cards, faulty males-only Spacer genetics, incorrectly projected limitations to deep-space radio communication, occasional examples of largely unquestioned male chauvinism) than I was continually impressed by its literate handling—in a popular, highly readable form—of this serious philosophical question: What is it in human nature that brings us again and again to the making of war?

As long as that question continues to trouble people of whatever age, I am sure *RFTR* will not lack for young readers. Within the dominant cultural discourse of patriarchy and power, *RFTR* (sometimes almost despite itself) gives voice to repressed or marginalized discourses involving the role of women in society, as well as the necessity for compassion and a nonviolent approach to conflict resolution if humanity is to survive "to maturity." It is a story that concerns itself with the limitations of the masculine adolescent viewpoint, particularly on women and war—a story of the painful adolescence not only of Tom and Joyce and Ben, but of the entire human species.

RFTR is science fiction that is prophetic not in the sense of literally foretelling the future, but in the sense of warning us what might happen "if this [sort of immaturity] goes on." By showing us both a dangerous future and a way of avoiding that future, the novel may help us to prevent that dangerous future from happening in the first place. It is not a "self-fulfilling" but rather a "self-destructing" prophecy, a self-consuming forewarning that is the more successful the less the actual future looks like the story's foretelling. Despite Ronald

Reagan's Strategic Defense Initiative, there are (at least for now) no orbiting battleforts like those in Nourse's book—at least in part because such orbiting battle forts and *Star Wars* Death Stars had appeared previously in science fiction and, even when advanced earnestly by an American president, could be rejected as "bad sci-fi."

Finally, works like *RFTR* help influence the actual future not only negatively, but also positively, In the years since *RFTR* was first published, the Cold War has ended, Americans and Russians have begun to work cooperatively as they did in the history of Nourse's Spacers, and some small steps have even been made in recognizing the rights of women. Could it be that these are early hints that humanity's suicidal adolescence may at last be coming to a close? That the mature potential of the species (so important to Nourse's alien Searchers) may at last be coming into view?

One can hope . . .

BIBLIOGRAPHY

Biskind, Peter. *Seeing is Believing: How Hollywood Taught Us to Stop Worrying and Love the Fifties*. New York: Pantheon, 1983.
Nourse, Alan E. *Raiders from the Rings*. New York: McKay, 1962.

7

Masters, Slaves, and Rebels:
Dystopia as Defined and
Defied by John Christopher

K. V. Bailey

John Christopher's juvenile science fiction novels followed his adult genre novels
of the 1950s and early 1960s, and have formed a large and significant part of his
subsequent output. Those adult novels had often depicted basic struggles to
survive or to create stability in the aftermath of some catastrophic occurrence—
the planet-wide destruction by virus of graminaceous plants in *The Death of Grass*
(1956) or the breakdown of civilized *mores* throughout earthquake devastated
terrains in *A Wrinkle in the Skin* (1965).[1] In each of these examples the action
follows a group, or groups, traveling over arid and hostile territories in search of
security: in the former case from the south of England to the north; in the latter over
the seismically drained and exposed bed of the English Channel. Any relief
achieved appears fragile: Much of human life has become poor, nasty, brutish, and
short; stark necessity often overrides any willed generosity.

In Christopher's juvenile (more specifically for both young and older adolescents) science fiction of the past twenty years, harsh and even catastrophe-
affected environments are certainly portrayed, but the lights of hope and idealism
glimmer more brightly. The oppressive controls become less those of abandonment or starvation and more those of smothering uniformities—which are none
the less oppressive and dystopian in effect, however adroitly administered or
smoothly adaptive. The novels are written to appeal to the rebellious and resurgent
nature of youth, with marked emphasis on such attributes as enterprise, self-
reliance, loyalty, and cooperative action.

* * *

A novel central to Christopher's juvenile oeuvre, and a prestigious one in that
it won both the *Guardian* newspaper award for the best children's book of its year

and the German Jungendbuchpreis, is *The Guardians* (1970). The locale of its future is the Thames Valley and the London Oxford Bristol Southampton quadrilateral, an area sharply divided between the Conurbs, separated from each other only by Green Belts, and the County.[2] No catastrophe has afflicted the land other than a deterioration of community that has produced, on the one hand, semihelot populations, partisanly obsessed by Byzantinelike stadia games, whose lives, reasonably well provided for but physically and socially debased, are spent in the segregated security of the Conurbs, and on the other hand, "back to the Golden Age" rentier, residually aristocratic and commuter populations, who enjoy artificially sustained atechnological lives of hunting, fishing, and gymkhanas in the County. Oxford and Bristol are the urban focuses of the County; London and an extended "Solent City" complex are the great southern Conurbs.

Rob, the story's orphaned protagonist, suffers in his London Conurb the alienating effects of individuality-crushing restrictions. He burrows beneath an electrified fence to escape from Conurb to County, becomes familiarized with the seductively gracious manor-house existence of those who protect, adopt, and educate him but is then almost fortuitously caught up in a movement, at first abortive and then surviving clandestinely, that has originated in part with the youth of the County, in part from within the Conurbs. Its purpose is to eliminate by rebellion the physical and social barriers, the fakery and conditioning, that have made virtually two nations of what might more justly, with freedom, be reshaped as one.

The British "Two Nations" theme is as old as Disraeli and Mrs. Gaskell. The future possibility of a machine-debased/pastoral-hedonistic duality was explored by H. G. Wells in *The Time Machine* (with an evolutionary twist as to who preyed upon whom). A conditioned proletariat motif, in even grimmer or in more satirical forms than that in which Christopher presents it, is central to novels by Zamyatin, Huxley, and Orwell. Revolt against an authoritarianly and technocratically maintained status quo informs a range of science fiction from Wells's *The Sleeper Awakes* to John Brunner's *The Shock Wave Rider;* while the problem of reconciling opposed socio-economic structures is a concern of Ursula K. Le Guin's *The Dispossessed,* significantly subtitled *An Ambiguous Utopia.*

It is not, of course, the case that John Christopher in *The Guardians* is attempting systematically to brew from such ingredients an ideological distillation for teenage consumption. Such ingredients do, however, variously color his narrative, giving it historical and contemporary relevance for a readership growing into awareness of the world and its societies. As a means to this, he adeptly uses techniques of "distancing" and perspective by including pseudodocumentary allusions and images; for example, a bramble-overgrown anti-aircraft gun site used as a boys' secret "den" is vaguely identified as "something out of the Hitler war. . . . Maybe older" (66); and the pointing out of meadows fringing Oxford as having been the scene of a one-time, but contemporarily obsolete, car manufacturing industry, "one of the biggest in England. Perhaps the biggest" (121). Among the most telling of these "echoes" in *The*

Guardians is Rob's reading (a rare Conurb pursuit) of G. K. Chesterton's satiric/romantic *The Napoleon of Notting Hill,* seen by Rob as "a novel about Victorian London in which local patriots fought pitched battles in gas-lit streets" (27). This, in fact, is the first specific indication that the events of Christopher's narrative are taking place between 2050 and 2060. Chesterton's work appeared in 1904, and Rob realizes when reading it that even 150 years before his time London would have been sufficiently a Conurb for such strife to have been conceived only as fantasy. (It is a matter of literary irony that Chesterton placed his future neo-medievalism at eighty years after 1904!) Rob thinks, however, that, in contrast to the mindless fighting between the Games terraplane factions of his Conurb, a parish "would have been something worth fighting for" (27). The idea comple-ments his other reading preference—the action-romantic Musketeer novels of Alexandre Dumas *père.*

The Notting Hill motif, in addition to functioning thus to link the centuries, prefigures what is to become an important element in Rob's new life in the County. Mike, the son of the befriending aristocratic Gifford family (and the persuasive voice in the matter of this befriending), has naturally grown up under the sway of the County ethos. Rob has to be remolded to act according to that ethos. He is Eliza to, in particular, Mrs. Gifford's Professor Higgins; and he assumes quite readily the role, taking well to archery and riding and admitting to a conversion from the Conurb plebian soccer to the County game, rugger. Although he at first thinks chasing a fox not quite fair, he exults in the hunt when he is a participant, finding in its rituals "a sense of belonging" (110); and the richness and tradition of Christmas festivities appeal to him so strongly that he shudders at the memory of the falseness of the succession of tawdry Christmas parties that had been paraded before him on Conurb holovision. These experiences build in him a County loyalty for which his earlier attraction to the banners and blazons of Chesterton's fantasy may have predisposed him; and this loyalty, strongly focused on his champion, Mike, becomes later redirected to Mike's cause of Conurb freedom.

It is when he and Mike are at school that Rob's two-way facing loyalties are tested. The school is Winchester, removed from inside the Southhampton Conurb to be rebuilt in the County around the ruins of an ancient monestery. [3] Among some of the older boys, including Mike, there exists an ethical aversion to existing inequalities and a determination to bring about change by force. Rob is conscious of a more or less contented equilibrium on both sides of the divide. He experiences a positive satisfaction with his own acquired social and material environment, and he is sensible of the debt he owes the Griffords for their trust and kindness. He disagrees with Mike's involvement in the movement, but when the premature revolt fails, he is loyal to him, helps him, and conceals his whereabouts. Rob is then brought before the Guardians, the country gentry who covertly rule and order both worlds, ensuring peace and security all round, shipping off the violent and misfit to an unending far-off war in China and maintaining in the County, for their own kind, a "Golden Age," free of obtrusive technology. It appears that they have rumbled Rob's deception from the start, but now they earmark him as a likely recruit. It is a solution he is happy to accept until he understands that he will be required to play Judas and that if caught Mike will, like other rebellious young aristocrats before him, be deprived of any nonconforming initiatives by an otherwise unharming measure of brain surgery. The Guardians claim that they are humane, though "not limited by the moralities [they] lay down for others" (149). It is the realization that Mike, whose initiative and humaneness had rescued him when he was a lonely refugee, would be deliberately deprived of an essential strand of his humanity for the purpose of maintaining a manipulated stagnation, that decides Rob, as the story ends, to return secretly under the barrier fence to join Mike and the hidden insurgents in the Southhampton Conurb.

* * *

In the three novels—*The Prince in Waiting* (1970), *Beyond the Burning Lands* (1971), and *The Sword of the Spirits* (1972)—collected as *The Prince in Waiting Trilogy* (1983), there is a partial shift away from the "freedom from conformity" theme toward picaresque and dynastic adventuring acted out within the narrative frames of myth and romance. Margery Fisher wrote of the juvenile historical novels of Henry Treece that "rationalization of myth was an essential part of Treece's approach to the distant past" (24). It is also a part of John Christopher's approach to the distant future. In the first novel of the trilogy, the focus is on initiation; in the second, on heroic questing; in the last, the pattern is one of broken loyalties, reminiscent of Arthurian tragedy. The trilogy has in common with Christopher's Tripods novels (to be considered later) far-journeying and crusading elements, in common with *The Guardians,* the concealed activity of a controlling and directing power—though in this case with perceptible, if ambiguous, authorial endorsement. The trilogy's setting is a postcatastrophe landscape extending over southern England and the borderlands of Wales. The catastrophe is of a somewhat indeterminate nature. Fluctuations in solar radiation have caused devastating terrestrial changes, vulcanism, occluded skies, and, as a physiological concomitant, mutations giving rise to dwarfs and polymufs (polymorphs), regarded as inferior in breed and status, the latter indeed considered to be subhuman by the dominant "pure" humans, and segregated for servitude. The deteriorated environmental state is believed to be a punishment by supernatural Spirits for the use of "magic" (i.e., technology); consequently, in this new medievalism, all machines are banned.

The political structure of postcatastrophe southern England is analogous, in part and on a small scale, to the Anglo-Saxon hegemonies and, in part, to the petty war-gaming rival princedoms of Italian city-states. Walled towns—Petersfield, Romsey, Salisbury, and preeminently, Oxford and Winchester—command a climatically harsh but habitable terrain separated from a virtually unknown north by the almost impassable Burning Lands of volcanoes, lava flows, and geysers. A superstitious religion of prophesies, prohibitions, and seances at which the voices of the Spirits are heard is in the hands of the Seers, who selectively recruit novice Acolytes to become members of their controlling elite. In the ancient capital and now again provincial capital city of Winchester, Luke, the young protagonist of all three novels and dispossessed heir to the Princedom of Winchester, is initiated by the Seers into knowledge of the real nature of their manipulative "mysteries" at a hidden operational center near Stonehenge. They hold and use the secrets of forbidden technology, including radio and television. With the aid of these, and by various Machiavellian strategies and apparently miraculous deeds enacted by their local Seer agents, they aim to return communities to a scientifically enlightened and technologically supported condition.

Let me refer back briefly to my account of *The Guardians*. The boy protagonist Rob, it will be recalled, was in the course of his reading fascinated by the Musketeer novels of Dumas and by the temper of Chesterton's warring London boroughs. There runs through the *The Prince in Waiting Trilogy* the companionship and separations of a teenage three, Luke, Martin, and Edmund. Also the between-cities parochial strife and leadership rivalries have often something of that Chestertonian complexion. Moreover, although the thrust of action in the trilogy is more toward heroic and legendlike adventure, the "ideological" and psychological elements and motifs of *The Guardians* do to a considerable degree persist. There is an "illuminati" element, there is the existence of an "underdog" population, and on the psychological and personal levels, issues of loyalties are pervasive. The arena of action in the trilogy is a more remotely future one than that of *The Guardians*, but linking and framing allusions and images are similarly made to relate it to the reader's known world. For example, in the first novel of the trilogy, *The Prince in Waiting*, the boys, sequestered in their den under the ruins of Winchester Cathedral (comparable functionally to the overgrown gun-site "den" in *The Guardians*), pore over a limp, mildewed book, a rarity found under ancient rubble, and can read its faded title, *POPULAR MECHANIX*, not understanding the second word, but frightened, yet intrigued into speculative argument, by an ill-defined picture that they recognize as being of some kind of machine, "a forbidden thing" (*The Prince in Waiting Trilogy* 61).

In *The Prince in Waiting Trilogy*, Christopher achieves an excellent carryover effect from past through (reader's) present to the future by incidental topographical references, such as that to the plinth, washed by floods from the Itchin marshes, on which still stands, in future Winchester, remnants of the statue of "a great Prince of ancient times"—recognizable, maybe, to readers as the well-known King Alfred statue prominent in the center of the present city (91). The device of intriguing and "distancing" by inference and oblique description is particulary effective when, in *Beyond the Burning Lands*, Luke is entertained at the court of King Cymru (a court comparatively tolerant of machinery). By means of a hand-cranked, acetylene-lit projector, a torn and scratchy film is shown of animals "too ridiculously drawn even to be taken for polybeasts" (*The Prince in Waiting Trilogy* 241). It depicts a cat, constantly assaulted but always unharmed, forever pursuing, but never catching, a mouse!

Beyond the Burning Lands has taken Luke on a mission, by way of a secret and foot-scorching pass through the volcanic range that lies north of the warring cities, to the court of the King of the Wilsh at Klan Gothlen. Behind the rather crude "distancing" phoneticization, the location of Llangollen is easily apparent, and it is intriguingly described. The Wilsh court is more liberal in its attitude to polymufs, dwarfs, and machines than anything Luke had known, and dwelling there reinforces his Seer-inspired disposition toward change. This second volume of the trilogy has very much the pattern of the questing voyage into lands of marvels and unexpected dangers, combined with the "good/brave prince rewarded" motif of such *Märchen* of the Brothers Grimm as "The Queen Bee" or "The Skillful Huntsman"—the type of story in which, as noted by Padraic Colum in introducing *The Complete Grimm's Fairy Tales*, "heroes and heroines moved towards and gained an absolute worth in life," on the way perhaps encountering "giants and dwarfs who threatened or helped them" (Grimm and Grimm xii). Christopher's science fictional equivalent of giantslaying is Luke's heroic ridding Klan Gothlen of a huge, mutated, maningesting amoeboid polybeast, the Bayemot, which emerges from a valley lake "like quicksand, but quicksand which was alive, and hungry" (*The Prince in Waiting Trilogy* 258). The Perseuslike reward is betrothal to the princess Blodwen, who is to visit him after his return to Winchester. Luke himself only reaches Winchester (where he has to establish his princely right through trial by combat) after typical "perilous journey" encounters with various breeds and broods adapted to postdisaster environments: the Building Rats and the Sky People.

In the last novel of the trilogy, *The Sword of the Spirits,* the mood is at first idyllic, with feasting and minstrelsy celebrating Blodwen's visit to Winchester, but it turns sour with jealousies and betrayals, brought to a head following the court performance by an itinerant band of actors, headed by the Player King, of *Tristram and Iseult.* The description of this episode makes it clear that, as during its performance "a strange uneasiness" takes possession of Luke (*The Prince in Waiting Trilogy* 370), some element of Shakespearian pastiche is intended. The tragedy that subsequently develops has echoes of Hamlet, of Fortinbras, of Lancelot and Guinivere, of the breaking of the Round Table companionship. No such allusions are direct, but whether they are specifically sensed by readers or not, the exile of Luke at King Cymru's court, the love for Blodwen of Luke's friend Edmund, son of a deposed and slaughtered former Prince of Winchester, the return of Luke with a cannon-equipped army, bent on revenge and in league with King Cymru, Luke's indecision and turning away from his purpose (persuaded by the now Christian counsel of his old comrade Martin) are all structurally resonant of such age-old, literary, and archetypal motifs. At the conclusion of *The Sword of the Spirits,* and of the trilogy, Prince Luke is left with his establishment and his memories at King Cymru's court, a hero without a kingdom brooding sadly on the past. He is accompanied, however, by Seers, now overtly scientists, who are busily reinventing and constructing not only seagoing ships, railways, automobiles, and aircraft with which to reconquer the south and the savage lands, but also the more surely all-conquering weapons of technological ease and affluence. Luke says of such a future: "It will happen because it must, but I am in no great hurry to see it" (*The Prince in Waiting Trilogy* 458).

This ambivalence, which colors so many of the novels, is given striking expression in the episode in *The Sword of the Spirits* depicting Luke's solitary journey to virtual exile. He and his attendant, the loyal and "elevated" dwarf, Hans, are saved from death in a blizzard by the Bell People, a primitive hunting folk who delight in the tintinnabulation of adorning bells. The tribe's close-to-nature way of life heals Hans's wounds and half-heals Luke's bruised soul; but when urged to remain and offered "an end to loneliness and misery" (*The Prince in Waiting Trilogy* 422), he refuses to let either revenge or ambition die and presses on toward the destined technological and personal climax/anticlimax of the romance.

* * *

I have raised the question of the extent to which Christopher may presume a perceptive literary awareness on the part of his young readers. His contextual interweaving of the kinds of theme I have noted is sufficiently skillful to ensure them impact in their own right, but undoubtedly that impact will be strengthened by appreciation of the author's occasional oblique—or open—allusions. *Empty World* (1977), a juvenile flagged by the publisher's note as "for older readers," is a narrative offering scope for such strengthenings. It elaborates thematically Mary Shelley's *The Last Man*, bringing, from diverse environments, three survivors, a boy and two girls, of a race-annhilating plague to meet, explore, and attempt to subsist in a deserted and decaying London. For "older" juvenile readers versed in science fiction, stronger than any thematic reprise of Shelley, there may be certain Wellsian reverberations. When Christopher's protagonist, Neil, comes from the Sussex coast into London, his mazelike wanderings, the skeletons, and the ruinous buildings encountered create much the same apocalyptic effect as Wells achieves when in *The War of the Worlds* his narrator comes from Surrey to undergo like experiences in "Dead London," with its stillness, its plundered shops, and "mighty desert of houses" (429-30). While Neil is combing Harrods for provisions, Christopher takes him into the book department. The whole scene, a promenade through floors of now useless artifacts, develops into something not at all unlike the Traveller's passage through the Palace of Green Porcelain in Wells's *The Time Machine*. Neil, coming across shelves of science fiction broods on "hundreds and hundreds of exciting futures for the human race. All boiled down to one. Or rather, none" (88). The Traveller of *The Time Machine*, confronting "the decaying vestiges of books," is struck by "the enormous waste of labour to which this sombre wilderness of rotting paper testified" (87).

Elsewhere in *Empty World,* specific literary contrasts and comparisons are made, as when Neil comes across a despairing suicide's diary and discovers that he had started the diary because when sickness struck he had, ironically, been in the middle of reading Daniel Defoe's *Journal of the Plague Year,* and as when Neil, in his lonely Princes Gate refuge reading *The Swiss Family Robinson,* realizes that the family's desert island situation mirrors his in reverse, he having endless food and shelter but no companionship. The element of "Robinsonade" in the narrative is emphasized when, foraging in Harrods, Neil finds in a freshly spilt and still tacky pool of some cosmetic the clear imprint of a girl's shoe. That is the start of the uneasy threesome menage. It has its traumas and jealousies, and in a very qualifiedly upbeat ending, it presages fresh beginnings in a return to rural England. Hope appears more possible among the hills and farmhouses of the Cotswolds, where "they would grind corn and make their own bread" (32), than in the the dead and decaying city. That ending, in fact, embodies a symbolic polarity.

Such antithesis, once more and variantly transformed, exists in *Wild Jack* (1974), a novel of the twenty-third century. We are back here in what is defined as a post-Breakdown era, with a scene not wholly unlike that of *The Guardians,* save that now the sybaritic, affluent, and ordered life is lived, slave-supported and energy-oppulent in walled-in garden cities, while the Outlands, forested and populated by the excluded so-called Savages, are a wilderness without ordered civilization, though free of the totalitarian dictates of the sterile cities. The story's hero, Clive, is, in the course of dynastic rivalries involving his family, framed as a suspected egalitarian subversive and sent to a penal offshore island, from which he escapes with one American and one Japanese companion (a musketeer motif once more) to the English mainland. There, after various adventures and initiatory trials, the boys become members of a band headed by a renegade city man, a Robin Hood figure, the legendary Wild Jack. Clive had from birth been conditioned to the city's way of life, but disillusioned by betrayals and brutalities, he turns against its machine-and-slave-maintained easeful existence to enjoy, at grips with nature, Wild Jack's freedom of the Outlands. "We have no power, no machines. We're forced to live by the strength of our arms and the sweat of our brows" (116). That is what the outlaw offers and what the boys accept.

* * *

Freedom and self-determination are the values informing John Christopher's perhaps most popular creation, the Tripods trilogy comprised of *The White Mountains* (1967), *The City of Gold and Lead* (1967), and *The Pool of Fire* (1968). These novels preceded and in many respects foreshadowed *The Guardians.* In them the authoritarian and controlling Masters are extraterrestrials, the invasive Tripods, living in cities they have built to meet their biological requirements but stalking the Earth in tentacled capsules, carried high on sixty-foot mechanical legs, to maintain their rule and to ensure a docile (and generally contented) human slave reservoir. This they achieve by the ceremonial grafting on to children's skulls, at puberty, of a "cap" receptive of and ensuring obedience to their coercive orders. Will, Christopher's first-person protagonist, directed by "resistance" agents and having evaded being capped, travels with two similarly uncapped boys to the hideout of a cap-free remnant of mankind, situated in an ancient railway tunnel within the Jungfrau mountain, a headquarters later shifted to the limestone caves of central France and then to a remote coastal castle. From these sites the insurgents spread their message, penetrate and eventually destroy the alien cities and, having done so, establish a free human society of renascent nations with a renewed technology. In a later retrospectively scene-setting novel *When the Tripods Came* (1988)[4], a human Tripods' mouthpiece is said to think the caps "are passports to paradise" (55); but the resistants' counterphilosophy is voiced by the first-person boy narrator in a sentence that epitomizes the ethical substance of this and other of John Christopher's juveniles. "The peace and harmony [the capped ones] claimed to be handing out in fact was death, because, without being yourself, an individual, you weren't really alive" (57).

What in such a code may sometimes appear oversimplistic is offset by that strain of ambivalence that for Christopher's readers challenges any too easy acceptance of his "political" and social generalizations. Although the persuasive bias is ever toward a combination of free individualistic initiative with cooperative loyalty, the attractiveness and even the advantages of a stable conformity are depicted and not underplayed. For example, in *The White Mountains,* when the three companions on their journey through France to Switzerland have reached the Loire Valley, Will is laid low with a fever. He is nursed to health by members of an aristocratic family (homologues of the Giffords in *The Guardians*) who press him to stay with them. The chapter, "The Castle of the Red Tower" (6), is an idyll of the neo-medieval. The round of the seasons, the flowery meadows, the hunting and falconry and tournaments, the days on the river with the fair Elaine— these as described have the appeal of a tapestry or a Book of Hours illumination. The castle's people, though capped, indeed partly because of this, are gentle and generous. It is only loyalty to his companions, strengthened by a revelation of the horror of the Tripods' methods of domination, that persuades Will to forsake the tempting conformable life of the tradition-bound Loire community. Even at the close of the trilogy, when in *The Pool of Fire,* the Tripods having been defeated and their capping undone, the representatives of newborn nations gather in unity to engender a free world, there is an ambivalence. Discord breaks out, generosity disappears, old sentiments of jealousy, suspicion, and isolation prevail in ways that in the capped world would not have been possible. The "musketeers" in the book's last paragraph are left facing the necessity of a new campaign "to try to get men to live together in peace as well as liberty" (155-56).

* * *

In two novels, *Dom and Va* (1973) and *The Lotus Caves* (1969), Christopher pursues themes of indivudal initiative, courage, decision, and achievement through more than usually exotic settings. His prehistoric protagonists in *Dom and Va* are a boy and a girl, each surviving the conflicts of, respectively, an aggressive patriarchal hunting tribe and a gentler matriarchal herding tribe. "In the dawn of human history, he was our father, she was our mother" (142). This archetypal status makes more acceptable their anthropologically impossible progression through a quick succession of technoeconomic stages on the path of civilization. The cooperative and complementary actions and decisions of each work toward the winning of culture from chaos.

The moon is the exotic setting for *The Lotus Caves*. The boy heroes of an exploratory expedition follow an urge to adventure that soon tests their inventiveness, judgment, and will—particularly when they encounter an alien being and (in a reprise of a familiar Christopherian motif) find themselves compelled to choose between hazardous freedom and seductive subjugation. By locating his story on an unexplored planet, Christopher is able to mingle speculative fantasy with a modicum of science. The existence of the moon creature described as the Plant-God has no empirical basis. It is, in its attributes (telepathy, etc.), a being of fantasy, though a "scientific" rationale is provided for its origin. In this respect the novel is science fantasy, standing at what has been termed "the locus of intersection" between the two subgenres of science fiction and fantasy (Malmgren 260).

Christopher avails himself in this creation of the licence proposed by C. S. Lewis in his essay "On Science Fiction" that what matters about the "far worlds" of fiction is not so much any of the scientific probabilities involved as "their wonder, or beauty, or suggestiveness" (69). Nevertheless, Christopher's initial account of life within the moon-prospectors' Bubbles is excellent and credible. The restrictions, economies, and frustrations that weigh on two chidren, aggravated by punishment for a wasteful prank, seem to justify their boldness in bending rules and taking a "crawler" to explore further afield. They become marooned when their vehicle accidentally breaks through the moon's crust into a system of air-filled caves, where they encounter Thurgood, the unaged one-hundred-year-old, lost survivor of an early moon mission. The boys see him as a "Robinson Crusoe" (105). He has been fed and sustained by the story's central creation, the Plant-God, which manifests itself through a marvellous and beautiful variety of botanic phenomena.

The Plant-God had millenia earlier arrived from a distant galactic point of origin and had contrived for itself a suitable habitat below the moon's surface (this, though fanciful, is "scientifically" established most ingeniously). By a half-hypnotic communion, and through the effects of Thurgood's consumption of the various fruits of the caves, the Plant-God holds him in a form of symbiotic relationship, and when the boys experience the ecstatic peace and contentment this offers, in an idyllic but undemanding environment, there is temptation to follow Thurgood's example. Eventually, however, recognizing that their minds would become will-less and that there could be no future freedom of decision they determinedly escape back to the real world of action, trial, punishment, and reward; but Thurgood stays.

The allusive symbolism of this semiallegorical story is implicit in its title and is made explicit when one of the boys, realizing that the cave experiences are making memories of the Bubble seem progressively less real says, "Remember the lotus-eaters in the *Odyssey*" (129). A convergence of imagery, rather than any direct emergence of allusion, becomes apparent if we compare the episode of the boys' summons to the actual presence of the Plant-God with that of Cavor's summons to the presence of the Grand Lunar in H.G. Wells's *The First Men in the Moon*. Just as Cavor is taken by water to the cavern of the Grand Lunar, so are the two boys to the cave of the Plant-God. In both cases the sight encountered is impressive. Cavor records that the Grand Lunar "was seated in a blaze of incandescent blue" (250); the boys see the Plant-God as "a column of golden light that hung down from the cave roof" (113). In Wells's novel it is finally implied that Cavor is destroyed lest his messages to earth result in the advent of a technologically equipped human aggression.[5]

In *The Lotus Caves,* the boys realize that the Plant-God will be motivated against letting them return to the Bubble—the resources of the cave, its life-prolonging fruits and waters, are exploitable and the Plant-God "has no means of protection. The rock is no defence against explosives and rock drills" (117). The boys discuss the analogous fate of the whale, and after escaping, they deliberate at length as to whether their consciences will allow them to reveal the secret or will demand that they invent a believable story to account for their absence and thus protect the Plant-God. They conclude that the inevitable destruction by scientists of so wise and beautiful a being after its eons of life would be evil, and they decide to stay silent. Thurgood has escaped back into his cave-paradise. (There is a platonic, and ambiguous, recurring image that the boys associate with him, of a prisoner chained in a cell and excluded from all knowledge of the real world.) Yet in the story's final paragraphs the boy Marty thinks that when he himself is a very old man Thurgood will still be unchanged; will still be worshipping the Plant-God's splendor and wisdom. "He was glad to be on his way home, but there was a glimmer of something underneath the gladness. Only a hint of feeling, but he wondered if it could be envy" (156).

* * *

The stimulating ambivalence of Christopher's "messages" to the young is typified in those uncertainties of the closing chapter of *The Lotus Caves.* Typified, too, in the boys' "conservationist" dilemma, is the skill with which Christopher feeds a little didacticism, a little pedagogy, into accounts of adventure without diluting the appeal and force of his narrative. This appeal, which failing extensive quotation it is difficult to convey, accounts greatly for his continuing popularity and reprintings. Two distinctive characteristics of his writing, both particular aspects of the general skills I have mentioned, call for further comment: his ability to create exotic landscapes and creatures of the imagination and his outstanding ability to lead his readers to recognize and vicariously to explore features of their own country or planet by "distancing" these features, placing them at an imaginative remove.

First, then, to instance Christopher's exotic landscapes and their denizens. Some comparison of *The Lotus Caves* with *The First Men in the Moon* is permissible, but Christopher's lunar subterrain—the spinning leaves, the coiling stems and tangles of branches, the mossy carpet that "glowed green, mauve, dull amber" (*The Lotus Caves* 71)—is distinctive and compelling. The effect he achieves is almost psychedelic and is certainly poetic—an atmosphere suggestive of Coleridge crossed perhaps with Erasmus Darwin! In *Beyond the Burning Lands* Christopher's description of the Eyrie of the Sky People and their "High Thinking" is an inventive attempt to represent not only the appearance of that bizarre life-environment, but its concomitant semiotic codes.

The "High" part referred not only to the fact that they were sitting among the tree tops, but to the quality of the thoughts. One of them would say something such as, for instance, 'A man is like a tree', and off they would go, taking turns to toss in supposedly clever remarks on this subject. (*The Prince in Waiting Trilogy* 285).

So empathically involved may readers become that, although the cruel destruction of the Eyrie is necessary to save Luke from a grim (and, to pun significantly—for the whole episode is a "Hansel and Gretel" variant—a Grimm) fate, they are likely to share Luke's revlusion at its occurrence. A rather similar sentiment may be evoked when in *The Pool of Fire* the Tripod Masters are totally destroyed in their City. True, the Masters are the detested slaveholding aliens from whom the world must be set free, but in the preceding novel, *The City of Gold and Lead,* and particularly in reading such chapters as "My Master's Cat" (*CGL* 99-101, 105-6)[6], where the pyramidal architecture and the golden ball game are described, and "Under the Golden Wall" (*CGL* 159-78), in which the massive technology of the City is revealed, enough admiration may be awakened in readers to occasion some distress at the genocide of the creators of such wonders.[7]

Second, in order to illustrate further John Christopher's topographically and historically oriented terrestrial excursions, I will draw on his recent trilogy comprised of *Fireball* (1981), *New Found Land* (1983), and *Dragon Dance* (1986). In these novels he opens up a parallel Earth into which his boy protagonists are transported. They find themselves still in the 1980s, but in the Londinium of a Roman imperium persisting through the millenia; this as a consequence of Julian the Apostate's having, in *that* universe, survived to defeat the Persians and to reorganize the empire. The narrative abounds in the kind of "discovery" I have indicated. For example, in *Fireball,* the boy Simon finds himself on a hillside overlooking a small river and, he believes, standing on the site of (his own world's) suburban Brixton or Clapham. Now "the road ran arrow-straight beneath them, a long ribbon of black cutting through green, south to Venta Belgarum [Winchester], north only a few miles to Londinium." He knew of no river there, but this could possibly mean that, in his own world, "it had gone underground, part of the drainage system of the megalopolis" (113-14).

A Christian-inspired Spartacuslike revolt succeeds only in establishing an intolerant theocracy from which, in *New Found Land,* the boys escape trans-Atlantically to a Norseman- and Amerindian-peopled continent, innocent of both Columbus and Cortes. From the empty beach of an island, which Brad, the American boy, identifies as Nantucket, remembering it "jammed with tourists, hot dog vendors, ice cream vans" (35), their adventures take them via an extended and flourishing Aztec empire to California.

From there, captured by Chinese raiders, they are carried in *Dragon Dance* to the Celestial Kingdom, where an incipient technology, a ruthless conservatism, and a form of Buddhism (without Buddha) coexist. Here much action centers around the Great Wall, "no crumbling ruin but an artefact in good repair and in use" (88). In this book, as in *The Lotus Caves,* Christopher introduces a quasi-metaphysical dimension. Toward its close the Master of the Bonzery tells the boys, who have often nostalgically thought and dreamt of home, that the cosmos of parallel worlds is like a spinning wheel with countless spokes and that if he sets them loose "there is that within your soul which will take you (home), as a pigeon, over great distances, returns to its box" (27). The boys, in fact, elect to be launched on an exploration of other worlds, a difficult decision exemplifying those tensions between the exotic and the familiar, the dangerously challenging and the cosily supportive, which structure much of Christopher's juvenile science fiction.

In this last respect Christopher exhibits an aspect of the British "scientific romance" of which Wells was the definitive and defining writer who, as Brian Stableford puts it, "helped to create the niche that was colonised by the other writers" (4). Wells was a master of the Home Counties apocalyptic. The advent of his Martians in *The War of the Worlds* is given greater depth of horror as their depredations are traced through the trim gardens and lanes of Surrey—"this was the little world in which I had been living securely for years, this fiery chaos!" (276); and the stature and menace of his Herakleophorbia-fed giants in *The Food of the Gods* are accentuated by their despoilation of the rural London fringe of the North Downs, which became a "space of God's earth that was once sweet and fair, torn, desecrated, disembowelled" (219). It is a narrative ploy often pursued by Christopher. The Tripods are introduced to us in *Empty World* in a placid, almost folksy, country-town setting; the plague strikes amidst the byways "green and flowery" of a seaside village, with "the theme music of BBC television news heard faintly on the evening air" (12), and at an Old People's Home in suburban Croydon.

There are in the novels many variations on the Eden-desolated motif that betoken structures lying deeper than, though consonant with, the more readily observed "political" and ethical presentations. The womblike environment of *The Lotus Caves,* with its nourishlng waters, is only exited traumatically; yet it is a paradise that the freely active individual *must* leave. In the Tripods trilogy, the limestone caves (like the Jungfrau tunnel) where the uncapped insurgents hide and plan the future before issuing into a hostile world, constitute a similar ambience. The caves are full of the sound of water, are safe and rock-wall protected against the weather, are of even temperature day and night and throughout the seasons.

The later escape of the boys by watery vents from the vast dark cavern below the Tripod city graphically parallels processes of birth, and in their violent emergence from a condition of near-death, they are reborn to life. Landmarks of the passage from childhood to adolescence and on to postadolescent experience are also represented through powerful image and metaphor. There is, for example, in *The Prince in Waiting,* a point at which the boy Luke, after crossing a bounding ditch, is introduced into the underground Sanctuary of Initiation beneath Stonehenge. When he leaves it, in the guise of a special Acolyte, he has fresh knowledge and a life-purpose "to help create the conditions in which knowledge could be brought from hiding and the cities made safe against the sea of barbarism which lapped all round and must otherwise rise and drown them" (158).

A significant boundary symbol is that of the electrified fence in *The Guardians.* It divides Conurb from County, and Rob crosses it twice: first, as an alienated boy, to enter the County, scene of his adolescent turmoil and decision making; and again to leave that scene to enter upon a new phase of life in the Conurb, having decided where his loyalties and responsibilities should lie. "The fence glittered away in the distance, a barrier easily crossed except in men's minds" (154).

* * *

That such structures are discernible does not necessarily mean that they are of conscious significance to young readers—though at some level of understanding they may have awareness of them. In the course of a novel readers will primarily enjoy fast-moving adventure but may also be appreciative of stimulating games of locale exploration and identification. They will be made more keenly aware of their own environments, geographical and temporal, as these contrast with or relate to other actual or imagined environments, and their understanding will be focused on the role of a free and responsible individual in contexts of environment and society. The adolescent protagonists whose exploits they follow are often motivated to command nature. At the same time, as in *The Prince in Waiting,* there may be represented a technocratic *hubris* followed by a decline toward the kind of condition in which, as described by Oswald Spengler, "nature becomes exhausted, the globe sacrificed to Faustian thinking" (II: 505). Counterecologies and cultures are half or wholly sympathetically displayed in the lunar ambience of the Plant-God or in the community of the Bell People. Thus, in being responsively involved in "problem" situations, the resolutions of which may often occasion some degree of ambivalence, young readers will be pleasurably, but challengingly, introduced to that experience that Coleridge, in writing of *The Tempest,* registered as a "genuine excitement [which] ought to come from within,—from the moved and sympathetic imagination" (401).

NOTES

1. *The Death of Grass* was published and filmed in the United States with the title *No Blade of Grass,* and *A Wrinkle in the Skin* was published in the United States with the title *The Ragged Edge* .

2. Christopher uses here the concept "the County" not with reference to any existing single county, but to denote his larger imagined territory to which that phrase, used in its colloquial sociological sense, may be applied—a sense that, complete with nuances of class structure, accords with the *Shorter Oxford Dictionary* secondary definition: " the county families or county gentry collectively."

3. Winchester College, founded by William of Wykeham in 1382, is situated ten miles beyond the present Southampton city limits. Christopher is here giving some idea of the extent of his future Conurb. G. N. Trevelyan in his *English Social History* notes that Winchester became "a model for foundations of equal splendour, like Eton" and that at its foundation "a proportion of its scholars were to be 'sons of noble and powerful (*valentum*) persons.'"

4. One circumstance explained in *When the Tripods Came* is how resistant humans came to establish their sanctuary/headquarters in the Jungfrau tunnel. This novel, written in the same decade as the repopularizing of the trilogy by its television version, serves similar purposes to those of Isaac Asimov's "retrospective" novel *Prelude to Foundation* (1988) and Anne McCaffrey's *Dragonsdawn* (1988).

5. The "imperialist" human Weston, in C. S. Lewis's *Out of the Silent Planet* (1938), is likewise a menace to the harmonious Martian ecology and is forcibly returned to an earthly quarantine by the tutelary spirit of Mars.

6. "My Master's Cat" is one of the most resonant of Christopher's concepts. Human as captive "pet" has a Swiftian flavor; and the privileged "pet" acquiring the knowledge to destroy its master and so to escape evokes, for example, "Hansel and Gretel" and "Jack the Giant-Killer."

7. The Tripods in their traveling machines have obvious similarities to Wells's *War of the Worlds* Martians. Unlike them, however, they are eventually defeated not by any fortuitous biological circumstance but by human initiative and perseverance. Like them they exhibit a technology that commands their victims' awe, if not admiration.

BIBLIOGRAPHY

References to Christopher's works are to Puffin Books editions when these are listed.

Christopher, John [Christopher Samuel Youd]. *Beyond the Burning Lands.* London: Hamish Hamilton, 1971. Rpt. in *The Prince in Waiting Trilogy.* London: Puffin Books, 1983.
_____. *The City of Gold and Lead.* London: Hamish Hamilton, 1967; Rpt. Puffin Books 1984. 1988, 2nd edition.
_____. *The Death of Grass.* London: Michael Joseph, 1956.
_____. *Dom and Va.* London: Hamish Hamilton, 1973.
_____. *Dragon Dance.* London: Viking Kestrel, 1986.
_____. *Empty World.* London: Hamish Hamilton, 1977. Rpt. Puffin Books, 1981.

_____. *Fireball.* London: Gollancz, 1981.

_____. *The Guardians.* London: Hamish Hamilton, 1970.

_____. *The Lotus Caves.* London: Hamish Hamilton, 1969.

_____. *New Found Land.* London: Gollancz, 1983.

_____. *The Pool Of Fire.* London: Hamish Hamilton, 1968; Rpt. Puffin Books, 1984.

_____. *The Prince in Waiting.* London: Hamish Hamilton, 1970. Rpt. in *The Prince in Waiting Trilogy.* London: Puffin Books,1983.

_____. *The Prince in Waiting Trilogy.* London: Puffin Books, 1983.

_____. *The Sword of the Spirits.* London: Hamish Hamilton, 1972. Rpt. in *The Prince in Waiting Trilogy.* London: Puffin Books, 1983.

_____. *When the Tripods Came.* London: Viking Kestrel, 1988.

_____. *The White Mountains.* London: Hamish Hamilton, 1967. Rpt. Puffin Books: London, 1984.

_____. *Wild Jack.* New York: Macmillan, 1974.

_____. *A Wrinkle in the Skin.* London: Hodder and Stoughton, 1965.

Coleridge, S. T. *Coleridge: Select Prose and Poetry.* Ed. Stephen Potter. London: Nonesuch Press, 1972.

Grimn, Jacob, and Wilhelm Grimm. *The Complete Grimm's Fairy Tales.* Introduction by Padraic Colum. Commentary by Joseph Campbell. London: Routledge & Kegan Paul, 1975.

Fisher, Margery. "Henry Treece." *Three Bodley Head Monoqraphs.* Ed. Kathleen Lines. London: Bodley Head, 1969.

Lewis, C.S. "On Science Fiction." *Of Other Worlds: Essays and Stories.* Ed. Walter Hooper. London: Geoffrey Bles, 1966. 59-73.

Malmgren, Carl D. "Towards a Definition of Science Fantasy." *Science-Fiction Studies* 16 (Nov. 1988): 259-81.

Spengler, Oswald. *Der Untergang des Abenlandes.* Munich, 1918-22. *The Decline of the West.* 2 vols. Trans. Charles Francis Atkinson. 2 vols. London: George Allen & Unwin, 1934.

Stableford, Brian. *Scientific Romance in Britain 1890-1950.* London: Fourth Estate, 1985.

Trevelyan, G. N. *English Social History.* London: Longmans, Green, 1942.

Wells H. G. *The Time Machine* (1895), *The War of the Worlds* (1898), *The First Men in the Moon* (1901), *The Food of the Gods* (1904). *The Works of H. G. Wells.* Atlantic Ed. 28 vols. London: T. Fisher Unwin, 1924-27.

8

Danger Quotient, Fiskadoro, Riddley Walker, and the Failure of the Campbellian Monomyth

Millicent Lenz

Danger Quotient, by Annabel and Edgar Johnson, *Fiskadoro*, by Denis Johnson, and *Riddley Walker*, by Russell Hoban, share post-nuclear-catastrophe settings and adolescent male protagonists struggling against chaos, longing to recover, reinvent, or restructure a fragmented humanness. My wish to look at them in tandem, even though this entails a cursory treatment of them all, grows from my perception of a certain progression in their relationship to the mythic tradition of Western literature, particularly as this tradition has been shaped by what Joseph Campbell terms the "monomyth" of the hero's adventure, encompassing the three rites of passage: separation, initiation, and return (30, 245-46).

The progression I see may be briefly sketched. In *Danger Quotient*, the monomyth is played out in the context of implicitly affirmed "old order values;" its elitist, materialistic heroic exalts paternalistic values at the expense of nature. *Fiskadoro*, in contrast, portrays the collapse of the old order and, further, exposes the violence underlying the myth of heroic sacrifice. Sacrifice, violence to the self, it is worth recalling, is central to Campbell's concept of the monomyth. *Riddley Walker*, in many ways the ultimate nuclear novel, similarly shows how violence, the corrupt element in the old order, has roots in what Daniel C. Noel has called in a brilliant metaphor, the "hounding of nature" ("The Nuclear Horror," pass.). Hoban's myth-rich text goes far beyond the other two narratives: first, because his protagonist refuses to embrace a re-ascendant mythology of violence and opts instead for creativity and intellectual playfulness; and second, because out of the chaos surrounding him, he constructs a way of being human, a personal mythology, an original "pattern-that-connects," in anthropologist Gregory Bateson's term (Capra 71-89).

Among these three works only *Riddley Walker* holds promise for addressing the contemporary Western psyche's troubled relationship with the Feminine inherent in the Campbellian monomyth and indeed in Western heroic tradition per se. Only Hoban's novel, I believe, transcends the pitfalls of Platonic dualism, undercuts the pretentious egoexaltation of the predominant Western heroic patterns, and clears the way for a mythology capable of supporting a whole relationship with the natural world. This is because *Riddley Walker* presents the conscious choice of a creativity-centered mode of human relationship to the "other," the nonself.

Let us look at the three texts in more detail. *Danger Quotient*, by Annabel and Edgar Johnson, is a light atomic adventure novel for teenagers, with a slight romantic subplot. Set in the year 2127, 130 years after World War III, it depicts survivors who "live like earthworms" (4) in an underground complex in Colorado. Humanness as we think of it today has been compromised. Casey is a test-tube and laboratory-nurtured eighteen-year-old whose genetic material has been cloned from those who sought shelter in the bowels of the earth when nuclear radiation shredded the delicate ozone layer and made survival above ground impossible. A superintelligent genetic hybrid, Casey undertakes a quest to find why supergeniuses like himself are dying at a young age. Starting from the assumptions of Darwinian evolution, he theorizes that since humans evolved in an environment of danger, they need a "danger quotient" to survive. Life in a secure, controlled subterranean "womb" robs them of longevity.

Casey's mythic ancestry is mixed. In a Campbellian context, he is the Great Hunter, but his hunt depends on his ability to time-travel. This ability of magical flight, granted him by advanced technology, suggests a relationship with Mercury or Hermes. Since he is superhumanly endowed, Casey cannot be taken seriously as a representative of the human condition. He is a literary construct, the stock-in-trade hero of the adventure romance, who *must*, by the rules of the genre, finally triumph.

Casey lives out the three stages of the Campbellian monomyth—separation, initiation, and return—in a simplistic fashion. He is doubly separated from others, first by his clone nature and second by his backward movement in time. His initiation comes when he is introduced to human emotions, affection, and feelings of vulnerability. His final return as the technologically gifted savior of his race relates him to the Captain America paradigm familiar in science fiction. He discovers his previous existence in the twentieth century as the multimillionaire Midas Forsythe, a developer who transformed Cinderella City, an enormous Donald Trumpish shopping mall, into the underground complex where a privileged remnant has survived the ravages of nuclear holocaust. The assignment the twenty-second century Casey has been genetically engineered to carry out—to find a solution to the ozone-layer depletion that imprisons his race underground—is forgotten.

In archetypal terms, Casey's achievement of maturity in the future society of the novel rests upon action that requires the talents of an all-American entrepreneur, but these are magnified beyond normal human proportions. The Captain America myth is made explicit in the description of Midas Forsythe:

Midas Forsythe, a man without a past, a mystery figure who came from nowhere, complete with plans, money and the dedication to show a desperate populace how to face devastation and live through it. (198)

This is Casey, a peculiarly American savior, who possesses astounding managerial abilities (the complete plans), King Midas-like riches, and technological know-how, augmented by his access to the supercomputer of the twenty-second century, Pinocchio, whose artificial intelligence far exceeds the brain power of mere humans. Casey discovers a 1996 speech of Midas Forsythe's, declaring that war and its aftermath are "nature's impassive way of testing our viability, to see whether we can evolve into a species that can dominate its ancient killer instinct" (134). Note the contradiction: Killing is assumed to be instinctual, thus natural; at the same time, nature is supposed to be a moral teacher. A dualistic view of human nature is implied: When our higher nature can dominate our lower nature, our species can presumably live in peace.

Read as sheer entertainment or mock epic, *Danger Quotient* is harmless enough. Some books are intended to fly below critical radar, and this may be one of them. Nevertheless, elements of the novel's mythic pattern may disturb some of us who find shortcomings in the Western tradition of heroic myth. The shortcomings manifest themselves in several ways. First, the capitalistic and patriarchal overtones of the Captain America paradigm may be less valid than their assumption presupposes. Second, there is the neglect of biocentric, ecological values that results when the Feminine is reduced to being no more than the "prize" for the "hero." Casey, I should point out, is rewarded with success in his romantic quest.

Third—and this is a weakness *Danger Quotient* shares with many novels designed for a youthful audience—is the failure to question received cultural values. The text's conformity to the prevailing, comforting cultural assumptions and the ego-aggrandizing myths so strong in the war mythologies of Western tradition is obvious. Underlying it all is a failure to value an abiding, harmonious relationship to the natural world. Both the gods above and the gods below have been banished, and Casey (alias Midas) has usurped the godlike preogative, solving the crisis with his self-sufficient, cloned artificial intelligence. A thinking reader may come away feeling the gods will have their revenge on this pseudogod (who is also a pseudohuman) who has dared to encroach upon their territory, for though he is rewarded with worldly success, the ozone layer grows, all the while, quietly and ominously larger. Casey's progeny face a continued underground existence, hardly human as we understand the term. Mother Nature, ignored, patronized, and outraged, will take a terrible revenge.

Both *Fiskadoro* and *Riddley Walker* were intended for adult audiences but are accessible to literate young adults (both made the *Booklist* and *School Library Journal* bibliographies of adult books recommended for young adult readers). Superior in literary quality, they also raise basic existential questions and reflect concern over the need for a new mythic paradigm based on biocentric ideals.

Fiskadoro Hidalgo is a thirteen-year-old black boy whose mythically significant first name derives from *pescadore*, fisherman, and *fisgadore*, harpooner.
Hidalgo, his last name, means a "man of the lower nobility" or a "man who owns
considerable property or is otherwise esteemed" (*Random House Dictionary of
the English Language*) and thus endows the boy with a noble ancestry, underscores the irony his present destitution; his personal fall from high estate is the
microcosmic expression of the decay of the entire civilization. Sixty years after
a nuclear holocaust, Fiskadoro lives in a Twicetown in the Florida Keys, so named
for having twice escaped incineration when "dud" nuclear weapons came down
nearby and failed to detonate. The impoverished and illiterate boy cherishes his
one legacy from the past, his clarinet. He seeks out the middle-aged Mr. Cheung,
of mixed Chinese-British descent, who, in an effort to preserve art and culture, has
assembled a ragtag band of musicians named, ludicrously, the Miami Symphony
Orchestra.

Fiskadoro's experiences fit the Campbellian three-part monomyth well.
Seeking identity and purpose, he encounters the pains of mortality: His father is
killed in a senseless boating accident, his grieving mother suffers from radiation-
induced "kill-me," a cancer caused by the radiation-poisoned environment. His
psychological separation is compounded by physical isolation when, lonely and
full of frustrated sexual longings, he tracks a girl of the Quaraysh (a swamp people
immersed in bizarre occult beliefs) and, in a brain-washed state, undergoes
subincision, their traumatic male initiation rite. A remarkable flashback, related
as a dream sequence, tells in vivid detail how a shaman conducts the rites whereby
the boys are drugged, psychically enslaved, induced to maim themselves, and left
without memory.

Fiskadoro survives separation and initiation but is robbed of his past. Cheung,
who cherishes all surviving tokens of the ruined preholocaust culture, panics when
he realizes history can be obliterated. When Fiskadoro returns to his own tribe, he
seems endowed with a magical intelligence; for the first time, he can play the
clarinet expertly, like some musical idiot savant, and read with ease. He has
presumably tapped into the shamanic powers of the collective unconscious.
Cheung reluctantly accepts the seemingly inevitable; and in an epiphany of
enlightenment, he sees himself and Fiskadoro standing between two civilizations.
He tells Fiskadoro he will be a "great leader," for he has unburdened himself of
a past weighted with intolerable guilt. In the world after the bomb, knowledge of
history is, Cheung now thinks, a liability.

All the old structures are obliterated. Cheung and Fiskadoro provide music
for a celebration to mark the end of "Babylon" and the beginning of a new era,
whether for good or ill, the reader must guess. The closing image of the novel, a
mysterious and ambiguous floating shape on the horizon, may prefigure either a
coming Peaceable Kingdom or another Armageddon.

Mythically, Fiskadoro is the sacrificed Fisher King figure, whose sexual
wound represents the lost fertility of his radiation-sickened world. Ironically, he
lacks a Parsifal, whose help is needed to restore blooms to the desert. The myths

of the past are fractured beyond repair, and the text does not supply any new "pattern-that-connects." The impoverished language, a patois of English and Spanish, suggests the difficulty of articulating a coherent myth to explain the nucleated world.

The mythical richness of *Riddley Walker* can be only glanced at in this short analysis. Riddley is the twelve-year-old protagonist of "a fable-like story about a hunting-gathering culture" (Myers 5) living in a Stone Age following a nuclear war.[1] Separated from human history by his birth into a dismembered world, Riddley experiences the death of his father in the first scene of the novel. On Riddley's "naming day" (1), his dad is killed when a group of men foraging for scrap metal accidently drop upon him a "girt big thing," some machine whose very name is now lost, crushing him before Riddley's eyes (10). Riddley inherits his father's role as "connexion man," the shamanistic storyteller-puppeteer, the mythmaker of his pathetically disconnected world. The wasteland he inhabits is the ultimate demonstration of the failure of a mythology that valued technological power over creative human capacities to sustain biological, psychological, and spiritual wholeness.

Riddley's imaginings are shaped partly by Lorna Elswint, a shamanistic older woman who tells him some of the major myths of his culture; her stories teach him to value the Feminine, dream side of consciousness, called the "1st knowing." The sacrificial aspect of heroic myth is exposed in its violent aspect in the sequences relating the reinvention of gunpowder. The violence of the life processes themselves is evident as well in images of life feeding on life in the Punch and Pooty sequences.

Riddley, however, rejects violence and shows compassion, at the risk of his own life, as when he rescues Goodparley from his torturers (175). His game-playing, improvising imagination goes beyond the constricting boundaries of the blood-drenched mythologies of power based on explosives—gunpowder and the "1 Big 1" (the atomic bomb)—and beyond the violent acting out of Punch and Pooty to suggest a creative way of being in the world. For Riddley, this means the creative artist's way of improvising "on the road," a process of making "reality" up as one goes along—by linguistic means. Inherent in Hoban's mythic novel is the power to move forward, through the invention of stories, into the future. Riddley's openness to innovation accommodates the shifting quality of con-sciousness, and his respect for the chthonic powers of nature (evident in the Greanvine sequence) shows his openness to the wisdom of goddess tradition.

Riddley's way of storymaking contrasts positively to the monomyth's model of male maturation, which views life as a Great Hunt, stressing achievement, inherently demanding the violent self-sacrifice of the hero, and relegating Woman to the status of prized object. Campbell fails to critique this patriarchal model of adulthood, despite his sensitivity to the way myths and rituals of male maturation mask the attempt "to deny the mother's power or to take it from her" (King 79). (A good example occurs in the puberty rite in *Fiskadoro*, where the male shaman gives 'birth' to the man by inflicting a wound on the boy.) Campbell persists in seeing Woman as a "mystery" to the male, but he cannot appreciate how she experiences herself and thus limits her to a fertility goddess figure (Downing104).

Hoban's text, on the other hand, though still presenting the Feminine as Mystery, also shows its male protagonist as experiencing the powers of the Feminine within himself—expressed in the novel as the power of the intuitive "1st knowing" (18). *Riddley Walker* thus helps to answer the need of a post-nuclear-holocaust world for myths with an ecological dimension, imaginative constructs with the ability to "remind us of our emotional and erotic bonds with the natural world and of the interdependence of all that lives" (Downing106). In short, Riddley as protagonist is attuned to the "biocentric" myths, celebrating diversity and intimacy, valuing storytelling as a mode of life characterized by "playfulness, not contest, [by] giving, not giving up" (Sexson 146). In Riddley's improvisatory spirit, Hoban gives us a model for creative mythmaking in a world otherwise deprived of structure. In the deconstructed spiritual wasteland of Hoban's bleak world, Riddley seems to have the rare artistic and psychic resources to compose a human life out of remnants of language and art.[2] He is also a living metaphor for the creative writer's (and it may be the creative reader's) structuring consciousness.

NOTES

1. The novel's much-praised linguistic innovation is a brilliant mix of phonetically spelled fragmented, regressed English, "Middle-English scatological slang" full of "obscure catch phrases" (Noel, "The Nuclear Horror" 291) and sly puns, worth reading for Hoban's witcraft alone. The mythic abundance has been explored notably by Daniel C. Noel in "The Nuclear Horror and the Hounding of Nature," a lucid approach through archetypal psychology to the Eusa myth and the central image of the novel, drawn from Pisanello's painting of *The Vision of St. Eustace*. Riddley's quest for "knowledge of self and psychic wholeness" in the "postapocalyptic" fantasy setting of Kent, 2400 years in the future, has been admirably interpreted in Jack Branscomb's "The Quest for Wholeness in the Fiction of Russell Hoban."

2. In an instance of the phenomenon known to Jungian psychology as the *principle of synchronicity*, "a meaningful relationship with no possible causal connection between a subjective experience within the human psyche and an objective event . . . in the outer world of reality" (Harry A. Wilmer, *Practical Jung: Nuts and Bolts of Jungian Psychotherapy*, Wilmette, IL: Chiron, 1987, 169-72), Mary Catherine Bateson uses the metaphors of "composition" and "improvisation" for the meaning-making process in women's lives. See her *Composing a Life* (New York: Penguin/Plume, 1990).

BIBLIOGRAPHY

Branscomb, Jack. "The Quest for Wholeness in the Fiction of Russell Hoban." *Critique* 28 (1986): 29-38.

Campbell, Joseph. *The Hero with a Thousand Faces*. 2nd ed. Princeton: Princeton UP, 1968. ["Dismemberment" and "Crucifixion" are at the center of the diagram of the mythological adventure.]

Capra, Fritjof. "The Pattern Which Connects: Gregory Bateson." *Uncommon Wisdom: Conversations with Remarkable People*. New York: Bantam, 1988. 71-89.

Downing, Christine. "Masks of the Goddess: A Feminist Response." *Paths to the Power of Myth*. Ed. Daniel C. Noel. New York: Crossroad, 1990. 97-109.

Hoban, Russell. *Riddley Walker*. New York: Summit, 1980.

Johnson, Annabel, and Edgar Johnson. *Danger Quotient*. New York: Harper, 1984.

Johnson, Denis. *Fiskadoro*. New York: Random House/Vintage, 1986.

King, Karen L. "Social Factors in Mythic Knowing: Joseph Campbell and Christian Gnosis." *Paths to the Power of Myth*. Ed Daniel C. Noel. New York: Crossroad, 1990. 66-80.

Maynor, Natalie, and Richard F. Patteson. "Language as Protagonist in Russell Hoban's *Riddley Walker*." *Critique* 26 (1984): 18-25.

Myers, Edward. "An Interview with Russell Hoban." *Literary Review: An International Journal of Contemporary Writing* 28.1 (1984): 5-16.

Noel, Daniel C. "The Nuclear Horror and the Hounding of Nature: Listening to Images." *Soundings: An Interdisciplinary Journal* 70 (Fall/Winter 1987): 289-308.

_____, ed. *Paths to the Power of Myth: Joseph Campbell and the Study of Religion*. New York: Crossroad, 1990.

Pisanello. *The Vision of St. Eustace*. The National Gallery, London.

Sexson, Lynda. "Let Talking Snakes Lie: Sacrificing Stories." *Paths to the Power of Myth*. Ed. Daniel C. Noel. New York: Crossroad, 1990. 134-53.

9

Growing Home: The Triumph of Youth in the Novels of H. M. Hoover

Thom Dunn and Karl Hiller

As recently as 1979, Peter Nicholls could with accuracy lament the lack of "generic purity" in children's literature: "Much children's fantasy contains SF elements and, conversely, much children's SF is written with a disregard for scientific accuracy, whether from hauteur or ignorance, which effectively renders it fantasy." By way of example, Nicholls notes that time travel in children's fiction is "an essentially magic device used in the service of fantasy" instead of being explored in and of itself as an intriguing subject for scientific speculation (113). The decade of the 1980s has, however, seen a dramatic and positive change in the situation with several writers offering to young minds works that challenge the scientist in them, and none has done this consistently with greater force than H. M. Hoover.

For the past two decades, Hoover has been turning out juvenile science fiction of very high quality with a dozen titles that belong on the shelves of every junior high school library. Hoover has written that science fiction's presentation of ideas as images makes it important as a teaching tool, since imaging is the very thinking process Einstein and other great thinkers used to generate new ideas ("SF—Out of This World"). This literary philosophy born to fruition is quite enough to make Hoover an important writer for young adults, but as we hope to show, Hoover's importance is even more profound: In her fiction, we find not so much a "product" turned out effectively for the instruction (and pleasure) of young minds as *the record of a true literary search* on her part, an attempt to solve, or at least explore, the mystery of growth in the individual, set against the relatively slower growth in society, and the inevitable conflicts and adjustments engendered by this contrast. There seems, thus, to be a kind of high mission and consequent development in Hoover's youth fiction, such as we find in such masters of the genre as C. S. Lewis and Ursula K. Le Guin. So it is that we find in her tales provocative images of scientific concepts and a liberating experience for the human spirit. Hoover always manages to showcase the struggles of her young protagonists to achieve acceptance in a world as troubled and challenging as our own.

We do not argue that Hoover's is a major talent, but we do assert that she has not yet received her due share of recognition and critical attention for the considerable skill and power of her work, nor adequate praise for her struggle to mirror the nature and humanity of childhood in its more painful vicissitudes. Those who study science fiction have a requirement to consider her work more closely, and those who teach young people have a responsibility to acknowledge the profound values to be gleaned within the realms of science fiction.

* * *

In most of her fiction, Hoover effectively uses the future as a background against which to consider themes that in contemporary settings would seem dark indeed. Her fictive worlds teem with incompetent, neglectful, and uncaring adults; in them, children are ignored, sometimes abused, often left to shift for themselves in ugly, sometimes hostile, environments. This is not to say, however, that Hoover is a poet of despair. The situation is never hopeless, nor do her protagonists even flirt with giving up; instead, they soldier on with a grim determination adults might envy. Again and again, Hoover finds in childhood and adolescence a tenacious strength all but forgotten by the adults of her future worlds. If the landscapes of her imagination are blighted by adult battle commitments and other preoccupations, her young people always manage to find the strength to snatch the reins of power and establish a newer, freer world for themselves.

So it is in *The Children of Morrow* (1973) and its sequel *The Treasures of Morrow* (1976). Tia and Rabbit are telepaths ill at ease in their wasteland home, "The Base"; but a visit to the more advanced and enlightened community of Morrow proves ironically that home is not a simple matter to define. Here and in all her subsequent novels, Hoover's children must struggle to find—or make for themselves— a "home" worthy of that title.

In *The Delikon* (1977), the Delikon, like John Christopher's Tripods, are an alien species ruling Earth as they see fit. Hoover takes Christopher's premise one step further: What if the aliens, not simply invaders and slave masters, were truly concerned with compassionate rule? Would they rule well and wisely? As expected, since this is a science fiction novel, the answer is "No," because something is very wrong. The rigid social order with its almost Confucian discipline is repugnant to Earthlings who live a much shorter lifespan than the Delikon. One of the latter, Varina, experiences an extreme form of reverse culture shock when she tries, in human disguise, to comprehend human discontent so strong it boils into revolution. In Varina's groping to understand what we readers already know full well, children can experience the cognitive disonance hitherto limited largely to adult science fiction and experience in extrapolated form the kind of cultural conflict that arises constantly among different societies of our own world in our own time—altogether an Einsteinian thought experiment in social anthropology. Such sophistocation of subject matter and such complete lack of condescension are the unvarying hallmarks of Hoover's fiction for young readers.

Anthropocentrism is examined in *The Rains of Eridan* (1977) when Theo, a young naturalist, and Karen, a child-orphan of conflict, team up first to survey and later to explore planetary life-forms. Often the clear-eyed vision of children is instrumental in the process. The story of exploration provides a background for their developing relationship. Karen learns to trust her new parent, and Theo learns that the child is skilled beyond her years—both with a laser gun and in the handling of fear and grief. Here and throughout Hoover's work, characters grope toward friendship across gender and/or generation, searching for clues to enlighten their immediate situations and solve the larger mysteries that imprison those about them.

By 1979, Hoover hit full stride as a writer of clearly definable works of science fiction for children, books that established four elements of the Hoover novel: 1) a clean, spare style with attention to select detail rather than atmospheric effects; 2) an abiding concern for environmental integrity and protection; 3) a keen interest in presenting children with the full range of promises that had become the staples of adult science fiction; and 4) a firm, at times painful, insistence on the realistic portrayal of childhood as a time fraught with loneliness, psychic isolation, and hard choices in a bewildering environment created largely by preoccupied adults and difficult circumstances of survival.

The concept of the conscious emotional disconnection for the purpose of psychological survival occurs frequently in Hoover's tales. In *The Lost Star* (1979), the young hero is ignored by parents who have adopted emotional reserve as a policy for working together as off-Earth astronomers over long periods of time. Her ability, born of youthful innocence, to recognize intuitively the intelligence and intrinsic worth of alien creatures is reminiscent of Ursula K. Le Guin's *The Word for the World Is Forest*, but Hoover's is a lighter and more hopeful tale. Also, the refreshing constant of her work is her depiction of realistic youth—not precocious kids in a fantasy world solving the problems of bumbling adults with their superior intellects. Youth, rather, is depicted as a special state, a passage of life whose clean slate allows its happy possessor to see through adult tangles for lack of vested interests. So we seem to have come 180 degrees from that "Father Knows Best" mentality, which yielded a literature of spoon-fed morals, a fatuous invitation for youth to join a perfect adult world.

This Time of Darkness (1980) utilizes the familiar idea of the escape from a hermetic environment to explore in depth the struggle of children to receive the affection and acceptance that should be theirs by right. Ostracized for their ability to read, Amy and Axel are two children in a Big Brother-style underground hive community so benighted that it has left scars on their bodies and has lost sight of any concept of a better world outside. Readers of science fiction will see in this story a children's literature counterpart of E. M. Forster's classic *The Machine*

Stops, and teachers may find it worthwhile for the hope it provides the abused child of the real world striving for psychic survival. As with the other adverse conditions in her future worlds, the children react to abuse with pragmatic defensive maneuvers free from the horrified reactions we might expect from adults, and the futuristic settings allow young readers to consider the issue of physical and sexual abuse as an abstraction that may or may not apply to their this-world situations.

In *Another Heaven, Another Earth* (1981), once more youth is hardly a paradise wasted on the young but rather life at its most confusing; adults are not monsters but battle-scarred survivors playing out a hand of settled compromise made by earlier generations in order to survive. Outside of science fiction per se, Hoover is one of a whole new generation of writers—like Judy Blume, Paul Zindel, and S. E. Hinton—whose work accepts alienation as a condition of youth itself, a baptism of ice water, a first horrific glimmer of the human condition. Each of us can surely remember such a dunking, the shock of it to the system, and if we are honest, we may admit that we could not take it now—that only the young can withstand youth.

All this is not to suggest that Hoover is in any way despairing of adult society and that children are for her the only hope for a better world. The situation may be quite otherwise: All human life, all life in general for that matter, may be viewed as a struggle against entropy within which humanity—by its very tenacity to adapt, hang on, and grow—is quite literally unnatural. In this context, each of us must "grow" a home (or in Virginia Woolf's less ambitious metaphor, a "room") of his or her own, carve a niche where there has been none provided, battling even with adults of our own species on occasion for living space and life support. Adaptation is, thus, not only a key ability of the human species, but an essential requirement for survival. Few of us can expect to be adopted by friendly wolves.

* * *

The novels of Hoover's first eight years of publication have mostly clean and simple plot lines, even traditional ones; but her next two, *The Bell Tree* (1982) and *The Shepherd Moon* (1984), find Hoover grappling with greater fictional complexity, extending her range and depth of mimesis, and probing the human heart and finding therein greater ambivalence and ambiguity.

In *The Bell Tree*, Hoover uses the device of archeologists exploring an alien world to study the relationships of a young woman, her father, and her first boyfriend. In background, motivation, and relationships, these three chartacters are all more sharply delineated than Hoover's earlier protagonists. Jenny Sadler is a fifteen-year-old with a B.A. degree and is set up to inherit the family business. Dr. James Sadler, her father, takes care of the family business, a research firm founded by his grandfather, but spends most of his time taking long, solitary trips in search of relatively impractical things. Sadler describes himself as a dilettante.

Eli (as he has named himself) shuns human contact, believes that people are untrustworthy, and hates to be touched. He has an unfortunate history: Abandoned by his father before his birth, Eli was originally named Gigo (garbage in, garbage out) by his mother, who told everyone that he was named for his father. This unpleasant woman died when Eli was three, leaving him to be raised by a robot "drone nurse" and taught by computers. He eventually went off to live by himself in the wilderness—small wonder that he is "damaged" and considered a bit "crazy" by those who know him.

The story line of *The Bell Tree* contains many by now familiar Hooverian elements. The discovery by Eli of an ancient scroll in the wilds of Tanin (a frontier planet inhabited mainly by miners, prospectors, and research scientists, including a Sadler Institute base that is developing crops for future settlement in the vast inhospitable wilderness) brings Dr. Sadler to Tanin on another quest despite the majority opinion (held by the institute director and staff) that Tanin was never inhabited. Sadler brings Jenny along for once, hoping to teach her some new things and to improve their relationship. Along with Eli, the pair head out into the wild.

Here, then, is a much richer setup for adventure than, for example, the earlier *Rains of Eridan*, and reviewers greeted *The Bell Tree* with appropriate enthusiasm. Writing in *The Science Fiction and Fantasy Book Review*, Gary Acton remarked on Hoover's increase in power.

Jenny is no precocious boy/girl à la Heinlein. She is a believable 15-year-old girl capable of vulnerability, toughness, intelligence, and näiveté all at once. The love interest with Eli is adroitly handled by Hoover. She develops a complex relationship between two young people based more on mutual respect and interest in each other as persons than on sexual attraction. The author has a knack for creating a believable alien environment. The reader can almost feel the descent of night and the simultaneous change in the texture of the vegetation and pitch and timbre of the animal sounds in a jungle/forest on a far planet. That sense of setting is one of the most compelling aspects of the novel. (43)

And M. B. Becker's review in *Hornbook* concurred with Acton's overall finding that "Hoover is one of the bright spots in science fiction writing for the adolescent market" (43):

The substantial theme is subtly developed through the plot and also through the gradual evolution of the principals: James Sadler, a curious blend of the romantic and the pragmatic; Eli, the child of nature; Jenny, the link between the two. Precise and descriptive, the writing is characterized by phrases such as "migraine-neat" which linger in the memory. (658)

In *The Shepherd Moon*, the loneliness of Merry, a thirteen-year-old of the forty-eighth century, is set against a background of terrorist intrigue. The fictional setting is Earth in the year 4752; history has developed as follows: By the thirty-first century, mankind had built almost a hundred artificial moons, each one a microworld in its own right, as stepping stones to the stars. These colonies eventually revolted and attacked Earth. In the ensuing chaos, all of the faux moons but four were destroyed, and Earth was plunged into a Second Dark Age, with burned cities and environmental disaster (in the form of melted ice caps). Civilization eventually recovered on Earth to a level of technology not much higher than that of the twentieth century (aircars, video programs, intercoms). The undefined leaders of forty-eighth-century Earth, however, possess far more information about science and history than they are willing to share with the general population. A privileged overclass lives in aristocratic luxury while the masses are ordered and herded about.

Meanwhile, a strange society has evolved on the remaining moons, which are regarded as real moons by most of Earth's population. Governed by the Shepherd Moon (the first artificial moon built, which acted as an administrative center for the others—hence the "shepherd"), the moons have become a hermetic society under totalitarian control where infants are genetically engineered and raised by machines ("mamatrons"), programmed from birth to respond instinctively to orders given in the form of wailing songs, and taught to shun tactile contact with others. There is a rigid chain of command here as well, with Masters obeyed unquestioningly by their lessers, including the elite "Life Cadets," who possess what might be termed superpowers—the ability to manipulate molecular energy to heal or to incinerate.

The catalyst for this story is the destruction of one of the four moons by a meteoroid. The scientist-rulers on the Shepherd Moon detect the impending disaster but deem it too costly to evacuate. Instead, they send out five experimental "life-pods" carrying Cadets to ride the wave of the explosion to Earth and test the waters for future invasion.

Merry Ambrose is the daughter of a wealthy family, granddaughter of General Ambrose, a government official. Vacationing at her ancient and massive family estate, Merry is beginning to wonder if her parents have forgotten about her. She has refused to go on a boring cruise with them (and their boring friends), insisting on being left at the estate until they returned. Now they are late, leading her to believe that they are being spiteful or, even worse, have actually forgotten about her (the latter appears to have been the case). Now, Merry is not actually alone. The estate has a permanent live-in staff, and Merry has a full-time bodyguard, a burley woman named Worth; but class distinction keeps Merry from befriending anyone of a lower station.

As a result, Merry feels alone and is the only person to witness the arrival of the scouts from Terra II (the Shepherd Moon). She finds their pods down on the beach and rescues the inhabitant of one, a young man of thirteen named Mikel, who reacts to his new surroundings in an almost infantile way. While Merry goes to get help, Mikel uses his powers to incinerate the other four pods (and his fellow scouts) so as to seem less of a threat.

In spite of their different origins, there are interesting parallels between the two young people. Both are the usual Hoover abandoned children, but Mikel is symptomatic of his entire culture, a slave to the upperclass totalitarian leadership, whereas Merry is an unwitting member of Earth's version of that same class. Her abandonment is personal; his is cultural. She recalls once hearing her father refer to her as a "nasty little bother and boring besides" (8).

The "shepherd" of the title telegraphs one of the novel's important themes: leadership versus dependency. Most of the book's people have become like sheep, willing to be led. Mikel obeys his Masters without question, and the people of Earth are not quite so programmed but still know their place. Later, there are twin epiphanies of dependence: Merry realizes that she has been blindly following her cultural doctrine, and Mikel does likewise. While all this is generally well done, Hoover seems for once in her career to have taken on too much. The complexities of the plot create not suspense but confusion. The point of view switches from Merry to an omniscient view of the Masters of the moons and to Mikel's reminiscing—all in the service of exposition. For the first time, reviewers jumped upon weaknesses even while giving overall high marks. Paul Heins wrote:

The novel speculates on a foreseeable disruptive intersection between life on Earth and life in space and in the end moralizes a bit on the cause. But despite an occasional narrative unevenness induced by a shifting point of view, the book is notable for its depiction of the innocent-appearing yet malevolent amoral space visitor. (337)

Allene Stuart Phy both criticized and praised at greater length:

Hoover . . . has some difficulty sustaining the brilliance of her initial ideas. Not all her themes are clearly delineated nor all her plot threads neatly tied. The narrative of terrorist intrigue contains a standard escape and a chase scene that suggests more readily the popular television of the twentieth century than the possible thrills of the forty-eighth.

Yet these flaws appear minor beside the book's merits. The real interest is generated by the courageous, inquiring, and supremely humane heroine. Merry's mood of loneliness is superbly conveyed. Despite servants who surround her with comforts and a grandfather who shields her from reality, she discovers the cruelty of the rigid social planning which makes possible the luxury she has neither requested nor desired. (40)

Clearly, by 1984 and with the publication of *The Shepherd Moon*, Hoover had reached that stage in her development as a writer at which tradition and individual talent begin to struggle.

* * *

It may be coincidence that Hoover's next book would appear three years after *The Shepherd Moon,* or perhaps this uncharacteristic passage of time marks a period of retrenching and regrouping of Hoover's forces. Whatever the case, in 1987, Hoover published another novel, *Orvis*, also based, like *The Shepherd Moon*, upon a trio of characters banding to rebel against convention; but this time her narrative grasp seems both more playful and profound.

This new and refreshing strength in *Orvis* is due, in part, to the focus given the book by its title character, a robot somewhat reminiscent of *Star Wars'* R2D2 but more endearing than his famous predecessor by the addition of a rebellious, recalcitrant, and finally dynamic character. By keying the tale on the intriguing paradoxes of robotic intelligence, Hoover has created a wondrous toy and teaching machine that, like Wallace Stevens' "jar" in Tennessee, gives order and perspective to her many solemn speculations about adult rigidity and entrenched vested interest as well as a humorous tone that younger readers can focus upon.

Orvis is a rich compilation of science fiction concepts and a fit subject for an extended illustration of Hoover's mature method. Mankind is expanding into space. Population pressures and the destructive results of the greenhouse effect have forced the creation of orbital (L5) habitats, Moon and Mars colonies, and deep-space ships (that prove Einstein right by allowing generations to pass while one is going to and fro). Cities on Earth have been domed to protect against solar radiation, and most of the planet has been adandoned. Even when scientists discover a way to reverse the greenhouse effect, most people sold on the media-hyped images of romantic living on the new frontier prefer space or the comfort of the cities to the vast, agorophobic "Empty" to which only a small minority of recluses, outlaws, and crazies have gone.

Hillandale Academy is an exclusive "character building" boarding school for children of rich ex-Terrans who feel that living on Earth will be a good experience for them, helping them appreciate the comforts of space habitat life. This is the initial stage for a trio of discoverers. Tabitha (Toby) West, the daughter of a rich family, is shuttled from school to school and rarely sees her parents. Thaddeus Hall, a naive young man born on an interstellar spaceship, has been left at the school by parents who have headed off on another long research voyage. The third member of the trio is Orvis, a self-aware robot. Originally used to explore distant planets, Orvis is now outdated (newer robots are more sleek and pleasing) and unwanted (its defensive systems are considered dangerous). Orvis is much smarter than most robots (and most adults), has developed a personality of sorts, and is the speculative ingredient that lifts the book to the level of thought-experiment.

Toby, about to be transferred to school on Mars, is wandering in the woods near the academy when she meets Orvis who is walking to the dump to scrap himself according to orders given by his last owner. Toby tells Thaddeus about Orvis, and Thaddeus identifies with Orvis's plight and insists on looking for it. When the children find Orvis in the dump, Toby suggests that the robot could go and live with her grandmother near Lake Erie (Toby has not yet met her grandmother as her mother and grandmother do not get along).

On their return to campus, Orvis gruffly refuses to communicate, but later that night, it appears at Toby's door and asks to be let in, claiming to have been frightened by a bear. There are complications with Hillandale's administrators, who are more afraid of Orvis because it can think than because it possesses weapons, and Orvis is ordered back to the dump. Toby discovers that her grandmother is quite a delightful person, and Toby and Thaddeus rescue Orvis from the dump (again) and thus begin an odyssesy of mutual rescue and discovery. In Orvis, Hoover has created an endearing combination of the brilliant and the childish, and she has created a situation that allows the young people and the robot to explore various topics—whether robots have souls, the nature of responsibility for one's creations, and the like—that take on multiple overtones because Orvis is there.

The unbiased perception of the children permits them to see Orvis as a thinking being worthy of caring and sympathy, rather than as a dangerous machine. The adults, particularly the staff of the academy, cannot see past the "outcast" categorization, while the children, being castoffs as well, identify strongly with the robot. Both children begin without real homes, and the obstacles on the way to the sort of home to which a child is entitled include survival in the wilderness (in which they are aided by Orvis in its "friendly adult" role) and escape from a cloying, artificially homelike spacer village (which is too desperate for children to be a good home). Throughout, Orvis plays a dual role: As an abandoned thing, struggling to understand interpersonal responsibility, it is like a child, but its formidable defensive capability and vast computerized memory also put it in the role of guardian (its memory banks contain huge amounts of data from its 400-year existence).

In her more recent novels, Hoover appears to have accepted and dealt with the challenge implicit in her earlier fiction: If the ideal world does not exist, then the young protagonists of today—whenever "today" might be—must in turn make some compromise with it as did their elders. And if they do, then along with talents conferred upon them by youth must exist one less happier ability, the ability to adapt to perverse conditions by themselves manifesting some permanent gnarls and twists of character—as the existing trees were bent, so must the new twig be, if it is to develop in the same forest. Here is a challenge rarely met in youth fiction; indeed, even John Christopher's White Mountains trilogy and Tolkien's Hobbit novels do not pose it (in these, the world is reshaped by the efforts of the protagonists). But how many children's novels go beyond the successful conclusion of the Adventure to show the humbling, even crippling, effects of childhood?

In *The Dawn Palace* (1988), Hoover retells a classical myth, informing it with many of the same ethical and developmental concerns as in her science fiction. Medea starts out with a good home, loses it because of the ambition of her father (who is not really indifferent or even wicked, but simply suffers from the blindness of his world views; he holds the same viewpoints as the other males in the book, namely, that rulers should be male, preferably Greek—he does, however, love his daughter, judging by the rage/guilt he feels when she elopes; he just does not think that she should be a ruler), and heads out into the real world to find a better home.

She finds that the rest of the world is not that much better; that ignorance, prejudice, and blind ambition exist everywhere; that she, through no fault of her own, is a member of several underclasses (female, non-Greek, and schooled), which makes it impossible to even have the kind of home she once had, much less the sort she dreams of. The message is long in coming, being hidden by the illusion of Home she finds with Jason in Corinth. Only when she flees that city with the knowledge of Jason's betrayal burning her does she comprehend the ugly truth. Her final disposition, in Colchis once again, is as the mother of the future king (her son, Medeius), rather than as queen. She has accepted the diminishment of her dreams in order to gain stability. What she wanted was probably impossible, and in any case, she failed in her quest to find it—and so she compromised.

It is tempting to apply Medea's compromise to the current situation of women, for the resonance is strong; but a broader view reveals it to apply equally well to both genders. Do not all of us give up on some of our dreams in order to achieve life equilibrium or to attain other, lesser, goals?

* * *

There is an irony in the fact that Hoover is all but unknown to academic students of science fiction while at the same time widely hailed by enthusiasts of children's literature. Once again, different fragments of the University have not been communicating well with each other.

Hoover's science fiction is serious and intelligent young adult fiction, not escapist fare. Typically, an alienated child appears in a home that lacks some essential component that we might regard as any child's birthright. And so the young protagonist has no choice but to choose the way of adventure, no choice but to seek fulfillment in a less-than-perfect world. Hoover writes children's science fiction without condescension, and her children are blessedly free of that precocity that blights so much fiction written for children by adults. Instead, they are presented as having that special strength of youth: a clear-eyed view of their surroundings. If their steps are unsure, they are nonetheless unhindered by adult baggage, uncommitted to any crippling, constraining ideology.

Nor do her children inhabit a kids-only world. Instead, they form alliances with sympathetic adults whose acquired knowledge complements their own youthful vigor. Hoover's fiction—whether futuristic, fantastic, or mythic—is most realistic in presenting what any child may expect to face in our less-than-ideal present. This is the kind of refreshing perspective given us by such mainstream writers as S. E. Hinton and Paul Zindel, but with the added cognitive component possible in science fiction, a perspective worthy of young minds that were, in decades past, greeted with such works as *Mrs. Pickerel Goes to Mars*.

Most recently, Hoover has returned, in *Away Is a Strange Place to Be* (1990), to the theme of escape from a hermetic environment, which she developed in inchoate form in the Morrow novels and then depicted in horrific detail in *This*

Time of Darkness. The emphasis in *Away* is less on running and more on ratiocination as her young heroes go about in a strange world they had no business making.

Hoover's basic extrapolation, then, is to take us forward and away to that exotic situation of a past time every human has experienced—do not *all* children do their best to carve coherent essence from an absurd existence? Didn't we? Hoover reifies a most significant step in human growth—having learned that we have no sure home to return to, we face the westward sun and set out to grow our own. We can never again look through childish eyes, but we can all, perhaps, recall that time of alienation when we did not "travel" but were "taken" places, there to be overlooked or patronized (Oh! And this *must* be Helen!), and we can rejoice that Hoover writes a galactic guide for the shanghied rather than for the hitchhikers, for it is that beleaguered readership, her proper critics, who can most use her assistance in the big job of taking care of the future and amending the present.

BIBLIOGRAPHY

Acton, Gary. Rev. of *The Bell Tree,* by H. M. Hoover. *Science Fiction and Fantasy Book Review* 13 (April 1983): 42-43.

Becker, M.B. Rev. of *The Bell Tree,* by H. M. Hoover. *The Hornbook Magazine* 58.6 (1982): 658.

Heins, Paul. Rev. of *The Shepherd Moon: A Novel of the Future,* by H. M. Hoover. *The Hornbook Magazine* 60.3 (1984): 337.

Hoover, H. M. *Another Heaven; Another Earth.* New York: Viking, 1981.

_____. *Away is a Strange Place to Be.* New York: Dutton, 1990.

_____. *The Bell Tree.* New York: Viking, 1982.

_____. *The Children of Morrow.* New York: Four Winds, 1973.

_____. *The Dawn Palace: The Story of Medea.* New York: Dutton, 1988.

_____. *The Delikon.* New York: Viking, 1977.

_____. *The Lion's Cub.* New York: Four Winds, 1974.

_____. *The Lost Star.* New York: Viking, 1979.

_____. *Orvis.* New York: Viking, 1987.

_____. *The Rains of Eridan.* New York: Viking, 1977.

_____. *Return to Earth.* New York: Viking, 1980.

_____. "SF—Out of This World." *Language Arts* 57 (1980): 425-28.

_____. *The Shepherd Moon.* New York: Viking, 1984.

_____. *This Time of Darkness.* New York: Viking, 1980.

_____. *The Treasures of Morrow.* New York: Four Winds, 1976.

Nicholls, Peter, ed. "Children's SF." *The Science Fiction Encyclopedia.* London: Roxby, 1979. 113-14.

Phy, Allene Stuart. Rev. of *The Shepherd Moon: A Novel of the Future,* by H. M. Hoover. *Fantasy Review* 71 (Sept. 1984): 40.

10

The British Science Fiction of Louise Lawrence

Marilyn Fain Apseloff

Louise Lawrence, a talented and optimistic British writer for young adults, first made her reputation with books of fantasy before she began to experiment with science fiction in five books: *The Power of Stars* (1972), *Star Lord* (1978), *Calling B for Butterfly* (1982), *Children of the Dust* (1985), and *Moonwind* (1986). In each book her characters often begin as one dimensional beings until circumstances bring out other sides to their personalities. Her plots, too, appear at first to be predictable, but the reader is in for unusual events, for Lawrence is an imaginative as well as a skillful writer. A common technique that she uses is to shift the narrative focus from one character to another so that the reader sees a variety of viewpoints. This blending of skillful characterization, intriguing plots, and a distinctive style, often full of imagery, combines to make her a contemporary science fiction writer worthy of attention.

The Power of the Stars was Lawrence's first use of what can be called science fiction rather than pure fantasy. William Sleator, himself an author in both genres, stated in "What *Is* It About Science Fiction" that "my own definition is that science fiction is literature about something that hasn't happened yet, but it might be possible some day. That it might be possible is the important part; that's what separates science fiction from fantasy" (4). He adds, "Once you have a scientific principle going for you, you can then slyly stretch it beyond the limits of reality without the reader being aware of it. What science fiction does is to take scientific laws—which have built-in credibility—and use them to make nearly anything possible" (5). These theories can be found in *The Power of Stars*. One evening a bright object flashes in a quarry followed by a scream. A bloodied rabbit appears, and when Jane, fifteen, helps him and holds him, she is fiercely bitten. From then on the stars have a strange power over her. Only one person, Miss Cotterel, quickly learns what has happened and attempts to save Jane; two of Jane's peers, Jimmy and Alan, are also concerned and suspect Jane of being the source of mysterious mechanical failures due to a massive surge of power. What is discovered and how Jimmy tries to prevent disaster for Alan and Jane build to a surprising, unexpected (except in hindsight), yet plausible conclusion.

Some of the techniques Lawrence uses in this novel appear in her later science fiction works. Shifting restricted third-person narration occurs throughout as she focuses on various characters even within chapters; the breaks are usually delineated by a wavy line. Individuals emerge gradually from almost stock characters presented at the beginning, taking on colors and depth. Although handsome Alan, down from London with his mother and stepfather, appears to have everything and Jimmy seems uncouth and harsh beside him, their true natures surface as the story develops and they learn more about Jane and what is controlling her. Jane is initially presented as awkward, rather plain, and opposed to killing anything. She is the one whose true nature is often submerged, taken over by the "neurons" that have entered her body and that gain their power from the stars. For that reason, there is constant repetition about that power and the beauty of the stars, a repetition that adds to the atmosphere and tension as do the references to the owl's hooting and to the cuckoo's song.

Hilary Crew, in her article "From Labyrinth to Celestial City: Setting and the Portrayal of the Female Adolescent in Science Fiction," wrote that "science fiction writers have used settings to symbolize the entrapment of the young adolescent" (86), and there is a strong sense of that in this novel. Lydcroft, where Jane and the others live, is rural, isolated, and near mountains and quarries, bogs and bracken and ravines. Jimmy cannot wait to get away to see cities, to leave the loneliness behind him. Alan is trapped there by circumstances; his mother has had a breakdown, and his stepfather feels that the isolation will be good for her after the bustle of London. Jane experiences a different form of entrapment, both from within and from those outside who want to help her.

Lawrence is skillful in directing her plots, which seem to be headed for a standard denouement, toward unsuspected endings. They are not, however, brought in abruptly. For example, in *The Power of Stars*, Jane's final dramatic act, true to her own nature and the creatures within her, and Jimmy's horror are perfectly logical, and the reader is left to shiver and ponder the gruesome possibilities. Sleator would approve, for he has said that "I always end my books on a note of ambiguity. . . . My hope is that after finishing the book the readers will be stimulated, even compelled, to use their own imaginations to continue the story" (6). Readers of *The Power of Stars* are left with much to ponder.

In *Star Lord*, Louise Lawrence's next venture into science fiction, there are heavy overtones of fantasy and myth. Janice Antczak, in her book *Science Fiction: The Mythos of a New Romance*, calls the combination "science fantasy" (173). The setting is Wales, primarily on a farm in a valley and on the neighboring mountain believed by many of the village inhabitants to have supernatural powers. Hywel Thomas, the grandfather, describes the effect that the mountain has:

He knew when the Mawrrhyn called. . . . She was more than just a mountain, rock scarred by glaciers, heaved up from the stone-dead land. She was alive. The soul of her lived, wild and untamed and ruthless. The Mawrrhyn was a place without pity. (7-8)

"The old man told stories of winter nights, how there were legends about those hills. How, if you listened, you could hear the voice of the Mawrrhyn in the wind. Magic, he said" (16). Rhys, his grandson, feels the same call, the magic. One day when he is on the mountain, a growing noise, maddening in its intensity, precedes a crash. The impact is horrendous, setting off a landslide, and then silence. "Something terrible had happened on the other side of the Mawrrhyn" (12).

As the next chapter shifts to Rhys's mother and sister returning from the village, more information about the "thing" that hit emerges: It had to be "some kind of machine" (17). They feel the shock waves through their feet when it hits the mountain, as do many others. Rhys is the first on the scene to see the crater, but "there was no wreckage, no clue to what it had been" (19). As he looks more closely, he finds tiny shards of an unfamiliar metal, and a feeling comes over him that someone has escaped from the carnage "and was needing to be found" (20). The dog, Blod, feels it, too.

Rhys and Blod are not the only one who thinks that someone survived, for the army quickly takes over the region (they have detected radiation), intent upon capturing the stranger. Gwyneth, Rhys's sister, remembers her grandad's tale of the young lord who went to the mountain with the faery, and when he returned home after what he thought were two days, he discovered that two centuries had passed. She thinks about the people in the area.

They went to chapel every Sunday but they were not Christian. They believed in something older than that, powers that were deep and dark. They planted rowan by the door to keep away fey spirits, and they would not walk the moors at twilight or bring May blossom into the house. . . . The dark living land was all around Gwyneth, the silence of earth and stone, and it was not hard to believe. (48-49)

The stranger is found in the Thomas barn, a boy covered in blood after having been shot by one of the soldiers. When he is carried into the light of the kitchen, they see that he is beautiful. "'Aye,' said Hywel Thomas grimly. 'Beauty it is, but not of this world. He doesn't belong to our kind'" (61). The boy tells them that he comes from "Eridani Epsilon. Eleven light-years away across space" (68). Although he looks young, "he is ageless but mortal, a star-lord" (Antczak 187). The rest of the novel explores the reactions of the family members to him as they try to protect him from the soldiers who come hunting him. Hywel and Rhys, with the dog, Blod, eventually get Erlich, the strange boy, back up the mountain. There Rhys finally understands the price that must be paid to get Erlich safely away.

Lawrence skillfully weaves in other events known to the reader to give verisimilitude to her fiction. "Don't question. Don't ask why dozens of boats and planes went missing in one triangle of ocean off the coast of Bermuda. Why voodoo happened" (148). Erlich claimed that Mawrrhyn had caused his ship to crash because he had invaded her power zone. "His power was not like hers. To her, Erlich was destruction on a scale hardly begun on earth.... Erlich could build cities from her rubble, dams across her streams, cabbage where the sundew grew. He could destroy her utterly" (148-49). Erlich muses, "I use pure and applied science, but what does she use? Mysticism! Once we scorned it as rubbish, but eons ago we came to accept that there were some things we could not understand, forces that defied science" (142-43).

Erlich's power reaches into Mawrrhyn, and through it a door opens and Rhys carries him inside the mountain, realizing too late that the door is closing behind him. Antczak has said that "the hero journeys to the mountaintop or descends into the dark spaces of the underworld in order to pursue the quest" (7). Rhys has done both. Erlich is rescued by one of his spacecraft; as Antczak has noted, "Space vehicles have replaced the beanstalk as the link between universes" (169). The faithful Blod, shut outside the mountain, remains there until her death many years later. When Rhys eventually awakens, he finds a passage through the rock and discovers Blod's old, weather-beaten gravestone. The farmhouse is a crumbling ruin. "His time was dead, dead like Blod's grave, dead like Gwyneth and Enid and the old man" (167). But the star lord has not forgotten him or his sacrifice; he returns for Rhys.

"We are cruel," Erlich murmured. "Natural forces pay no heed to the pains of people. She is mountain born, her soul rooted in rock, and I belong to the stars. But my power is not like her power, uncontrolled and indiscriminate, destroying all in its path, by earthquake, fire, and avalanche. Science gives me the ability to choose. So I choose not to destroy. I choose to come back for you." (169)

Then it is Rhys's turn to make a decision.

Lawrence is fine at creating mood through the Welsh atmosphere and landscape and the increasing references to the magical and mystical. Science fiction blends with fantasy. Thus, the reader knows little about the star lord's home or his spaceship; in fact, the reader knows very little about Erlich. He seems singularly vulnerable on Earth until the end on the mountain. Lawrence has created a contrast between the two opposing forces, constantly referring to the beauty of the lord and the brooding, dark nature of the mountain. Yet both, in the end, can be equally cold; Erlich does not hesitate to let Rhys give up everything for him. Unlike Mawrrhyn, however, he has pity and recognizes that without Rhys's sacrifice, he would have died.

Fortunately, Lawrence has crafted her human charcters much more fully. Enid, the mother, is attracted to the army captain and wants to look her best when he might appear. She has a mind of her own, too, for it is she who fetches the doctor against the wishes of the others, certain that Erlich will die without his help. She also has a bit of mysticism in her, for she is able to enter a trancelike state and feel the power of the mountain; through her trance she knows that Rhys will not return and that Hywel is dead. Even then she waits at the farm for two years for Rhys before leaving to marry the captain. Each character is developed well, even the captain whose role is pivotal but smaller.

Imagery is everywhere. For Rhys, "the mountains were hooked in his nerves, tugging him" (7). Later "the silence touched him, sharp as a claw, thick and cold with the mating of sky and stone" (9). A room comes vividly to life under Lawrence's description:

Gwyneth's dirty tights were stuffed down the side of the armchair. Her cardigan was draped over it, her magazine under it. Lipstick, mascara, hair curlers, clips, brush and tissues were left on the cabinet. Her slippers were on the floor by the stove, her satchel on the floor by the cabinet, and the slop bucket needed emptying. (41)

Into this room that Enid is trying to put to rights unexpectedly comes the English captain, and she is humiliated by her appearance and the state of the room.

Lawrence's third science fiction novel, *Calling B for Butterfly,* is a complete departure from the first two except in its focus on a variety of characters rather than primarily on one person. A spaceship carrying 1200 people is hit by a huge asteroid and almost totally destroyed; only four teenagers and two young children survive and get to Life Ferry B where personalities clash and problems mount. They know nothing about operating the craft, but when Ann presses the right switch and uncovers the radio transmitter, their hopes rise. No one answers their calls for help until one of the small children, Caroline, manages to make contact with Ganymede. Then the problem is to bring the ferry safely there, first getting it out of a trajectory leading it straight for Jupiter and certain death.

When the characters are first introduced, the reader is given a one-dimensional glimpse of them: sour, bored Sonja, sixteen; timid Ann; morose, angry Glyn; Matthew and his preoccupation with butterflies. Caroline and her baby brother, Benjamin, sick with measles, are found by Glyn and Matthew when they check the cabins in their area for other survivors. There is also a mysterious ball of light accompanied by music that is later revealed as an alien life form. This is the group that the people on Ganymede try to rescue, using one of their hotshot pilots to tell Glyn and Matthew what to do.

How each main character holds up and develops under extreme circumstances is the focus of the novel, although much is made of the symbolism of the environment. The ferry, identified in radio transmissions as B for Butterfly, is also a cocoon, and the adults in charge on Ganymede can see the awakenings of the four adolescent "butterflies." Baby Benjamin is a one-dimensional character, and Caroline serves as an antagonist for several others with her constant demands and whining when she does not get her way. It is a while before the adolescents realize what has happened to all of the others and what their own position then is.

When Matthew discovers that Caroline has pushed his chrysalids through the airlock grill vent, he loses all control and attacks her; the others have to pull him off. When Ann is ordered to take charge of the crying Ben of whom she had been fearful in the past, she discovers that he is beautiful and that she loves caring for him. Horrified at his own behavior, Matthew locks himself in the only washroom where the alien form brings him sleep. He is eventually dragged out by Glyn who had to break the glass seal on the door, and all but Sonja see the strange light. The adults on Ganymede are afraid of it, want it destroyed, because in the past its presence has been associated with disasters, and the children argue about it. Ann assumes a major role here, against the killing; she has fully emerged from her cocoon of timidity and fear.

When Joe, the Ganymede operator, deliberately shuts off contact with them because of their bickering, Glyn begins to do some belated soul-searching. Noticing how well Matthew and Ann are getting along, he is determined to reform from the boor he has been. When radio contact is reestablished, he and Matthew are drilled so repetitively on how to take over the controls manually that Matthew develops a migraine and has to lie down. Glyn is left in charge of the controls, but when the ferry is caught in one of Jupiter's fierce storms, drawn into the vortex toward the planet, and loses contact with Ganymede, Ann, wrapped in the light and music, takes the controls and tells Glyn what to do to break free of the planet's deadly grasp. The moves are successful, but at a cost; they can now never land on Ganymede. When the light assumes the shape of a boy and offers them an alternative destination, all ends on an upbeat note. Even Joe, on Ganymede, distraught at thinking that the children were killed, learns that they survived, sees the alien boy as they go by, and is at peace.

Al Muller, in his article "Doomsday Fiction and the YA Reader," wrote that "the catastrophes are mere catalysts setting the stage for the characters to struggle to survive and prevail in a devastated and, essentially, an unfamiliar world" (42). Although he was discussing books with Earthly global catastrophes, his words apply to *Calling B for Butterfly*. The ferry serves to bring the protagonists together, but its sterile confinement also creates tension, for there is little room to retreat alone. Matthew attempts it in the washroom and is ultimately unsuccessful because it is a room needed by everyone, just as the control room is a room in which they all (except baby Ben) have parts to play. The ferry seems to shrink in size as the story progresses, and the confinement grates more and more on the teens.

Lawrence once more shows that she is adept at handling several characters, the narration moving from one to another just as it did in *Star Lord*. Only Sonja is very slow to change, staying vain and self-centered until near the end of the novel. When she finally realizes that they will not be going to Earth, she breaks down, is comforted by the others, and finally sees the light that they had spoken of, the alien presence that assumes a boy's shape. It is in the main cabin, now filled with yellow butterflies that are hatching from the air vents where Caroline had put the chrysalids, that Sonja realizes "he was the power that would take them traveling across the universe to another home" (208-9), and she is content.

Hilary Crew stated, "The female adolescent's arduous journey toward independence, maturity, and responsibility and her increasing role in shaping her own future and that of society are often symbolized by the physical nature of the settings in which the heroine is placed" (84). This observation especially applies to Ann. Originally she was found in her cabin, a smaller cocoon where she had curled up in bed waiting for her father, afraid to do anything on her own. Forcefully ejected and taken to the ferry, she again withdraws until the time is ripe for her to emerge, gradually at first through caring for Benjamin, until she begins to assume a more forceful role that even becomes obvious to Joe on Ganymede: "There was a quietness in her eyes, a depth and strength such as Joe had never seen before, as if she had absorbed the things that had happened and passed into a different state of being. . . . More than Glyn, more than Matthew, more than Joe himself, Ann could cope" (158). She is one of the golden butterflies.

In *Children of the Dust,* Lawrence again introduces a new situation. The novel is a fiction of life after a nuclear war. It is a tale of survival, of technology versus adaptation. The book is in three parts and deals with three generations. In Part I, Sarah experiences a nuclear blast with her mother, her younger sister, Catherine, and her brother in a sealed room; she comes to realize that of the foursome, ultimately, only Catherine will survive. In Part II, many years later, Ophelia, born after the nuclear war and raised in an underground bunker built to withstand a nuclear attack and to protect those inside indefinitely, meets her adult half-sister, Catherine, outside the bunker and is appalled by the conditions there. In Part III, Simon leaves the bunker fifty five years later, and he discovers that the horribly scarred old woman who cares for him is his grandmother, Catherine.

Al Muller states about a group of catastrophe novels that "while the characters are not trained survivalists, they are admittedly not without the innate abilities and strengths necessary to survive" (42). Such is the case with Catherine who is eight when the bombs fall; intuitively she stays in the protected "room" that she made for herself under the table, she will drink only bottled water, and she will eat only food that comes from a can. Sarah, fifteen, realizes that Catherine has a chance. When Sarah knows that she has little strength left, she takes Catherine to Mr. Johnson. "He had survived like Catherine because he took no chances" (59). Surprisingly, despite all of the devastation and misery he has seen, he is still hopeful. "This was the beginning of a brave new world. . . . We'll build a world from the dust, she and I. . . . A society based on human decency, free people, cooperating without violence, better than the old" (61). Pockets of life survive, both above and below ground. Eventually the two settings will be compared.

In Part II Ophelia knows only her bunker environment, a labyrinth of safety in contrast to the views of a ravaged earth on telescreens as outside cameras pan the landscape. There Ophelia sees "an outside world that was treeless and hostile, a landscape eroded by wind and rain and sun" (73). Everything was barren except for packs of scavenging dogs chasing the few surviving flocks of sheep. In other places, in valleys by water, vegetation grew and could be planted, but there were terrible deformities among the animals. "The only things that thrived in the land outside were lizards and flies" (74).

"Inside the bunker nothing ever changed. It was a constant environment"

(74). Yet there are visible signs of decay as equipment fails from time to time and the concrete has cracks and crumbles. Bill Harnden and his wife, Erica, argue constantly, for Bill believes that they "need creative thinkers" (76) while she insists that "we don't need dreamers. We need scientists and technologists. . . . They're the ones on whom our future depends" (76-77). He tells her that the future cannot be built without a knowledge of the past to spur their imaginations. Erica is scornful; genetic engineering is what is important to her so that eventually they can live above ground. Underground there can be no "beauty, and truth, and freedom, the pursuit of personal happiness" (77), and there is certainly no room for imagination. Bill reminds her, "It was science and technology that invented the bomb and devastated the earth" (78). This confrontation is a very old theme in literature.

Dissent arises in the bunker over how General McAllister has ruled it for twenty years. Even his son, Dwight, objects to his control and sides with Bill Harnden. When Dwight learns about an intended cattle roundup, he tells Bill, and they decide to leave the bunker to warn those outside. Ophelia joins them because of her attraction to Dwight. When they reach Johnsons's, where the cattle are, Catherine thinks Ophelia is her dead sister Sarah.

Ophelia is horrified at what she finds at the Johnsons': Catherine pregnant for the seventh time, with all but one of the other births dead; her mating at fourteen with the forty-year-old Johnson; the run-down, stinking buildings and primitive conditions; and the rats. "The land came first, Catherine said, food and necessities before material advancement and academic learning" (108). Ophelia talks to Dwight about the deplorable conditions, comparing them to the "decent standard of living" in the bunker and exclaiming, "At least we're still capable of civilized behavior!" (109). He retorts, "Like coming to steal their cattle?. . . We're dinosaurs in a bunker! We deserve to become extinct!" (109).

Johnson had envisioned a communal life, and now more than 700 people live in his group, working together for the common good. But he is dying from radiation sickness; others will have to carry on his work. Catherine's daughter, Lilith, is a mutant. More are being born like her, with snow-white fur and milky eyes with "black pinprick pupils" (118) to shield them from the relentless sun that now beats down through a depleted ozone layer.

In Part III Simon emerges from the bunker after fifty-five years and meets a mutant who has tools and who wears beautifully embroidered clothing complete with buckles. Simon is now one of a dying breed, a "dinosaur," and it grates on him. He thinks of the mutant girl, Laura, as an ape girl, a primitive, until he becomes aware of her talents. When he meets some children who question him about his appearance, he realizes that he is the freak. They have adapted to the new world conditions; he has not. The people in the bunker "had sacrificed their children's futures for a technological breakthrough that had never happened . . . mutants would inherit the earth" (154). As Hilary Crew observed, an underground city bunker with its labyrinthine tunnels can symbolize entrapment, while an alternative aboveground "can offer escape into a more idyllic milieu" (84). That is exactly what has happened in this novel, for the city with its cathedral is indeed shining, "celestial." Later Simon learns that the mutants use telepathy and psychokinetic energy, yet Simon is needed, too, for the technology he can give them before it is all lost. Because he was raised in the bunker, he will have to wear protective clothing whenever he goes outdoors, but at least he now has a future to look forward to after all.

In this catastrophe novel Lawrence has continued to use restricted third-person narration, limiting her focus primarily to the three people named in the parts so that the reader comes to know them well. Moreover, her writing is often graphic. Catherine is seen with "her weeping sunburn and rotting teeth, stringy hair that failed to conceal the radiation sores that festered on her scalp" (107). Others survived by eating "dead meat frozen in the snow, rats and corpses, insects and worms, rotting vegetables and even manure" (106). As Simon reflected, "They should have listened to the warning cries of the peace protesters before the war" (153).

The novel ends with praise for the mutants as "*homo superior,* the children of the dust" (183), ironic since water is usually the symbol for life. The tables are turned in other places, for the bunkers, built for protection, have done their job too well; the educated people within have not had to adapt, and only those who have adapted can ultimately survive in the new blasted environment. Moreover, despite the graphic presentation of the nuclear destruction and its aftermath, according to Muller "the settings [in catastrophe novels] . . . are not so bleak and inhospitable as might be imagined or supposed. The settings provide opportunity for the resourceful survivor to endure and re-establish a civilization. The settings provide hope for humanity" (44).

Lawrence's most recent science fiction novel, the futuristic *Moonwind,* is set on the moon. Two teenagers, Gareth from a poor section of Wales and Karen from a wealthy home in California, have won trips to the space station there through an essay-writing contest. Unknown to anyone at the station, a spaceship had landed near there 10,000 years earlier, and its only survivor, Bethkahn, is awakened from her cryogenic chamber now to fix the broken stabilizer before people from the station discover the ship. Gareth is a loner; Karen with her incessant chatter grates on his nerves. He is the first to spot the figure in the moonwind, a sudden swirl of wind and dust that seems to come up out of nowhere. Bethkahn is taken with Gareth and finally applies to him for help in getting the stabilizer fixed. As they get to know each other, Gareth finds himself drawn more and more to her. In the end he must make the choice of departing with her or returning to Earth.

Through a flashback in the beginning of the novel, the reader learns why Bethkahn is alone: The others went off to explore, leaving her to fix the stabilizer. When they did not return and she could get no one to answer her signals for help, she endured years of loneliness and eventual madness until she was put into the cryogenic chamber. The reader learns that she has an astral rather than a physical body, but that she can assume the body of something else, animal, bird, or human. But "flesh was never easy. . . . It was cruel always, a mixture of violence and beauty, bittersweet feelings that were difficult to bear" (15). The people on the space station are evidently descendants of those who left the spaceship, and they are not to be trusted, according to the voice of the ship, Bethkahn's only companion.

Bethkahn is shown the landing of the first men on the moon, hears their words ("This is a giant leap forward for mankind"), sees them planting the flag, and shudders at the sight of them. "Those are not advanced evolutionary beings. They are subhuman! Cavorting imbecilic monsters!" (20). Then fifty years pass on the screen, and Bethkahn is relieved to find the humans greatly advanced. She wants to go to them but is warned by the ship that they are corrupt, that there are "war and famine, cruelty and monstrous acts of destruction" (23) on their Earth. She must save the ship and herself before they are discovered and destroyed.

At the American station, Gareth is warned about being alone. "Solitude can be dangerous on the moon. . . . Human sanity is a fragile thing" (31). Karen wants to be with him, but his soul cries out for silence when she is around. Alone on the catwalk of the observatory he suddenly feels how insignificant he and humanity are, and he is terrified until his perspective shifts to the heavens and the stars. They "were calling him toward them. The Moon tugging his heart. Terror changed to ecstasy" (34). Then Karen enters and breaks the spell, one more reason for disliking her. She is also very gullible, and he cannot resist telling her all sorts of fanciful tales that she believes and tells others who know better; however, like the boy who cried wolf too often, when Gareth really does see something, no one will believe him.

Gareth discovers the sphere from the spaceship and hides it in his room, but Karen sees it and thinks it is beautiful. She will keep his secret. When it sprouts a tripod, he flees in terror, finds Karen to tell her, and kisses her in his need for comfort. Meanwhile Bethkahn has learned that she must assume a human shape in order to fix the stabilizer, and when the first person she tries to inhabit is accidentally killed, she tries to take over another man's body but is again unsuccessful. Ultimately she turns for help to Gareth, whom she has come to love, and he agrees. Although Bethkahn has never tried to influence Gareth to leave with her, he senses what life must be like on her planet. "She represented it—a beautiful being from a beautiful world. He knew now why men looked up at the stars and called them heaven. A part of them remembered, paradise echoing through generations of human dreams" (169). Convinced that he, too, has an astral body, he leaves with her in the end.

His mortal body is found lifeless, but when a spaceship blasts off and begins blinking a strange message in Morse code, Karen realizes that he has survived after all, for the message is in Welsh for her, a private saying that only she would understand. Unlike Rhys in *Star Lord,* who might choose to remain on Earth despite the loss of everyone he knew, Gareth wants a new freedom in a new world. The dinginess and sordidness of his Welsh home could not compete with the promise of a new world as could the flowers and the mountains of the Wales that Rhys knew and loved.

Narration again shifts back and forth from Bethkahn to Gareth and the station. Feminists will deplore Karen's depiction; she appears shallow and dim-witted, told repeatedly to call Gareth by his real name, not "Gary" as she persists in doing as the days pass. As already mentioned, she is gullible to absurdity, yet she remains determined to stick to Gareth because she is afraid to be there without him. If he is sent home early, then she will have to go, too. There is nothing heroic about her characterization. She is also a tattletale. On the other hand, there is an openness and friendliness that is admirable even if it is misplaced with Gareth most of the time. When the two of them are taken on the underground tour of the base, it is Gareth, not she, who becomes disoriented and ill. She is the one who tries to help him get adjusted so that he will not be sent back early.

Hilary Crew has said that "science fiction has the capacity to use settings to posit a new vision" (88). Lawrence has done that in most of her novels, yet not with one voice. Although Earth is seen as a beautiful planet (so much so that the ships that came to look for Bethkahn went right by the moon to look at the lovely blue orb), its dark side is also shown. For Gareth in *Moonwind,* hope for a brighter future and life cannot be found on Earth, and he takes to the heavens with Bethkahn. The children in *Calling B for Butterfly* have little choice, but they, too, seem happy at the prospect of going to a new environment. The "new vision" of *Children of the Dust* is of a new breed that has adapted to fit the changed environment brought about by man's determination to destroy himself and everything else. Only Rhys in *Star Lord* might choose to remain where he is.

Regardless of the varied settings, what Lawrence leaves the reader with in most of her books is hope for a better life, on this world or on some other. Although several of her protagonists are rather hostile personalities, as are Jimmy, Rhys, Glyn, Gareth, and Simon to some extent, each gradually assumes other traits as the books progress, and they all react to the peculiarities and difficulties of their respective environments. Sleator has said that "an area in which a lot of science fiction falls flat on its face—is characterization. The reader must know the characters are not fictional creations, but real people" (5). Lawrence has created samenesses in her science fiction characters, but differences, too. All of them find hope in one way or another. It is that hope for the future that remains long after the tales and the adventures have satisfied the readers.

BIBLIOGRAPHY

Antczak, Janice. *Science Fiction: The Mythos of a New Romance.* New York: Neal-Schuman, 1985.

Crew, Hilary. "From Labyrinth to Celestial City: Setting and the Portrayal of the Female Adolescent in Science Fiction." *Journal of Youth Services in Libraries* 2.1 (Fall 1988): 84-89.

Lawrence, Louise. *Calling B for Butterfly.* New York: Harper, 1982.

_____. *Children of the Dust.* New York: Harper, 1985.

_____. *Moonwind*. New York: Harper, 1986.

_____. *The Power of Stars*. New York: Harper, 1972.

_____. *Star Lord*. New York: Harper, 1978.

Muller, Al. "Doomsday Fiction and the YA Reader." *ALAN Review* 16.1 (Fall 1988): 42-45.

Sleator, William. "What *Is* It About Science Fiction." *ALAN Review* 15.2 (Winter 1988): 4-6.

11

The Debate Continues: Technology or Nature– A Study of Monica Hughes's Science Fiction Novels

J. R. Wytenbroek

> Once again we see the theme which Monica [Hughes] hammers home
> again and again with great gusto and invention: the necessity of
> knowing the interface between the wilderness and civilization, be-
> tween our past and our future, of knowing the interface and establish-
> ing intercourse across that border at all cost however inviolate that
> border may seem to be. (Wynne-Jones 51)

For some years, discussions have continued regarding the problems, even dangers, inherent in anti-technological, "back-to-nature" science fiction for adolescents. Perry Nodelman argues, in his article "Out There in Children's Science
Fiction: Forward into the Past" and again in his rebuttal to Jill May's response to
his paper, that this anti-technological stance is, in fact, regressive. He states that
such young adult science fiction novels "all hide a retrogressive vision under their
theoretically revolutionary fervor" (May and Nodelman 229).

Whether one agrees with the substance of Nodelman's arguments in these two
articles or not, his accusation that "at the . . . heart of [these] novels" lies an "anti-
technological and even anti-evolutionary bias" (Nodelman 288) that is an expression of a "clear prejudice against scientific knowledge" (290) that causes the
characters to embark upon a "curious descent into complacency" (289) is frequently heard, although it is more usually leveled against pastoral fantasies than
science fiction. On one level, the criticism is valid. Many science fiction novels
for young adults, including those set in postnuclear holocaust times, indicate that
the only way to either save the world from its current path of destruction or ensure
that destruction does not recur in the future is to retreat to a un- or even anti-
technological state in which humanity once more moves in tune with its natural
environment, an environment so often at risk or already destroyed in these novels.

Of course, the argument that humanity does indeed need to move back into a more balanced relationship with the natural world before we damage it irrevocably and, in so doing, destroy ourselves is also valid. This argument is gaining strength as we come to recognize the precarious situation our environment is now in after centuries of general abuse and decades of the intensive abuse of modern industry and technology. But do we, in fact, have to discard all technology to restore what we have almost destroyed and to save ourselves?

Monica Hughes's science fiction for young adults addresses this question again and again. Her central argument is that we must return to a more conscious and balanced relationship with the natural world if we are going to survive, not only on a physical level but, perhaps more important, on an emotional and spiritual level. However, she is equally adamant that it would be most difficult, maybe even impossible, for us now to survive on a physical level without technology: She argues clearly through her novels that technology used properly and wisely can enhance our lives and free us to explore the richness of our human heritage on the emotional, spiritual, and cultural levels.

Most of Hughes's science fiction novels deal with this issue in one way or another. In her early novel, *The Tomorrow City* (1978), Hughes explores the concept of a city computer, named C-Three, that, once unwittingly programmed by Caro, the teenaged daughter of its inventor, slowly takes control of the city it was meant to serve and improve. As it does, C-Three simply and literally eliminates the city's "undesirable" or unproductive elements, such as winos, the elderly, and pets, while programming the remaining citizens to accept and indeed desire the changes it brings. Refusing to watch the TV programs with their subliminal brain-washing messages, Caro and her friend Dave Sullivan eventually find a way to stop the computer, although both pay a great price. David loses his beloved dog in an early and abortive attempt to unplug Caro's family TV set, and Caro loses her eyesight when they finally and successfully manage to stop the computer altogether.

Two elements that appear again and again in Hughes's science fiction works surface in this early novel. One is the dehumanizing effect of technology run rampant, technology that takes control of its human masters. The loss of emotional concern and involvement with others is an immediate side effect of such control in most of the novels. For example, in *The Tomorrow City,* Caro's father, usually a caring and sensitive person, completely accepts the "necessity" of the city's driving David's grandmother out of her lifelong home so a playground can be built for the children, the "future" of the city that C-Three has been programmed to protect. Already under the influence of the subliminal messages, Mr. Henderson sees the old woman's house only as an impediment to the "progress" the computer envisions and refuses to help Caro and David try to save her home. The other citizens are in equally bad shape emotionally, and all relationships become distant and formal as C-Three programs people for efficiency and optimal performance to ensure its mandate, which it can fulfill on only the most superficial levels-the happiness and well-being of the children.

The other major theme that appears in this novel and that will recur is the theme of personal cost. Hughes is uncompromisingly realistic in her science fiction novels. She implies throughout them all that we cannot reduce our destructive overuse of technology without paying a price; the young people in her novels who confront tyrannical computers or overly technologically oriented societies must pay a price for their freedom, sometimes a heavy price, as David does with his dog and Caro does with her eyesight.

However, in this early novel we do not get a "back-to-nature" theme as a counterbalance to the tyranny of technology. Instead we get a "back-to-humanity" theme, which, given the setting of an ordinary twentieth-century city, works well. Here, where Hughes has not quite balanced the equation of technology and nature, she is neither excessive nor retrogressive in her vision. The Tomorrow City will become a city of today once more, and control of the city will return to the people who will then proceed to progress in their own way at their own pace, evolving naturally as opposed to evolving in the artificial fashion induced by C-Three. And Caro recognizes that the city's people may still not be mature enough as a whole to recognize the value of the gift that she and David have returned to them at the end of the novel:

Everyone in the city was still asleep, unaware of their new and hard-won freedom. Would they understand? Would they be grateful? Or would they just be angry because it wasn't going to be easy any more? (*The Tomorrow City* 137)

It is through this technologically induced trance that Hughes presents complacency, not in the more humane solution to it.

The Tomorrow City is, however, the only one of Hughes's science fiction novels that does not include the third theme—that of the importance of the environment. In *Beyond the Dark River* (1981), Hughes presents a post-nuclear world, in which the cities in Alberta, Canada, as elsewhere, have been destroyed, but both native Indians and the exclusive religious communities of the Hutterites have survived. In their search for a cure for a mysterious plague that is killing all the children of one Hutterite community, a Hutterite boy and a native girl travel through the nearby city, looking for information that will help them save the children. They find nothing there of help, only the evidence of decay and devastation, which has reduced the few remaining city people to diseased and decadent cannibals. They realize they must rebuild their world themselves, that there is and can be no help from the self-destroyed technological society.

But the Hutterites have also paid a price for their lack of technology, although not as heavy a one as the technological society they have spurned. They have no protection against such plagues, as they have not developed any advanced medical systems to deal with emergencies such as the one they face now, considering such illness simply "the will of God." They have kept no records of their own history through writing or song, and thus they cannot help the native healer when she discovers that the generation before her friend's one was wiped out by a similar plague. They have some technology, such as windmills, but no longer know how to create such things. And their loss of contact with the commercial center of the city has further deprived them of the few things they used to purchase that rendered their lives slightly easier and more comfortable. However, this theme is not explored fully in this novel, as the interdependence of the two young people and the need for additional interaction between the two cultures is more central.

Even in her earliest, seemingly anti-technological writing, Hughes is never against technology itself. She is against the control of technology over humanity. She is also against the use of technology to make a profit at the expense of other people or as a tool for the exploitation of others. The ecologically sound environment being engineered on the Moon in the early novel *Earthdark* (1977), for example, utilizes technology to its fullest extent in the force fields, airtight domes, and other technologies needed to make the Moon a more inhabitable environment for its colonists. Even the people in the undersea communities in *Crisis on Conshelf Ten* (1975) utilize the latest available technology so that they can live permanently and comfortably deep under the ocean while also using technology to help feed Earth's starving population and to reoxygenate Earth's oxygen-depleted air, depleted through decades of uncontrolled pollution. In both novels, technology itself is not evil. But Hughes all too realistically points out the flaws in human nature that make people misuse technology, thereby creating a monster. The multinational corporations in both novels are the ones misusing technology to exploit people. Their chief concern is profit at any cost, and human life is as expendable as the environment in their one-eyed search for more and more profit. These corporations use extensive technology in their quest for profit, using it to rape both the Moon and the oceans. Through a twist in *Earthdark,* however, Hughes shows that the technology being used to exploit the Moon and its colonists was, in fact, first invented by those colonists to ensure their survival on the hostile satellite. Thus, she clearly establishes from the earliest novels that it is *how* humanity uses technology, not technology itself, that can be so negative and have such devastating results.

Despite the appearance of these themes in the earliest novels, *Ring-Rise, Ring-Set* (1982) is the first science fiction novel in which Hughes really explores all three themes mentioned earlier: the dehumanizing effect of an overuse of technology, the price to be paid for freedom from this enslavement, and the need for a closer relationship between humanity and nature. *Ring-Rise, Ring-Set* is set on a future Earth that is just entering a second ice-age caused by sun-blocking rings left around the Earth by a disintegrated meteorite. In this novel, the importance of both the technological and the ecologically holistic perspectives is bought out very clearly. The scientific community that has been established just below the encroaching ice fields, along with other scientific communities of the same nature all over the world, is the only hope for the world. Without technological intervention, Earth is doomed to a second, possibly permanent Ice Age that will destroy everything outside of a narrow belt at the equator. Yet this scientific community has become a cold, emotionless group, in which women have been subjugated to purely domestic roles, children are raised in communal, nonfamilial units with little parental contact and no affection; the slightest deviation from the accepted norm is treated with open suspicion and hostility, and knowledge of a purely scientific nature flourishes at the expense of art, literature, and music, which have become dying luxuries, little mourned by this cold, rational community committed to survival at any cost.

Liza, a young adult in the community, refuses to accept her role as subservient, emotionless, and domestic; and through a series of misadventures, finds herself out in the frozen wastes near the ice field in winter, where she is rescued by a group of Ekoes (Eskimos) who have assumed that she is a long lost relative. This second community in which she initially stays for many months has the humanity that her city lacks. Love, compassion, sorrow, and anger are deeply felt and openly expressed. For the first time in her life Liza *feels* loved, welcomed, wanted. She becomes part of a community where all work equally hard and in very similar ways for the survival of the whole group, without a hierarchy of male intelligentsia and female servants. But theirs is a harsh life, and there has been little time for the development of art and music here, either, although they do have a rich oral tradition. Also the Ekoes, while emotionally and spiritually wealthy, are totally at the mercy of their deteriorating environment; although they have adapted naturally to it with remarkable success, unless the Ring is removed, the caribou will eventually perish—and once the caribou are gone, the Ekoes will die. Therefore, they need the technocrats to preserve their very lives. But the technocrats, who come up with one solution to part of the problem near the end of the novel, are now so dehumanized by their total reliance on technological solutions and a technologically based life-style that they are willing to sacrifice the lives or culture of the Ekoes to advance their solution to the problem rather than look for a less deadly alternative.

In this novel, then, Hughes shows once more the importance of the interdependence of peoples. The technocrats may be able to save the world from certain destruction. They may be able to save the Ekoes from more immediate destruction if they want to. But they need an infusion of the humanity still so alive among the Ekoes before they care enough to save the Ekoes and, also, to save themselves as human beings. Neither can really survive without the other. Each has something essential to offer the whole of humanity. But here, as in *Beyond the Dark River,* Hughes reveals clearly that the superior culture is the one that maintains its deepest human values, that remains both emotionally and spiritually engaged with its own humanity. At the end of the novel, by refusing to go into the protection of the city and embrace the technological life-style, the Ekoes choose their humanity and possible death over dehumanization and probable survival. Hughes explicitly indicates that the former choice is the better choice of the two. Furthermore, there is a great potential cost to Liza, who opts at the end to share the fate of the Ekoes rather than return to the safety of the city. But Hughes further implies that, by choosing humanity over survival, Liza touches the buried humanity of the city's scientists, one of whom is her own father, which causes them to find an alternative method of combating the ice *without* destroying the Ekoes, and Liza along with them. (This implication is substantiated as, part way through the novel, Hughes gives us a glimpse of the future when she states "in later years, when [Liza] told the story to her own children" (*Ring-Rise, Ring-Set* 79).

As with *Ring-Rise, Ring-Set,* Hughes's other novels usually end with hope. There is hope in the sweet rain that falls on Caro's blinded face at the end of *The Tomorrow City.* There is hope offered for the isolated community at the end of *The Guardian of Isis* and, particularly strongly, at the end of *The Isis Pedlar.* Hope for two communities, if not so much for the individual who sacrifices himself for those communities, is strong at the end of *Devil on My Back.* And hope is like a beacon by the end of the otherwise horrifyingly bleak *Invitation to The Game.* But these endings of hope do not support Nodelman's complaint regarding the "retrogressive vision" and "descent into complacency" in young adult science fiction. The hope in Hughes's novels is hard won through individual sacrifice and loss. And the hope depends on balance, on some kind of contact or bridging between the technological societies and environmentally based societies frequently set in opposition in the novels. Hughes attests that this hope arises from her deep conviction that "over all, pattern will emerge out of chaos" (Jones 13). This hope, however, like all her themes, is founded firmly on realistic principles. "True hope is . . . rooted in the hard facts of the past and the present, but it desires to transform—not to replace, nor merely rearrange, but to transform—their undesirable patterns" (Smedman 93).

The Isis books pursue this theme of hope and the balance essential to hope in a somewhat different way than does most of Hughes's other young adult science fiction. Beginning in *The Keeper of the Isis Light* (1980), Hughes shows the dangers that beset a community that starts off balanced with technological advantages that help them settle with ease into their chosen agricultural lifestyle on their new planet and then abruptly abandons all technology. In a study of human nature that is superb on many different planes, Hughes shows the potential devastation when a society deliberately turns its back on even basic technological aids in a hostile environment, which the planet Isis can be. By refusing all technology and labelling it as "evil," the human community on Isis becomes self-defeating, almost being destroyed by a series of natural calamities the people no longer have the capabilities to deal with in the second novel of the trilogy, *The Guardian of Isis* (1981). They are also almost destroyed again by purported "magic," which is simply forgotten technology, in the third novel, *The Isis Pedlar* (1982). Both times they are saved by the high technology of the robot guardian of Isis. Here technology is shown to be necessary for survival, as it was in getting the settlers from Earth to Isis in the first place, years before. But narrow-mindedness, prejudice, and fear have deprived most of the settlers of all the advantages of technology, causing them to become as imprisoned in their "simple" life as the people were mentally imprisoned by C-Three in *The Tomorrow City* and as the people are imprisoned on many levels in the sterile cities of *Ring-Rise, Ring-Set* and *Devil on My Back.*

The people of Isis do not lose their humanity to the extent that the city dwellers do in any of the three books above, but their narrowness sets up prejudices, suspicions, fears, and hostility among them that finally erupt into attempted lynchings, the first physical violence that has ever manifested itself in the society, near the end of *The Isis Pedlar*. The ones most free of these negative qualities, and thereby the freest creatures in general on Isis, are Olwen, the keeper of the Isis light, David and Jody N'Kumo, from the settlers' community, and the guardian of Isis, a very human robot. These four, all physically or emotionally rejected by society at one time or another, are the ones who save the community during its times of greatest danger, and they are also the only ones who can accept the importance and necessity of technology. Here Hughes is showing that prisons of mind and soul are not the exclusive problem of the sterile technological society, but that any society can become dehumanized if it is self-isolated and allows itself to become unbalanced. Technology is presented primarily as a good thing throughout the trilogy, something that is helping save the people of Earth and that could greatly enhance the chances of survival and the development of the Isis community, at least in its early stages. By the end of *The Isis Pedlar,* however, it is too late for advanced technological aids, and the community must learn a new humanity within its chosen course; thus, it still has the chance to break free from the self-imposed prison of fear, prejudice, and hostility, opening the possibility for technological development again in the future.

Like the early community on Isis, the forest community of free slaves in *Devil on My Back* (1985) depends for survival on higher levels of technology than it currently enjoys. However, unlike the people of Isis, the free slaves have not refused technology but rather have not had an option. Escapees from the inhuman, tyrannical, and totally computerized city of ArcOne, they left with what little they could take, which over the years has amounted to only one axe, one saw, and one knife. On the other hand, ArcOne has too much technology so that its people, like those of *The Tomorrow City,* are completely controlled by the computer, at least all except the slaves and the Overlord. But unlike *The Tomorrow City,* the people of ArcOne have not wrenched themselves free of the computer's oppression, and the computer has become a tyrant, dictating every aspect of every person's life, either directly or indirectly. Here the computer is the ultimate Overlord, beyond all but the most cursory control of the human overlord. There is no freedom of any kind in ArcOne, and the social structure of lords, workers, soldiers, and slaves accentuates the total dehumanization of the people in the city.

The bridge between the two communities is Tomi, son of the Overlord, who is ejected by mistake from the city during a slave riot. He eventually finds his way to the community of free slaves who help him find his personal freedom, including his own identity as a human being. Once he finds true freedom, he elects to go back into prison, into ArcOne, so that he can smuggle out to the forest community the tools and seeds they so desperately need, as they are unable to forge new tools for themselves from the depleted resources of an Earth raped and pillaged for centuries for her mineral wealth. Tomi pays a great price for the survival of the forest community, exchanging his newfound freedom for captivity and for the community's continuing freedom. However, in the process, he finds a new and unexpected freedom for himself. As he begins to help his friends achieve the needed balance, he finds a totally unpredicted chance to work toward the freedom of tyrannized ArcOne. At the end of the novel, ArcOne remains the cold, emotionally and spiritually sterile place it had been before Tomi's accident, but once again the humanizing force of Tomi and, unexpectedly, his Overlord father, begins immediately to affect, to counter, and (we are left with every reason to believe) to eventually undermine the dehumanization of this society, bringing it freedom, humanity, and a new, more balanced relationship with nature, as does indeed happen at the end of the novel's sequel, *The Dream Catcher.*

A much more frightening type of dehumanization takes place in Hughes's most recent novel, *Invitation to The Game* (1990). This time, she does not use the tyranny of the uncontrolled computer, or even the threat of extinction to dehumanize, but rather the novel is based on the simple human weakness for an easy life, an important theme in *The Tomorrow City,* as well. Hughes also reverses a pattern evident in both young adult and adult science fiction that Margaret Esmonde discusses in her article "From Little Buddy to Big Brother: The Icon of the Robot in Children's Science Fiction." Esmonde argues that "the negative aspect of the computer in children's science fiction exists in sharp contrast to the benevolent icon of the robot" (96). She goes on to say that "whereas in the robot stories the mechanical character is almost certain to be benevolent, in computer stories, the machine without exception poses a serious threat to man's free will and even his life" (94). She concludes that

one may speculate that the robot's anthropomorphic appearance somehow reassures us of some common bond while the impersonality of the computer banks with their flashing lights, or the repulsive, disembodied brain, both sealed in a sterile, protective environment, accents the differences between man and machine. (96)

Hughes herself has followed this pattern before with her negative computers and her benevolent robot guardian of the Isis novels. However Hughes has set *Invitation to The Game* on a post-pollution-crisis Earth, where, after most of the human population was wiped out by a pollution-based cataclysm, the remaining people created benevolent robots to help them reconstruct their world. But the efficiency of the robots has rendered them vital to the survival of a humanity afraid of returning to its old destructive patterns, and as the population increases, there are increasingly few jobs for humans. Vast slums are created in the cities for the huge number of unemployed, where most students end up upon graduation from the government-run boarding schools. In this novel, the robots themselves have not taken over. They have simply, as in many adult science fiction stories, become so indispensable that people are losing their own function in their society and are, in the process, becoming dehumanized.

The city Hughes depicts in *Invitation to The Game* is more frightening than those in any of the previous novels, for it is the city of nightmare, of gray, broken slums housing broken people who try to keep the tatters of their humanity together by living with dignity and true supportive community within this ugly world. Other inhabitants of this broken world cannot even maintain that much of their threatened humanity, sinking into gang violence, anesthetizing themselves with drugs or alcohol or both, or living for the wildly colored nightlife. The most frightening thing about the city in this novel is that, unlike any city in Hughes' other novels, it is already here, at least in part. One need only watch TV or walk some of the streets in larger North American cities to see the same numb despair on the faces of people in the tenements and listen to the news of the violence and substance abuse in such places to know that the nightmare has already begun, and we do not even have the excuse that the controlling powers do in *Invitation to The Game*. In other words, the more young adult science fiction she writes, the more realistic Hughes gets on many levels, and therefore the more frightening.

But hope is equally as strong as despair in this powerful novel. Through a lengthy process that is never explained to them, the members of the newly graduated group on which the novel focuses find themselves on a new, previously unpopulated planet, a completely pastoral planet, where they have the chance to begin again. They are not forewarned that they will be sent there, and they are given nothing with which to begin life on this new planet, except the advantage of their particular skills and training and having explored their area of the planet through induced dream states in which they were given realistic "tours" of their region where they found what growing things could be safely eaten, where there was water, and what dangers lurked.

The novel, then, seems to be one of Nodelman's "retrogressive visions," with the first ten Adams and Eves left in an idyllic paradise to simplistically regain what all humanity lost when it moved from its supposedly idyllic prehistory past, before the first technology—simple tools—changed the course of humanity forever. However, a closer reading shows quite the opposite. All the members of the team were highly trained before they left school and were more than competent in a field that will aid the survival of the team. One is a trained doctor, another a biologist, another a chemist, another a woodworker, and so on. Their technological society has given them all the skills needed for survival, as it has, in varying combinations, the other groups "seeded" on the new world at the same time as this group. As Lisse, the protagonist, states near the end of the novel, while she is making the first writing paper for the new colony, "we have been reliving the discoveries and inventions of our remote ancestors only speeded up enormously, so that we will move from the Stone Age to the Bronze in less than five years" (167). She goes on to

wonder how far we will go. Iron Age. And what then? Our memories hold all the discoveries of humankind: coal, gas, oil, electricity, fission power. Pollution. The end of the line. Pollution caused the sudden drop in fertility that nearly destroyed human life on Earth. It was only the robots that saved us, becoming our hands and feet and brains when there weren't enough humans left. Then we recovered and couldn't get rid of them. The Government was faced with a choice: get rid of the robots—or get rid of the young people. It's ironic that is was easier to get rid of the young people. It all has to do with the use of power. We hope we won't make the same mistakes. We are careful and we talk a lot about what went wrong on Earth. (168)

This is not a "retrogressive vision." This group has enough vision to desire a more advanced future, but also the wisdom born of bitter experience to know that there must be limits to technological advance. These young people have recovered their full humanity, at great cost, and have learned the importance of a true and good balance between technology and a natural life-style.

Through these novels, Monica Hughes offers young people and us all a chance, maybe a last chance, to see the necessity of this balance, to see the importance of preserving our own humanity by moving closer to a more natural life-style that will help protect and maintain our environment while utilizing the real benefits of humanized technology, a technology that works for us all, not one that controls or imprisons us on any level of our beings or that is used by some to exploit others. In all these novels, she presents the importance of human emotions, culture, and spirituality to help us keep that precious and precarious balance, so that we will not find ourselves, like Lisse and her friends, citizens of a nightmare reality come true, and come to stay.

BIBLIOGRAPHY

Esmonde, Margaret P. "From Little Buddy to Big Brother: The Icon of the Robot in Children's Science Fiction." *The Mechanical God*. Ed. Thomas P. Dunn and Richard D. Erlich. Westport, CT: Greenwood, 1982.

Hughes, Monica. *Beyond the Dark River*. New York: Atheneum, 1981.

_____. *Crisis on Conshelf Ten*. London: Hamish Hamilton, 1975.

_____. *Devil on My Back*. New York: Atheneum, 1985.

_____. *The Dream Catcher*. New York: Atheneum, 1987.

_____. *Earthdark*. London: Hamish Hamilton, 1977.

_____. *The Guardian of Isis*. New York: Atheneum, 1981.

_____. *Invitation to The Game*. Toronto: Harper Collins, 1990.

_____. *The Isis Pedlar*. Scarborough, Ontario: Fleet, 1982.

_____. *The Keeper of the Isis Light*. London: Hamish Hamilton, 1980.

_____. *Ring-Rise, Ring-Set*. New York: Julia MacRae, 1982.

_____. *The Tomorrow City*. London: Hamish Hamilton, 1978.

Jones, Raymond E. "The Technological Pastoralist: A Conversation with Monica Hughes." *Canadian Children's Literature* 44 (1986): 6-18.

May, Jill, and Perry Nodelman. "The Perils of Generalizing about Children's Science Fiction." *Science Fiction Studies* 39 (1986): 225-29.

Nodelman, Perry. "Out There in Children's Science Fiction: Forward into the Past."

Science Fiction Studies 37 (1985): 285-96.

Smedman, M. Sarah. "Springs of Hope: Recovery of Primordial Time in 'Mythic' Novels for Young Readers." *Children's Literature* 16 (1988): 91-107.

Wynne-Jones, Tim. "An Eye for Thresholds." *Canadian Children's Literature* 48 (1987): 42-54.

12

Myth in Action:
The Trials and
Transformation of Menolly

Patricia Harkins

Anne McCaffrey's Harper Hall series introduces one of her most engaging female heroes—Menolly. As the first book of the series, *Dragonsong,* opens, we meet a gifted but lonely teenager. Through a series of transforming trials she achieves "the conquest of fear" (Norton 299). The motif of the misunderstood adolescent, and the quest for a purpose in life, are as old as storytelling itself. But McCaffrey interweaves "universal values, desires, struggles and emotions" into a tapestry of fantasy and science fiction; what Jane Yolen, among others, has called "speculative fiction" (*Writing Books* 54).[1] It is a tribute to her power as a storyteller that the trilogy she began writing for young readers almost twenty years ago has retained its popularity with that demanding age group while steadily gaining new readers among critics, librarians, teachers, and parents.

McCaffrey engages both the heads and the hearts of her audience, all of whom share a mutual human "hunger for heroes as role models, as standards of action, as ethics in flesh and bones like our own. A hero is a myth in action" that "reflects our own sense of identity, and from this our own heroism is molded" (May 54). Menolly's story chronicles the progress of an insecure loner who learns how her individual feelings, aspirations, and capabilities can serve other people.

The Harper Hall books form part of a multivolume saga about Pern, the "third world" of six planets that orbit Rukbat, in the Sagittarian Sector, a "golden G-type star" (*The Dragonriders of Pern* Series Introduction). The entire saga is set sometime in the future, after "a committed and resourceful" (*Dragonsdawn* 4) group of men and women from Terra (Earth) and other worlds within the Federated Sentient Planets have migrated far into space. Searching for riches and freedom from the repression of the technocrats who dominate their societies, these adventurers colonized the planet they named Pern, and descendants of the original human colonists now inhabit Menolly's world. McCaffrey's trilogy for young readers is integrally connected with several of her Pern novels for adults through overlapping characters and plots.[2] All of her novels affirm specific human values such as "the need for faith and perserverance in the face of obstacles, the importance of personal and social responsibility, and the power of love and friendship" (Norton 296).

Dragonsong, the first book of the Harper Hall trilogy, is set in Pern's northern continent, where Menolly lives with her family in the important fishing settlement of Half Circle Sea Hold. Yanus, her father, is the leader of the Hold. In his blind loyalty to tradition, he represents those in his society who are unable to distinguish between customs that still make sense in a changing time and those that no longer work. In the role of middle-aged, conservative authority figure, he serves as the perfect foil for his youngest daughter. Menolly's mother, Mavi, is as conservative and tradition-bound as her husband. Menolly's tattletale sister, Sella, rejects the younger girl. Stella agrees with their mother that Menolly is troublesome, an impractical dreamer, yet "too clever by half" (2), and with their father that Menolly even looks odd, "too tall and lanky to be a proper girl at all" (1). The only one in her family who accepts Menolly is one of her brothers, Alemi. He admires her as an athlete who easily outruns boys her age and as a musician who outplays and outsings everyone else in the settlement. But since she is "only a girl" (1), they are seldom together except at community gatherings.

McCaffrey has skillfully set the stage for the drama of Menolly's quest for selfhood. As in many fairy tales, the protagonist is an adolescent and an outsider, "powerless, scorned" (Heilbrun 146). Although she is "animal-loving, kind, generous, affectionate" and hardworking, Menolly is "again and again rejected" by most of the people she cares about. As she herself acknowledges sadly to her mentor and friend, old Petiron, in Pernese society it is a long-established custom that "women can't be harpers" (4). No wonder then that Yanus and Mavi view Menolly's music as a form of stubborn rebellion that must be quelled for her own good.

In spite of custom and parental opposition, however, Petiron has such faith in his student's outstanding abilities that he makes a secret plan to ensure her future as a musician, sending a message to the powerful and respected Masterharper Robinton along with two of Menolly's original compositions. Unfortunately, Petiron dies before he receives a reply, and fourteen-year-old Menolly is left without an ally strong enough to counter her parents' determination to suppress their daughter's "distressing tendency toward tune-making" (10). They allow her to sing her teacher's Deathsong only because she is the sole person with the musical skill to properly honor the old Harper. They further decide to allow her to temporarily instruct the youngsters of the Hold in the basic Teaching Ballads through which the traditions of Pern are passed down. But she is warned, "Behave yourself while you stand in a man's place. No tuning!" (11). Meanwhile, they anxiously wait for Masterharper Robinton to send them a new male teacher from Harper Hall.

Yanus feels obligated to maintain the ancient beliefs and customs Pern harpers pass on, out of respect for the heroic dragonriders of Benden Weyr (or fort), led in this generation by Weyrleader Flar and Weyrwoman Lessa. The dragonriders have protected Yanus's people, and those in other settlements, from the dread threat of Threadfall for as long as anyone can remember. Thread is made up of mycorrihizoid spores that travel from the erratically orbiting Red Star to fall on Pern periodically, burrowing into the soil and devouring any organic material in their path. In order to protect themselves from invasions of Thread, the original colonists of Pern bred a highly specialized variety of indigenous flying "fire lizards" into "dragons" large enough to teleport empathic human riders instantly from one place to another. These "dragons" were trained to chew a phosphine-bearing rock so that they could emit flaming gas capable of killing Thread on land—water drowns Thread at sea.

Menolly is growing up in a period of great discontent and fomenting rebellion throughout the northern continent where her family lives. Due to the conjunction of Rukbat's five natural satellites, the Red Star has not passed close enough to Pern to drop the terrible Thread for nearly four hundred years. Supported in their stony, barren fortresses by the tithes and offerings from farmers, fisherfolk, and merchants, the dragonriders have generally fallen into disfavor as outdated and useless. However, there are those like Yanus who have been faithful to their traditional heroes. Their faith is justified when it becomes distressingly evident that Pern is due to suffer a new cycle of Threadfall. The Pernese must once again learn to cope with the perils of life during the years that constitute a Pass, a period when Thread is a potent threat.

Masterharper Robinton of Harper Hall recognizes that this time in Pernese history is crucial in safeguarding the future of the planet. "Many old ways need shaking up and revising" (45). He sends a vanguard of young, specially trained Harpers to the Holds and Crafthalls, each with the same mission to "provoke a change, subtle at first to get every Holder and Craftmaster to think beyond the needs of their own lands, Hall and people" (45). McCaffrey is well aware that adolescent readers want a hero who is not only close to their own age, but also "important," though "it may not be that the hero's importance is recognized immediately" (Whitney 91), and so Menolly will have a major part in the transformation of Pernese society.

Petiron's mission to the Masterharper has been successful; Robinton commissions his trusted aide, Elgion, to find out what has happened to his old colleague's mysterious apprentice. Her highly original and haunting melodies have convinced him that she should come to Harper Hall to receive the further professional training that she deserves. At this point, the Masterharper knows neither her name nor her sex, only her potential.

Elgion arrives at Half Circle Sea Hold full of hope that he will be able to quickly discover the brilliant young songmaker. But when he presses Yanus with questions, Menolly's father lies, telling Elgion that Petiron's apprentice was a fosterson who has recently returned to his home Hold. He is ashamed to admit that his youngest and most rebellious child is really the one for whom Elgion is asking. Besides, he reasons, Menolly has recently injured her hand and may never be able to play a harp or flute again. Yanus is sorry that the girl has cut herself so badly, "and not entirely because she [is] a good worker;" the fact is, he sometimes misses her "clear, sweet voice" (43). Still, it is best to keep her "out of the Harper's way until she [forgets] her silly tuning... you had to keep your mind on your work, not on dreams" (43, 45).

Menolly's injury is the indirect result of her first overt disobedience to her father, who is "doing what every father is tempted to do, namely overprotect his daughter," so "blocking her growth" (May 202). After Yanus refuses to allow her to sing anymore or to continue inventing her own tunes, Menolly initially obeys him although she is bewildered and angry. After all, in the past she had been encouraged to sing and had never been punished for creating new music. Soon, Menolly cannot resist the creativity that wells up in her; she resorts to hiding in corners and softly trying out new songs. Yanus overhears her one day. Not only does he beat her, but he takes away her gitar, thus symbolically crippling her.

Menolly's plight echoes that of many of her true ancestors, the adolescent protagonists of folk and fairy tales around the world. She suffers an unjust punishment, then passes through a series of increasingly difficult trials. Readers of varying ages find it easy to empathize with her as she struggles to understand herself and her world. This quality of empathy is the "final magic" that novelist Phyllis A. Whitney identifies as absolutely necessary for a memorable story (92). Whitney agrees with Rebecca West's definition of empathy as "our power of projecting ourselves into the destiny of others by fantasy" (qtd. in Whitney 92). Whitney writes that once readers empathize, they "will read with delight, knowing they are meeting" a character "as real as themselves," a new friend "they will want to keep, whose experiences they will profit by long after they have put [this] story down" (92).

Seeking solace for the emotional and physical pain her father's beating has given her, Menolly tries to earn her mother's approval by cleaning packtails, a tasty but smelly fish with sharp spines that ooze an oily, potentially dangerous slime. Brooding over her wrongs, she becomes careless. Her knife slips and gashes her left palm. Her sister, Sella, may be a jealous tattletale, but even Menolly admits that the older girl is always coolheaded in an emergency. Now she grabs Menolly's wrist and deftly stops the spurt of blood from the severed artery. Their mother, a skilled healer, stills her young daughter's panic and then stitches shut the long slice in the injured hand.

In this scene, McCaffrey shows her awareness of a basic rule of characterization set down succinctly by Phyllis Whitney in *Writing Juvenile Stories and Novels:* "No character must be goody-goody; no character must be thoroughly bad" (91). Both Sella and Mavi are Menolly's antagonists, yet they care about her and continually try to protect her from herself. Yanus, too, is no villain. In many ways, he is an admirable character, a stern but loving leader and father. On the other hand, Menolly's tendency to sulk and feel sorry for herself is understandable, but not admirable. She will pay a high penalty for her faults.

Menolly is left-handed, a common trait among the "maverick heroes" of myths and fairy tales. She is stunned when her mother pronounces, "with a shine of pity in her eyes . . . . Even if your fingers will work after that slice, you won't be playing again" (40). As the girl slips into a drugged sleep, "her last conscious thought" is of "misery, of being cheated of the one thing that had made her life bearable" (41). At that moment, she is certain that her recent decision to defy her parents by letting Elgion know she is Petiron's apprentice is now futile, and she is also certain that her fervent wish to continue growing and learning as a musician will never come true. However, Menolly's tale has really just begun. "In one sense," as Rollo May has noted, "every tale, every myth, every emergence of a new element in one's development starts with a wish . . . a longing for some fulfillment" (200).

With the resilience of youth and a strong, if sometimes oversensitive, spirit, the girl soon recovers from her wound enough to continue exploring the cliffs outside her home. More than ever, she becomes the loner, the outsider. Rebelliously she wanders further and further from the Hold in spite of the danger from a possible Threadfall attack. Like Briar Rose in Rollo May's analysis of the Sleeping Beauty fairy tale:

[The] growing girl [moves] out into the world. She does this when she's alone. . . . The word "alone" here is especially significant because this kind of development, this leap of freedom, must always contain some element of being alone, taking responsibility for one's own steps oneself. (203)

Menolly had begun the frightening, but necessary, process of "moving out into the world" even before her hand became crippled. It was while she was gathering greens for dinner at her mother's command that she first strayed beyond the invisible but strong boundaries that her parents had enforced for years. And by going beyond the limits they had so carefully set to protect her, Menolly gained an entirely unexpected reward—the sight of fire lizards darting and swooping at play, their wings flashing in the sun like jewels. "A mere girl had seen what all the boys—and men—of the seahold had only dreamed of seeing" (25). She wisely determined to keep what she had seen a secret.

After her accident, Menolly is exploring the seaside cliffs near the Dragon Stones, a famous landmark, when she receives another unexpected reward, but this time only after putting her very life at risk. The fire lizard queen is frantically trying to save a clutch of unhatched eggs from the unusually high, and swift, rising tide. Menolly scales the sheer cliffs, helping the little queen secure the eggs within a cave. Afterward, "torn between laughter and awe" at the "enormity of her adventure" (57), she flexes her fingers, which ache from unaccustomed exercise. Suddenly she realizes that she is almost completely extending the fingers of her injured left hand. "It hurt, but it was a stretchy-hurt" (59). Perhaps if she works her hand more she'll be able to play again!

That night she decides to emerge from her self-protective shell long enough to enjoy the evening's entertainment in the Great Hall. But when Elgion urges everyone to join in the choruses of the rousing songs he sings, Mavi pinches her youngest daughter so hard in warning that the girl cannot help gasping. Once more feeling unjustly rebuked, Menolly runs away the next morning.

Thread falls, and afterward it is Sella who first misses Menolly and reports her absence. Their parents are keenly annoyed and anxious, but Yanus decides not to initiate a full search although he does tell anyone who happens to be abroad to "keep a sharp eyes for any trace of her" (78). He feels that his first responsibility during this dangerous time is to his people, not to one girl—the one child out of his many children who is both a troublemaker and a cripple. Besides, as her closest brother, Alemi, asserts, Menolly is intelligent and able to fend for herself. The usually composed Mavi does "catch her breath in a sound very like a sob" when she understands that her child is in danger; yet accepts her husband's decision, Elgion notices, almost "as if the girl were an embarassment" (78). Alemi bitterly confesses to the Harper, "I think [Menolly's] alive and better off wherever she is than she would be in Half-Circle" (79).

Menolly's creator must agree with Alemi, for never once, in all the intervening years and books since *Dragonsong* first appeared, has she sent Menolly back home. Fortunately, Alemi's assessment of his sister proves to be correct. In fact, not only does she survive after she runs away from the safety and confining protection of home, she thrives. And as she grows increasingly stronger and more mature, Menolly learns to "walk through any doors that are opened" for her (Frances Perkins, qtd. in Heilbrun 120). Like the ideal hero that Carolyn Heilbrun describes in *Reinventing Womanhood,* Menolly is "almost always rescued or helped," but her "dependence on help is characterized" not by her "expectations of rescue, but by" her "openness towards others and before experience" (148).

When she is caught out in Threadfall, for example, far from either the Sea Hold or the cave where she has been living with her fire lizard friends, she refuses to panic. Urged on by the fire lizards, she does her best to outrun the dreaded gray spores. She is oddly exhilarated, feeling as if she "could run forever" (108) and is prepared to clamber down a steep bluff in order to reach the relative safety of the sea if she must. Instead, she is rescued by the great dragon, Branth, and T'gran, his rider. Elgion had alerted the dragonriders in the area of Half Circle Sea Hold to watch for a runaway. Wasting no time in indulging her astonishment at their sudden appearance above her, Menolly dives for the dragonrider's extended hand—and straight into her next adventure.

While at the fishing settlement, Elgion never discovers that Menolly is the apprentice he has been looking for, yet it is he who saves her life by alerting the dragonriders to look out for a runaway. He further helps Menolly when he does at last find and identify her, at Benden Weyr, where T'gan has taken her. Elgion is delighted and astonished, not only at who she really is, but by how she has managed to tame nine of the fire lizards that the dragonriders themselves have only recently discovered to be real, rather than mythical, and "much like dragons, only smaller" (82), capable of being impressed and trained. He encourages Masterharper Robinton to take her with him immediately to Harper Hall.

Through talent, determination, and the aid of Masterharper Robinton himself, Menolly of Half Circle Sea Hold becomes the first female apprentice, then journeyman, of Harper Hall. As she grows to young adulthood, Anne McCaffrey's female hero evolves into a dauntless protagonist, who makes "patently clear" to her readers "women's desires and determinations and their abilities to achieve, at least as much as men do, their goals" (Cornillon xl). The once shy and fearful adolescent not only learns to tame fire lizards and ride dragons in *Dragonsong* and its sequel, *Dragonsinger,* but she explores the wilderness of a vast southern continent in *Dragondrums.* By the time she appears in McCaffrey's adult novels, *The White Dragon* and *The Renegades of Pern,* it is no surprise that the grownup Menolly is in the vanguard of those Pernese men and women who are learning how to use the powerful telepathic gifts of the tiny dragon-cousins to help save their planet.

In her role as an adventurer and risk-taker, Menolly personifies the kind of hero in twentieth-century fantasies that may "help break the cycle of female commitment to passivity" that Karen Rowe asserts has doomed the protagonist of the traditional fairy tale to "pursue adult potentials in one way only;" she "dreamily anticipates conformity to those pre-destined roles of wife and mother" (qtd. in Heilbrun 147). Menolly does have a passionate love affair with a fellow journeyman-harper, Sebell, in *Dragondrums.* This affair, though freely entered into, comes as a complete surprise to the inexperienced, though by now nearly grown-up, protagonist. Certainly she has never had either the time or the inclination in her busy life at Harper Hall to "dreamily anticipate" becoming Sebell's lover. Whether she marries Sebell (or anyone else) or ever becomes a mother is left an open question at the end of the trilogy and is not addressed in any of the McCaffrey adult novels to date in which Menolly has a role.

We can be sure that she would never choose to follow the example of her mother or of any other woman she knew at Half Circle Sea Hold. On the other hand, she might consider following the example of Lessa, the beautiful and intelligent Weyrwoman of Benden Weyr, who enjoys the enduring love of the handsome Weyrleader, F'lar, and their son, Felessan, without abdicating her civic power and responsibility or the close relationship she has with her golden dragon queen. Menolly's story is, in some ways, like the fairy tale of Briar Rose, which, as Rollo May remarks, is a tale of awakening, of "emerging femininity" (196) with all of its attendant dynamics and problems. Menolly, however, unlike the fairy-tale princess, is not rescued by a "prince" but by her mentors. She is fortunate to have the help and guidance of a series of able and loving mentors—both female and male—while she is "in the proces of creating or discovering" her "wholeness . . . questioning and finding viable answers and solutions" (Cornillon xi). They serve as guides or exemplars "in dealing with the central concerns of her life" (Heilbrun 146).[3]

If Menolly feels lonely or misunderstood, she has the example of Lessa before her, the starvling slave girl who endured long years of poverty and despair before enjoying fame and fortune. If she needs more immediate mothering and under-standing than the somewhat remote Lessa offers, Menolly can turn to Silvina, the affectionate and practical headwoman of Harper Hall. From their first meeting, Silvina adopts Menolly as her foster child. Menolly, who so often bewails her state as a mere girl, becomes reconciled to, then grows to appreciate, her femaleness. From the women she admires, she learns to embody the "feminine" characteristics of nurturance and relatedness without losing the "masculine" qualities of questing, acting, and performing (Heilbrun 148) she has acquired. The men who mentor her, especially Masterharper Robinton, successfully combine stereotypical "feminine" and "masculine" traits as well. In spite of an impressive baritone voice and an imposing air of authority, Robinton, for example, is described by McCaffrey as having "kind eyes" and a warm, gentle touch (*Dragonsong* 175).

As Menolly continues to grow and change throughout the Harper Hall trilogy, her readers are never bored, for her story is marked by "disruptive energy, rapid and shocking experience, and persistent revelations of contradictions and strangeness at the core of personal, familial, and social life" (Frey and Griffith x). McCaffrey never forgets the "sobering truth about the imagination" that Charles Frey and John Griffith describe so eloquently in *The Literary Heritage of Childhood* (x). For her, as for them, the best fantasy writing often "tends to hover over the glowing border between good dream and nightmare" because "the wellsprings of the imagination" often "flow from pain" and "the imagination is, among other things, the mind's way of taking charge of unsatisfactory reality, of dominating it, and forcing it to yield to the meanings the heart requires but the world does not provide" (ix, x).

Menolly's unusual talents, her ever-active curiosity and her increasing determination to "do everything I can" (*Dragonsinger* 202) constantly attract jealousy as well as admiration, malice as well as generosity. It is like a good dream to Menolly in that she is allowed to study music at Harper Hall and to keep her fire lizards there with her. But it is a nightmare in that she is still often shunned, especially by girls her own age.

She enjoys a small, but personally significant moment of triumph when she is teased once too often by her smug rival, Pona, in *Dragonsinger*. Menolly decides that it is time to stand her ground—figuratively and literally. First, she challenges the other girl with words: "I claim insult from you, Pona" (190). Then, to Pona's surprise and dismay, she backs up the words with action, lunging past the prissy socialite's escort. Menolly enjoys a larger and more gradually realized triumph as Masterteacher Domick's prediction of her ability to touch other's lives with music comes true. Many Pernese find Menolly's songs "are a fresh voice, fresh new ways at looking things and people, with tunes no one can keep from humming" (233). In addition, her music has the power to "provide comfort" for "lonely minds and tuneless hearts" (233).

But one of Menolly's most gripping songs is a haunting piece that teaches and warns rather than comforts. It is inspired by the strangest and most shocking of her "nightmares." The restlessness of her nine fire lizard companions has waked her from a sound night's sleep. Through their touch and telepathic images, she learns that they are reacting to a fear whose source is some distance away. Terror overwhelms her as she receives an impression of slick, unbearably hot gray masses that churn around her. She hears a scream in her mind, which she later records in lyrics: "Don't leave me alone! / A cry in the night, / Of anguish heart-striking, / Of soul-killing fright" (129). Unaware of what she is doing, Menolly calls out in response. Before even the swiftest dragonrider can fly the message to them, Masterharper Robinton and the rest of Harper Hall find out from Menolly that a dragon has fallen from the sky. A messenger soon brings the news that dragonrider F'nor has tried to travel to the Red Star and has barely survived. What Menolly heard was F'nor's mate, Brekke, calling out to her lover and his dragon, Canth, once the mate of her own dead dragon queen. Menolly's terrifying experience, though caused by near-tragic circumstances, has a far-reaching, positive consequence: It alerts the Masterharper and other leaders to the possible importance of fire lizards as more than vastly entertaining pets.

The trilogy for young people that chronicles Menolly's adventures on Pern as she grows into young adulthood fits the definition of a masterpiece in *The Literary Heritage of Childhood*. It is a series of books that "people buy and read not merely because some teacher or professor has instructed them to, but willingly and with joy" (Frey and Griffith vii). As Jane Yolen writes, such books enchant their audiences with "ideas and the great treasure of story" (Yolen, *Touch Magic* Flyleaf).[4] "Begun as a dream or a vision," she adds, "the fantasy book moves beyond dreams and into craft. And there it is polished until it shines, ready for its audience, which is many miles wide and many years deep" (66).

The world of Anne McCaffrey's female hero in the Harper Hall trilogy is fantastic—an alien planet where fire lizards and dragons prosper. And, like many much older fantasies, the Harper Hall series may not "make direct contact with the world" that our young people must deal with today, fraught with the "very real problems of drugs, racism, poverty" (Yolen, *Writing* 66). However, "the best fantasy, by its very power to move the reader, by its dramatic—even melodramatic—morality finally does something else. It instills values" (Yolen, *Writing* 66), for such literature is almost invariably about "many things of fundamental concern to us—as children, as adults, as readers, as decision-makers, as seekers" (Frey and Griffith ix).

Anne McCaffrey's story of Menolly's trials and transformations works on many levels. Readers identify with, and learn from, her protagonist—a female hero whose quest for self-realization within her society succeeds against all odds. Menolly of Harper Hall is a "myth in action" (May 54).

NOTES

1. Jane Yolen argues that the phrase "speculative fiction" serves as "an excellent definition for fantasy in general. Fantasy is fiction that speculates that this, and other worlds, hold limitless possibilities" (54).

2. Two volumes in McCaffrey's Dragonriders trilogy for adults were published

before *Dragonsong;* they were *Dragonflight* (1968) and *Dragonquest* (1971). By the time the final book in this trilogy, *The White Dragon,* was published (1978), not only *Dragonsong* (1976) but *Dragonsinger* (1977) was in print. The final volume of the Harper Hall trilogy, *Dragondrums* (1979), was nearly ready for publication as well.

3. Carolyn Heilbrun discusses the etymology of the word *mentor* in *Reinventing Womanhood.* Originally a Greek word, it signified a friend of Odysseus, named Mentor. This character was entrusted with the education of the hero's son, Telemachus. "The word has come down to us, through the Latin, connoting now something more than a mere teacher" (146) .

4. Noted storyteller and critic, Jane Yolen, wrote this personal dedication to an aspiring writer at a book signing during the summer of 1986, while attending a conference at the University of Southern Mississippi: "For Patricia Harkins in the hope that she is not casting pearls but rather enchanting those who listen to her with her ideas and the great treasure of story" (*Touch Magic* Flyleaf).

BIBLIOGRAPHY

Cornillon, Susan K., ed. Preface. *Images of Women in Fiction.* Bowling Green, Ohio: Bowling Green UP, 1972.

Frey, Charles and John Griffith. *The Literary Heritage of Childhood.* Westport, CT: Greenwood, 1987.

Heilbrun, Carolyn. *Reinventing Womanhood.* New York: Norton, 1979.

May, Rollo. *The Cry for Myth.* New York: Norton, 1991.

McCafrrey, Anne. *Dragondrums.* 1979. New York: Bantam, 1980.

_____. *The Dragonriders of Pern: Dragonflight* (1968); *Dragonquest* (1971); *The White Dragon* (1978). New York: Doubleday, 1978.

_____. *Dragonsdawn.* 1988. New York: Ballantine, 1989.

_____. *Dragonsinger.* 1977. New York: Bantam, 1986.

_____. *Dragonsong.* 1976. New York Bantam, 1988.

_____. *The Renegades of Pern.* 1989. New York: Ballantine, 1990.

Norton, Donna E. *Through the Eyes of a Child.* 3rd ed. New York: Macmillan, 1991.

Whitney, Phyllis A. *Writing Juvenile Stories and Novels.* 1976. Boston: The Writer, 1976.

Yolen, Jane. *Touch Magic.* New York: Philomel, 1981.

_____. *Writing Books for Children.* 3rd. ed. Boston: The Writer, 1983.

PART III

Science Fiction as a Vehicle for Ideas

Science fiction has always been a literature of ideas—sometimes at the expense of the story; but as the "New Wave" took hold in the 1960s, one of its emphases was on incorporating ideas and themes from the soft sciences—anthropology, psychology, sociology, and the like—into novels and short stories of high literary quality. The four essays in this section examine science fiction in terms of the philosophical attitudes that the fiction seems to support if not actually espouse, and the authors of those essays generally refer to non-science fiction materials for their perspectives.

Raymond E. Jones, in "'True Myth': Female Archetypes in Monica Hughes's *The Keeper of the Isis Light*," uses essentially feminist theories from Annis Pratt's *Archetypal Patterns in Women's Fiction*, Carol Christ's *Diving Deep and Surfacing*, and Carol Gilligan's *In a Different Voice: Psychological Theory and Women's Development* to analize and help explain what happens to Olwen in the course of that novel. In doing so, he concludes that *The Keeper of the Isis Light*, in addition to being about Olwen's development as a woman and as a person, is also a truly modern mythic novel that "the more one reads it, the more one sees in it."

Judith N. Mitchell, in "Neo-Gnostic Elements in Louise Lawrence's *Moonwind*," looks to Gnostic philosophy, the beliefs of what was considered a heretical sect by the early Christian church, to help explain Gareth's choice to reject things of Earth, including his own body, for things of the Spirit, rendered in this novel as an alien life form, in what appears to be a suicide to those left behind. The contrast of the bodiless alien, Bethkan, with the materially oriented California teenager, Karen, is less clear-cut than it appears, but Gareth's decision to leave his body behind and go with Bethkan, Mitchell suggests, "asserts a primacy of the spirit and indicates that the brave and the loving will find their way to its triumph."

Joseph O. Milner, in "Captain Kirk and Dr. Who: Meliorist and Spenglerian World Views in Fiction for Young Adults," pulls together social theories from Mortimer Adler, Jacob Bronowski, Abraham Maslow, and Reinhold Niebuhr—to name but a few—to contrast Kirk's well-ordered search for the good to the Doctor's repetitive encounters with deteriorating societies. *Star Trek* and *Dr. Who* not only illustrate the two poles—Meliorist and Spenglerian—which Milner sees underlying science fiction for young adults, but in fact "demonstrate the pursuasiveness of the dichotomy in the genre" itself.

Millicent Lenz, in "Raymond Briggs's *When the Wind Blows*: Toward an Ecology of the Mind for Young Readers," combines the ecological attitudes of Gregory Bateson and the literary critical position of William Sheick to discuss a picture book that might well be used to help teach young people to think more clearly about the general nature of the world around them as well as the specific rhetoric to which we are all subjected by official government agencies. What happens to the Bloggses, and by extension all of us, as nuclear war approaches and erupts, Lenz suggests, is a result of a "bad belief system." What needs to happen, and what books like *When the Wind Blows* can promote, Lenz continues, is an "ability to start thinking critically about thinking itself."

It may not be that the authors discussed in this section had these specific concepts in mind when they wrote their fiction, but an understanding of these philosophical precepts certainly allows the reader to understand the fiction on a deeper level or from a broader perspective. The "ideas" in science fiction literature do not exist in a vacuum (in or of outer space); the themes, ideas, and attitudes in science fiction are very much a part of the larger culture. Science fiction for younger readers not only presents those readers with fictional characters in situations analagous to their own, but also places those characters within a cultural worldview of which the reader may well need to become aware.

13

"True Myth": Female Archetypes in Monica Hughes's *The Keeper of the Isis Light*

Raymond E. Jones

It is easy to consider Monica Hughes as but one more voice in the chorus of practitioners who have declared that "speculative fiction is the mythology of today." ("A Different Kind of Magic" 66).[1] Hughes, after all, writes for children, and many people who might tolerate, if not accept, the claims of adult writers, will find the term *mythology* too pretentious for children's science fiction. Hughes, however, unlike so many in the chorus trying to establish the respectability of science fiction, has created at least one work that actually displays the elements of what Ursula K. Le Guin, in "Myth and Archetype in Science Fiction," calls "true myth" (78):

Such myths, symbols, images do not disappear under the scrutiny of the intellect, nor does an ethical, or aesthetic, or even religious examination of them make them shrink and vanish. On the contrary: the more you look, the more there they are. And the more you think, the more they mean.

On this level, science fiction deserves the title of a modern mythology. (81)

The Keeper of the Isis Light (1980) is on this level. When she was writing it, Hughes thought of the novel as a study of the difference between being alone and being lonely ("The Writer's Quest" 16). Many readers, however, see the novel primarily as a study of prejudice, something its author considers an accident of her plot (Jones 10-11). Both of these powerful themes, though, can be seen as elements of another important one. Carol P. Christ cites Annis Pratt's assertion that "if there is a 'myth of the hero' there must also be a 'myth of the heroine'" (Christ 9). This is precisely what *Keeper* is. Symbolically, it traces the development of its central character through the central archetypal phases of female identity: maiden, mother, and crone. A novel intellectually and aesthetically far above most science fiction and worthy to be set alongside the best modern books written for children, its elements, like those of the true myths Le Guin describes, reward the deepest examination.

The story of Olwen Pendennis, an Earth girl surgically and genetically altered to permit her to survive the ultraviolet radiation of the planet Isis, *Keeper* is a complex myth about the development of female identity. Olwen develops from egocentric childhood, through an adolescence in which she considers sacrificing her essential identity and freedom, to a maturity in which she finds fulfillment and autonomy by rejecting the destructive demands of patriarchal society. To present this theme, the novel combines images and patterns that Pratt, in *Archetypal Patterns in Women's Fiction*, has shown to be common to many novels by women. *The Keeper of the Isis Light* interweaves archetypes from two forms Pratt has described, the novel of development and the rebirth journey, the latter being a pattern most commonly featuring older women (136). Connecting these inter-woven patterns are Olwen's changing relationships. To put the matter baldly, she grows to an understanding of herself only by discovering the limita-tions of others and of the relationships she has with them. Thus, she grows beyond dependent childhood only by recognizing the limitations of her seemingly perfect foster father, Guardian the robot, and the idyllic nuclear family he heads. And she grows to spiritual maturity only by rejecting her putative lover, Mark London, and the technological social life he represents. Ultimately, by recognizing the limita-tions of these males, Olwen grows spiritually and establishes a larger sense of family, one in which she can comfort and nurture others and yet retain her independent identity. Her development is tinged with pathos, but it is a victory of independent female identity.

As a novel of development, *Keeper* begins on the day that marks Olwen's transition from one stage to another, her birthday. Although only ten on Isis, she is sixteen in Earth terms. The dual accounting of her age symbolizes her position: She wants to remain a child of Isis, but the arrival of settlers from Earth, which she learns about on this day, will force her into mature responsibilities.

Initially, Olwen is a dependent child. Living alone with Guardian, she is completely self-absorbed, as is evident in the birthday wish she makes before hearing that the settlers are coming: "I wish that everything will go on being perfect, just the way it is now" (8-9). The chief perfection in Olwen's life is Guardian, the robot who raised her alone after her parents' deaths. Guardian clearly states his role: "I am your father and mother" (6). Olwen certainly sees him as such because, hypnotized to forget her biological parents, she does not know that he is a robot. All she knows is that he fulfills her every physical and emotional need so successfully that she has no desire for people beyond her nuclear family: "I don't want anyone else but you, Guardian dear. You're perfect" (10).

The second perfection in Olwen's life is nature. Occupied only by Olwen and Guardian, Isis is an Edenic garden of childhood, a place where she is completely happy. Guardian warns her that resistance to change is not just childish but suicidal: "Stasis is death" (9). Olwen nevertheless resents social change, and, for her, the natural world of Isis gradually takes on the features of what Pratt calls the green-world archetype. Pratt summarizes Simone de Beauvoir's description of this, the adolescent girl's "kingdom" of nature: "About to be conquered by 'human' society, she turns to something 'inhuman' about to be dwarfed at the moment of the first development of her energies, she feels that the natural universe as a whole is 'her kingdom'" (Pratt 17). This is precisely what Olwen feels shortly after the settlers land. Standing on a mesa watching them unload their equipment in the valley below, she rejects human society and the changes it demands in favor of the permanence of her natural kingdom: "I hate it, Olwen thought passionately. I wish they had never come. She turned her back on the southern end of the mesa top and looked out across the rest of her kingdom. It was all right. It was as perfect as it had always been" (20).

Olwen, however, cannot simply turn her back on change. Forced to make contact with the settlers, she herself changes from the contented child to the longing adolescent. This stage of Olwen's development establishes the central question of identity. As Hughes made clear to me in an interview, she tends to believe that "the feminine qualities are the nurturing qualities as opposed to making, wisdom as opposed to intelligence, caring and intuiting as opposed perhaps to finding out and thinking" (Jones 11). Throughout her works, she has identified the technocrat with a self-centered masculine view she believes developed during the Renaissance. In *Keeper* she uses an adolescent love story as the central element of the novel of development in order to explore the opposition between these masculine and feminine values.

This opposition is evident in the geography of Isis, which symbolically opposes the upper world, the green world of female freedom, and the valley, which becomes the confining world of masculine technological organization. The settlers, including Mark London, the boy with whom Olwen falls in love, can survive only in the valleys of Isis because the oxygen is thin on the uplands and the radiation is harsh. Olwen, biologically altered so that she would not be, as Guardian said, "'imprisoned in this valley'" (80), can go everywhere in safety. Nevertheless, she prefers the high ground because "Up there was freedom and peace" (63). For her, as she declares to Mark, "This valley isn't Isis at all. Isis is the mountains" (37). She equates herself so fully with the mountain world that she is mortified when the settlers reject her first eager invitation to see the mountains: "It had never crossed her mind that they might totally reject her beautiful world of upper Isis, and with it, her" (34).

This opposition evokes something like what Pratt calls the rape-trauma archetype: "the villain/rapist assault symbolizes the fulcrum of a world of enclosure and atrophy opposite the freedom of the green world" (16). The assault is evident even to Mark London when he first climbs up to the mountain to see "the true Isis" (48) and notices what the settlers' equipment has done to the valley: "It looked as if Isis itself had been wounded and had bled" (49). This parallels Olwen's earlier vision of the land being defaced with "muddy scars" (19), and it suggests, because she identifies herself so completely with the planet, the damage that will occur to Olwen herself.

Supplementing this symbolic geographical opposition is the opposition between masculine and feminine perceptions, an opposition developed through the symbol of the mask and the motif of seeing. In order to permit the altered Olwen, whose features are reptilian, to go freely among the settlers, Guardian makes her wear a suit and mask that conceal her transformation. Olwen, who has never seen herself in a mirror, does not realize that Guardian is trying to protect her from contamination by the settlers' prejudices, not their viruses. As Hughes told me, "Mark falls in love with the mask, not with the real Olwen, a common enough fault in teenage romances, too" (Jones 7). In developing what she calls "the whole Jungian thing of masks" (Jones 7), however, Hughes stresses that Mark's action is in keeping with his masculine, logical sense of perception. Mark literally needs to see with his eyes in order to know or believe.

Mark's reliance on seeing is stressed even before he sets foot on Isis. As the families are awakened from hypnosleep before landing, Mark feels that "it was good to see his family safe, with his own eyes" (25). The shallow logic implied by seeing is especially evident when Mark analyzes his feelings about Olwen: "Love? That was crazy, completely absolutely off. I've never even really *seen* her he told himself angrily. Just talked to her . . . shared some thoughts . . . felt . . . felt what?" (54). When Mark climbs the mountain and catches sight of Olwen without her suit and mask, he sees her from behind and calls her a "beauty": "He knew that she was the most lovely, the most graceful, the most desirable woman he would ever see in his whole life" (58). For a second before she turns, he actually sees her truly as part of the green world, part of the nature of Isis: "She was like Isis as she stood there. She was alien, like the wonderful tangy drink, like the scented golden flower, like the rolling mountains" (58). When she turns around, of course, his shallow mind cannot accept her as she truly is, and, overcome with "irrational horror" (59), he falls.

His physical fall from the place of Olwen's peace and freedom symbolizes his moral fall from innocent teenage lover to bitter man. Afterward, trying to convince himself that he was not at fault, he falls back on an archetype of male development, the need for independence, seeing Olwen as one who had cheated him and "had trapped *him* into loving her" (126).[2] He clearly reveals his value system: "He had shared his inmost thoughts about life and poetry and God and music. And, to be just, she had shared hers with him . . . but not the main fact. Not the fact of her inhuman appearance" (125). This "main fact" of her appearance dominates the masculine view of Olwen. Like Mark, Captain Jonas Tryon, for example, can see her beauty only by considering her as an alien. When he considers her as a human, he, too, finds her disgusting (96).

Thematically, the rejection of Olwen because of her appearance can be an example of racial prejudice, but symbolically, in the myth of female development, it represents the rejection of the Female Other, who will not or cannot conform to conventional patterns of behavior and of beauty. Speaking to Guardian about improving the lighting of the path that Mark must take to reach her upper-world home, Olwen makes a symbolically important observation: "I think my eyes are better than his—I mean, than theirs" (44). Olwen, however, does not realize the full import of the settlers' limited vision. In fact, she is just as eager to remove her mask as Mark is to see her: "I want Mark to see *me,* to know *me,* not a plastic imitation" (61). Guardian has withheld mirrors, telling her, "A mirror can only show you what *you* see as yourself. It cannot tell you what another person sees" (39). He later says, "Form and function should be as one. You function perfectly. You are beautiful" (82-83). Thus, instead of considering herself inferior to Earthlings, Olwen, because she alone can properly inhabit the planet, can begin to understand her truth worth: "I'm better" (82). Furthermore, when Olwen finally sees herself in the mirror, she stares at "the Other" (84) that it reflects and then gratefully thanks Guardian for her body: "It's beautiful. . . . You gave me Isis— the mountains as well as the valleys. I love you for it, Guardian" (85). Seeing herself through female eyes, that is, she accepts herself and rejects the superficial notions of beauty governing Mark's perception.

The love story in *Keeper* is thus an ironic variant of the "Beauty and the Beast" tale. Mark falls in love with the superficial Beauty. When he sees her actual features, he fails the traditional test of recognizing inner worth, instead rejecting her as a "disgusting creature" (110). For her part, Olwen doesn't completely judge with her eyes. Asked how she can love what she doesn't know, she says, "You take it on faith" (69). She even toys with the idea of having an operation to transform her into a being like Mark, something Guardian says would be a sacrifice of her freedom (112). As Carol Gilligan has shown in *In a Different Voice: Psychological Theory and Women's Development*, during one stage of their development, women have traditionally viewed such self-sacrifice as a natural part of a woman's morality (70-71, 74). Although Olwen doesn't at first agree with Guardian, she gradually does come to accept herself as she is. When Mark belatedly tries to pass the traditional test of worthiness by expressing love for the person inside the body of the Beast, Olwen recognizes that he speaks from guilt. She rejects him and the confining masculine world he represents, asserting her need for the green world: "We have nothing in common, not even the same appearance of humanity. Isis is mine, from the valleys to the mountain peaks, summer and winter and cosmic storm. You can't share that with me and I will not spend my life as a prisoner. I must be free" (135). She thus insists on the value of her own identity, rejecting sacrifice for a higher sense of duty to herself.

As a novel of development, then, *Keeper* shows Olwen rejecting the "world of enclosure and atrophy" that Pratt shows as consistently representing male-dominated social institutions in women's fiction. When it becomes a novel of rebirth, *Keeper* presents Olwen more positively as someone who is not simply rejecting society but is actively contributing to it without being compromised. In this strand of the novel, Olwen grows to spiritual independence by recognizing both the limits of the father figure who has shaped all of her previous decisions and the need to allow her feminine qualities, not masculine logic, to be her guide.

Outwardly, Olwen's relationship with Guardian does not change as dramatically as her relationship with Mark, but the change is significant and ends her role as a dependent child. Initially, Olwen believes in Guardian's infallibility, thinking that "everything Guardian attempted turned out absolutely perfect" (7) and that "he was always so right" (60). (In spite of his claims about being father and mother, the use of masculine gender pronouns clearly establishes Guardian as the symbolic father.) Olwen's beliefs are true only in an ironic way when applied to Olwen herself. In genetically altering her to make her function perfectly, Guardian has made it impossible for her to be a part of normal society, forcing her to remain within the nuclear family he heads. Until the coming of the settlers, Olwen is content. Afterward, as pain and rejection come to make her more aware of her own identity, she realizes how different Guardian is from her. The process begins simply, when, in reply to Olwen's protest against change, Guardian points out how insignificant their individual existences are to the planet. At the point Olwen realizes that "he seemed to have a viewpoint parsecs away from hers" (10). The most dramatic change comes after Mark falls. Guardian realizes his error in not telling Olwen the truth about herself and her appearance. Olwen, turning to him for comfort, finds only uncertainty (76), not the logical infallibility he had provided all her life. Thus, she too loses a kind of innocence when Mark falls.

The final shift in their relationship comes as a result of her symbolic rebirth journey, an archetypal journey that Pratt describes as a "quest into the unconscious" (135), the goal of which "is to integrate her self with herself" (136). This journey allows Olwen to take command of her own actions and, having recognized Guardian's limitations, to assume forceful direction of his. It includes all of the five phases Pratt outlines. Pratt titles the first phase the "splitting off" and notes that it "takes the form of an acute consciousness of the world of the ego and of a consequent turning away from societal norms" (139). For Olwen, this occurs when the settlers, frightened by the appearance of her pet hairy dragon, Hobbit, kill it and then point a gun at her. She storms into the village, declaring her hatred for the settlers and their norms: "You're spoiling Isis. . . . Go back to Earth where you belong. Isis is mine. Mine" (74). Acutely conscious of her identity because of the attack (which enables her to realize how alien she is to the settlers), because of the restoration of her memory of her biological parents, and because of the gratifying sight of her own body in a mirror for the first time, she receives the final blow when Guardian informs her that the settlers will not pay attention to him because "I am nothing to them" (88).

Because the settlers have rejected all of that is meaningful in her life, they have rejected her, emptied her life of meaning. In *Diving Deep and Surfacing*, Carol Christ notes the results of such situations, which she calls "the experience of nothingness": "Experiencing nothingness, women reject conventional solutions and question the meaning of their lives, thus opening themselves to the revelation of deeper sources of power and value" (13). This is what Olwen does. Choosing a relationship with Guardian rather than accepting the settlers' masculine, hierarchical vision, she rejects the settlers, vowing never again to go into the valley. Furthermore, she sets out on a physical journey that eventually leads to a revelation of her powers and a discovery of her own values.

This journey permits the second phase of the rebirth pattern, that of the green-world token, in which, Pratt says, "the hero is helped to cross the threshold of her adventure by some ordinary phenomenon that suddenly takes on extraordinary portent" (139). Olwen finds such a token because, living so close to the settlers and thus feeling "like a prisoner" (*Keeper* 89), an archetypal feeling of female entrapment, she sets out for "unknown territory" (89), the previously unvisited areas of the green world that symbolize the unknown depths of her character. She undertakes this journey in the appropriately symbolic season of late spring, and, once in nature, she begins "to find her way back to the quiet core of herself, the part that she had lost when Pegasus Two had landed" (90). For her, the ordinary phenomenon, the token, is a storm. Feeling uneasy, she goes to the uplands and takes shelter in an archetypal setting, a cave. This symbolizes her rebirth, and she begins to regain what she had lost.[3] For example, she regains a pet when she is joined by another hairy dragon, whom she names Little Hobbit. As Pratt notes, phase 3 of the female journey involves meeting the green-world lover. "Sometimes," she says, "the green-world lover is actually an animal" (140). For the reborn Olwen, the new pet gives her someone to love again, and its presence causes her to end her anger toward the settlers. In fact, she actually prays for their safety, indicating that she is no longer as alienated as she was when she set out.

Rebirth is not, of course, merely a restoration of what once was. In traditional male-focused literature, it represents the development of mature heroic identity. In *Keeper*, Olwen discovers both feminine power and her own heroic identity. This occurs because Olwen, unlike Guardian, whom she continues to insist is "much wiser" (96) than she is, did not, in spite of his scientific instruments, predict the damaging storm. Olwen, however, senses with her body the coming of another even fiercer storm. As Guardian notes, this indicates that Olwen is "becoming more and more one with the planet" (113). Indeed, it is at this point that her name becomes significant. In an unpublished portion of our interview, Hughes said that she chose the name because its Welsh and Cornish roots suggest "somebody who was a little in touch with the old parts of Britain" and that "it predates the Roman masculine takeover." The name Olwen Pendennis thus suggests for Hughes a spiritual and female relationship to life.[4] Olwen demonstrates her spiritual heroism by ignoring her own vow never to return to the valley. She goes out into the storm to find Jody, a little boy who is lost. In doing so, she inverts her relationship with Guardian, assuming authority over him because he is too limited in this situation. Against Guardian's masculine objections that her behavior is illogical, she offers a female moral imperative based on the ethics of responsibility and her firm sense of identity: "I have to go. I'm the only one who can" (116).[5]

Olwen's rescue attempt further defines her identity. Discovering that the planet contains sinkholes, she realizes that she could not do her lighthouse keeper's duty of warning the settlers because she had not known about them. Even more startling to her is the fact that Guardian, on whom she had depended for all her knowledge, had not known about them either, a recognition that leads her to modify further her understanding of him: "Guardian knew everything, or so it had always seemed" (119). Unable to depend upon the knowledge Guardian has given her, Olwen must rely on her own understanding. When she pulls Jody from a hole, she does not know if he is alive and wishes Guardian were there to help. Olwen, however, does not rely on appearances, on what she sees; she has her own sources of understanding to help her cope: "He *felt* alive" (120). Relying on her own experience, her memory of how she had revived Little Hobbit, she restores the boy with water and then croons while rocking him. The scene is thus a potent symbol of her achievement of the second of the major female roles, that of mother and nurturer, a role she achieves by listening to her own feelings, not the directives of Guardian. Furthermore, in "delivering" her "child," the only one who has not rejected her because of her appearance, she not only demonstrates her own compassion but also keeps alive within the settlement the potential for overcoming learned prejudice. Her actions thus establish her own worth and provide the opportunity for achieving a secondary aim of the rebirth journey, "the renewal of society" (Pratt 137).

This episode leads her into the fourth of the five phases that Pratt has identified, a confrontation with parental figures. Faced with a shocking new perception when Captain Tryon explodes, "He's only a damned robot, after all" (131), Olwen feels, for the first time in her life, "abandoned, alone" (131). She thus confronts Guardian with the fundamental question of his identity: "Am I seeing you as you are, or as you want me to see you? Which is real?" The question again brings forward the symbolism of seeing, the faculty upon which the males placed such value. For Olwen, who is functionally beautiful herself, the robot is his function, Guardian. For the settlers, however, Guardian is, as he says, only his appearance: "Captain Tryon can only see DaCoP Forty-three" (132). Guardian is, of course, both, and the ability to see both is a test of the heart. Just as they failed a similar test with Olwen, Mark and the settlers cannot pass this one; only Olwen, who extends her knowledge beyond the superficial logic symbolized by seeing, passes this test.

Because of this confrontation, Olwen now assumes a superior role to Guardian's, directing her own life by deciding that they will move away. A sign of the new relationship is that she is now the one who provides comfort, telling him when he blames himself for her problems, "You did what you had to for my own good. You gave me a great gift, the freedom of a planet" (135).

Olwen's final phase of development is symbolically equivalent to Pratt's fifth phase, the "journey toward the unconscious proper, the realm from which the green-world lover and the guide or token have summoned her" (141). Olwen decides to return to the green-world upland valley where she saved Little Hobbit. Although physically linear, this journey is symbolically circular as are the plots of many women writers (Pratt 11; Spivack 9). Olwen's journey here represents a circling back to the time of her childhood. She regains the green world, her pet, and her existence in a nuclear family with Guardian. Olwen is not, of course, returning to childhood egocentrism. She is now aware that her unique female qualities make her superior to Guardian, who must depend upon technocratic, masculine logic: "I 'feel' a cosmic storm brewing before even your instruments do" (136). Olwen is thus in touch with both her inner being and the natural world, something Pratt suggests is the primary goal of the rebirth journey (137). She does not, however, cut herself completely off from society. Her decision to use her ability to warn the settlers of coming storms gives her success in her goal, "To be part of them, just a little" (136). Thus, her moral commitment to them maintains the web of relationships, which Carol Gilligan sees as central to female morality and development (62-63), instead of the male hierarchy, which had caused the settlers to dismiss Guardian. Olwen goes off to assume the last of the major female roles, that of the crone, the Wise Old Lady, who, although physically remote, provides them with the knowledge they need to survive.[6]

Olwen's story is thus truly mythic, the story of female spiritual growth. Olwen begins as dependent child, who views the father figure as perfect. With the coming of Mark London and the settlers, she becomes the maiden who is so eager to avoid loneliness that she is willing to sacrifice herself through surgical transformation to preserve her relationship. After Mark rejects her, she undertakes the rebirth journey, during which she discovers her own powers. She then becomes the mother and nurturer with the rescue of Jody from the sinkhole. Finally, she becomes the crone, the woman who wisely knows the value of her own experience and can offer it to others. She has discovered the depths of her own humanity, as is evident when Guardian declares that he can never be lonely and she whispers, "Poor Guardian" (136). Her painful journey is a triumphant one, for it symbolizes her coming into full power as a female through her development of her relationship to nature, her understanding of her inner being, and her acceptance of her physical identity. Olwen's meaningful and moving story meets the criteria Le Guin set out for true myth: The more one looks at it, the more one sees in it. Its very richness suggests that, at least as far as *The Keeper of the Isis Light* is concerned, Hughes is absolutely correct in declaring that "speculative fiction is the mythology of today."

NOTES

1. Notable voices promoting this idea include members of the Science Fiction Writers of America and Science Fiction Research Associates, two groups who jointly sponsored an introductory anthology titled *Science Fiction: Contemporary Mythology* (New York: Harper Row, 1978).

2. See Chapter 2, "Images of Relationship," in Carol Gilligan's *In a Different Voice*, which discusses male images of heirarchy and the fear of entrapment, most notably the male perception of "a danger of entrapment or betrayal, being caught in a smothering relationship or humiliated by rejection and deceit" (42) and female images of the web of relationships and consequent fears of isolation.

3. A couple of animal images, which strengthen her connection to nature, foreshadow this ultimate rebirth. When she is given back memory of her biological parents, her mind

stirs "like a fledgling bursting out of its shell" (79). Just before she sees herself for the first time in a mirror, "she had the painful feeling that she was growing inside so fast that she was going to split and shed her skin, the way a snake does" (84). The experience of rebirth here resembles what, in *Diving Deep and Surfacing,* Carol Christ calls "awakening. . . . a coming to self, . . . a grounding of self-hood in the powers of being" (19).

4. Similarly, Mark London's name, redolent as it is of the Roman takeover, suggests his symbolic role as representative of the technological, patriarchal society.

5. Note that Meg Murry, Madeleine L'Engle's female hero in *A Wrinkle in Time,* makes a similar statement when she is about to rescue a male, her little brother: "I see, I see, I understand, it has to be me. There isn't anyone else" (177). Gilligan talks about the ethics of responsibility throughout Chapter 3, "Concepts of Self and Morality," of *In a Different Voice,* but note especially her summary of the developmental stages of ethical stances (74).

6. In the second volume of the Isis trilogy, *The Guardian of Isis* (1981), which is set a number of years later, the embittered and elderly Mark London fosters a religion in which the long-absent Olwen becomes, ironically, "That Old Woman" and "The Ugly One," the "nameless" one who "brings darkness and death to all people in the end" (85).

BIBLIOGRAPHY

Christ, Carol P. *Diving Deep and Surfacing: Women Writers on Spiritual Quest.* 2nd ed. Boston: Beacon, 1986.

Gilligan, Carol. *In a Different Voice: Psychological Theory and Women's Development.* Cambridge: Harvard UP, 1982.

Hughes, Monica. "A Different Kind of Magic." *Quarry* 34 (Winter 1985): 65-68.

_____. *The Guardian of Isis.* London: Hamish Hamilton, 1981.

_____. *The Keeper of the Isis Light.* London: Hamish Hamilton, 1980.

_____. "The Writer's Quest." *Canadian Children's Literature* 26 (1982): 6-25.

Jones, Raymond E. "The Technological Pastoralist: A Conversation with Monica Hughes." *Canadian Children's Literature* 44 (1986): 6-18.

Le Guin, Ursula K. "Myth and Archetype in Science Fiction." *The Language of the Night.* Ed. Susan Wood. New York: Putnam's, 1979. 73-81.

L'Engle, Madeleine. *A Wrinkle in Time.* 1962. New York: Laurel-Leaf, 1976.

Pratt, Annis. *Archetypal Patterns in Women's Fiction.* Bloomington: Indiana UP, 1981.

Spivack, Charlotte. *Merlin's Daughters: Contemporary Women Writers of Fantasy.* Westport, CT: Greenwood, 1987.

Warrick, Patricia, Martin Harry Greenberg, and Joseph Olander, eds. *Science Fiction: Contemporary Mythology.* The SFWA-SFRA Anthology. New York: Harper, 1978.

14

Neo-Gnostic Elements in Louise Lawrence's *Moonwind*

Judith N. Mitchell

It still astonishes me when I run full-tilt into ancient themes or issues reappearing in what I think of as contemporary literature. Most recently, I experienced a crisis of recognition stemming from a reading of Louise Lawrence's science fiction for young adults, which presents to the late twentieth-century adolescent the key tenets of Gnosticism, in particular a disdain for flesh and an exaltation of spirit. The Gnostics had pre-Christian roots but really came into prominence as a heretical sect, which was stamped out by the early Church precisely because it held beliefs that threatened everyday assumptions about the value of Earth-based human existence. Gnostic themes run through all of Lawrence's works, but they show up most starkly in *Moonwind,* and it is by moving through the text of *Moonwind* that we are able to trace them to their chilling conclusion.

Moonwind presents the reader with two teenaged characters, Karen, the naive Californian, and Gareth, underprivileged and Welsh, whose prize-winning essays have earned them a trip to a space station on the Moon. Already on the moon and just waking from an eons-long sleep is Bethkahn, sole survivor of a starship crew and, for all intents, a third adolescent. Bethkahn is lonely and curious about the humans who have evolved from the breeding of her crew mates with an indigenous species on a nearby planet (Earth) long ago. As a prelude to what will shortly follow, Lawrence has Bethkahn recall what it was like when her astral body took possession of a deer and a hawk, prey and predator, initial twin images for fleshly existence. Sickened, she was counseled by a senior crew member:

Flesh was never easy, Mahna had said. It was cruel always, a mixture of violence and beauty, bittersweet feelings that were difficult to bear. Their kind seldom stayed enfleshed for long. They experienced it briefly and were glad to be free. (15)

Now abandoned and alone, Bethkahn is instructed about the nature of the human interlopers by her ship, which has amassed a great deal of information and opinion. "'Flesh can corrupt,' the ship voice said. 'It can subordinate the spirit within it. They are not beautiful, Bethkahn, nor is their world'" (23). Bethkahn is appalled by what the ship tells her; her own society, where there is no flesh, only spirit, represents a higher rung on the evolutionary ladder, a state of being in which the nasty, corruptive influences of flesh are unknown. Yet both Bethkahn and her mentor/ship recognize that contact will have to be made with humans if the ship's broken stabilizer is to be mended. This sets the stage for confrontation.

We meet Gareth and Karen in Chapter 4; significantly, he, like Bethkahn, is dreaming. Left behind, his body has no influence on the voyages of his mind in sleep, and he regards Karen's waking him up, bringing him back, with undisguised hostility. Both talented writers, Gareth and Karen identified the parameters of the emotional affect of the Moon before they actually reached it. Gareth's essay examined "The Lunacy Syndrome," an intriguing phenomenon that deepens the religious feelings of those who have spent time on the Moon, while Karen's essay predicted the role of Bethkahn by postulating the existence of an incorporeal female presence who is driven to unwitting cruelty. Yet, despite the commonality of their talents and sensitivities, the two do not get along, and their differences are exacerbated when Gareth gets a hurried glimpse of Bethkahn, who then becomes Karen's foil. Where Karen is voluble, Bethkahn is silent; where Karen is gauche, Bethkahn is elusive. All in all, Gareth finds the disembodied idea of a girl infinitely preferable to a girl in the flesh. Hiding from the human girl and recoiling from the world that has produced her, Gareth has a moment of transcendent awareness as he waits for the sun to rise.

It was . . . as if the fragment of being he had become detached itself from his body . . . and Gareth did not belong to earth. (34)

But this moment of at-oneness with the universe is shattered when Karen joins him, and Lawrence makes the intrusion all the more jarring by employing a succession of images whose cumulative effect is to tie Karen to the existence Gareth is coming to despise. Her smile is "a white gash," and her breath "makes mist." Her voice echoes "hollowly," and her casual touches enrage Gareth, even as the constant click of her camera destroys his peace.

Gareth's revulsion spreads to encompass the whole moonbase, depicted as a set out of nightmare. "Low sunlight . . . turned Drew's red hair to a peculiar shade of puce. Faces looked gray and ill. . . . J.B.'s face was hatched with lines, a Tenniel illustration come to life, smile creased and heavy-jowled" (41). Inevitably, the ramifications of Gareth's own body increase his sense of despair and alienation. On a camping trip, "he sweated in the heat of his sleeping bag and could smell the stench of his socks" (87), while back in the main base, "his room . . . smelled of sleep and staleness" (103).

Turning to the *Zen Buddhist Handbook,* Gareth sees its exposition of transcendence as deliverance of a sort (and as a possible key to the riddle of

Bethkahn's existence). "'I was reading about it . . . ,' he tells Karen. 'Everybody has an astral body'" (124). But anchored to life, Gareth sees himself "trapped in a prison of flesh [where] he would serve out his sentence" (160). Urged to eat, he utters his need with naked candor: "'What I need is food for my soul,' Gareth muttered" (164). He sees himself, "a soul evolved from the stars," held captive by "a body evolved from the beasts of the earth . . . torn between spirit and flesh, between Earth's bleak reality and Bethkahn's universe, fear and faith" (166).

Bethkahn herself, left alone for thousands of years, finds Gareth intriguing. As these feelings deepen, she confides to the ship, "I happen to love him." Appalled at this development, the ship reviews the human track record—its wars, famines, and murders—and responds, "You cannot love flesh." But Bethkahn, seeing the flesh only as vehicle, believes she "can love the spirit within it," though the ship insists that Gareth is too different, "not spiritually evolved" (119-20). But Bethkahn's accidental killing of a convoy driver fills her with self-doubts, and her unsureness about the complementary functions of soul and body cause her to be very cautious in the face of Gareth's similar confusions: "It would have been easy to tempt him, but she had held her tongue. . . . She could have persuaded him that his flesh did not mean very much . . . but she would not take him from the planet of his birth" (146-47).

From Gareth's perspective, however, whatever doubts and fears he may have entertained about the self-sufficiency of his spirit retreat under the twin onslaughts of memory and anticipation. In memory he goes back to Wales, to its grinding poverty, its lack of opportunity, its stultifying materialism:

Come tomorrow he would be going home, back to . . . the gray hills of Wales, Mom and her lover, and the housing project in Aberdare where vandals ruled and dog muck fouled the pavements. . . . It was not life Gareth would be returning to, but a kind of dying. (153-54)

As Lawrence drives Gareth closer to suicide for his soul's survival's sake, all that humans do with their bodies seems to be dirty, corrupted, unredeemable. Flesh pollutes, and Gareth, by the end, would agree with what the ship had told Bethkahn in the beginning, "Flesh can corrupt. It can subordinate the spirit within" (23). On the way to his death "he felt like a ghost, sitting inside himself and looking out, uninvolved with what went on, not caring about their hopes and fears or the planet they came from" (171).

The effect of Gareth's death on Karen is catastrophic. She is at the window when his canvas-shrouded body is put on the shuttle for its long voyage to what had not truly been Gareth's home. He has made the final, definitive rejection of the world, the flesh, and perhaps of the Devil; and Karen is his bewildered, grief-stricken survivor. Enlightenment comes painfully. "Suddenly, clear and terrible, Karen saw the world through Gareth's eyes in everything he had talked of—the cruelty and injustice, the squalid streets of Aberdare, his mother living with a man he had not liked" (175).

But the repudiation is only half of the Gnostic equation; the other half is the exaltation of the purely spiritual, and in *Moonwind*'s resolution, the tandem relationship between neo-gnosticism and transcendence holds fast. At the very last, Karen's mourning is interrupted by a bravura gesture from Gareth's newly liberated spirit, who, as Bethkahn's ship lifts off, signals "Nos da, cariad" ("Goodnight, darling" in Welsh).

Karen stared at the sky, at the colored lights flashing off and on, off and on. *Nos da, cariad, Nos da.* The colors whispered deep in her mind, glorious with meaning. Gareth has fooled them, just as she had said. Wild with joy, Karen pushed past the security guard and hurled herself at the window. Two hands waved back at him and her voice was screaming.
"Nos da, Gareth! Nos da!" (179)

Gareth, like the early Gnostics, has traced out a path for himself involving a choice and priorities that few (we hope) will be inclined to follow. For Gareth, as for the Gnostics, the pearl without price is secret knowledge, involving the preeminence of that immortal component of human personality that the poets call the soul. But Lawrence, like the Gnostics again, is on the receiving end of controversy. Our lengthy examination of what happens in *Moonwind* crystallizes some hard questions. Is Lawrence, by presenting the suicide of a dissatisfied teenager as heroic, saying something to depressed and unhappy youngsters to whom all the world seems dross? And does the survival of Gareth's vital essence, or spirit, say to adolescents that death is not a final, binding choice? Depending on how one answers these questions, the triumph of spiritual values—which is what *Horn Book* reviewer Ann F. Flowers singled out as memorable—is either a vindication of enduring values in an era of blatant materialism or a seductive come-on that encourages adolescents to disparage the status quo and may, in fact, be seen by them as permission to check out metaphorically and, most frighteningly, literally.

To answer these questions, we need to take one more look at *Moonwind* and to assess *Moonwind*'s place among other Lawrence novels to see if Gnostic themes are consistently expounded and if there is a unifying similarity in their development. Since we have just finished talking about Karen's moment of truth in the conclusion of the novel, it seems clear that Karen at least has a kind of conversion experience. When we first meet her, she is almost a caricature of the American tourist, well-heeled, intrusive, and overwhelmingly complacent. Although the text does indicate that Karen has a sensitive side, it has not occurred to her to question the culture that produced her or the materialism that has produced the culture. She is good-heartedly oblivious to issues of social justice or to questions of spiritual significance. Faced with an enforced companionship with the deprived Gareth, her immediate response is to Americanize his name (Gary) and to give him one of her unused cameras; in other words, she wants Gareth to be like her, and this, she thinks, ignoring his critique of wealth, will eliminate his discontent. Later, when she and Gareth have reached a better accord and he blurts out his reluctance to go back, she employs the same logic to offer him a home with her in Santa Barbara, where, significantly, nobody wants for anything—or just *wants* anything that cannot be touched, bought, and collected. But in trying to come to terms with Gareth's death, Karen sees another side to the American dream: "She could remain untouched by it all. But Gareth had despised wealth as much as he had despised poverty. He had turned down the opportunities she had offered because he could not close his eyes to things. . . now she was ashamed. . . guilt mixed with grief" (176). Karen, then, learns by the end of the novel that affluence dulls perception, the perception to recognize the New Testament secret truth about the world: "It is the Spirit that gives life."

Bethkahn's change is not nearly as dramatic. She is attracted to Gareth before she ever really knows him, and although it is possible that Lawrence seeks to present a balanced message about flesh by dwelling on this attraction, it is more than outweighed by Gareth's willingness to be bodyless. In fact, Bethkahn, like Karen, is sometimes treated satirically. She is bound to remind the adult reader of the adolescent who copes with depression by sleeping, even though her body *is* astral. Her real function, besides providing a colossal getaway for Gareth, seems to be to register horror at what she learns of human nature and history. Her fellow crew members, she considers, have unutterably debased themselves by uniting with inferior beings, and it is only Bethkahn who has the perspective and background to conclude: "If the spirit was not strong enough, flesh could become dominant. . . . Trapped within flesh a soul could lose sight of its origin and purpose, even lose sight of itself" (16). Still, she has the courage to let herself trust and love Gareth.

Gareth would seem to move on a direct course toward negation of flesh and affirmation of spirit. But a careful reading reveals that Lawrence creates shades of ambivalence within even Gareth. At first he feels violated by Karen's use of touches to extend language; as his sense of isolation deepens, however, he regrets having rebuffed her proffered warmth, and just before he removes his helmet, killing himself, he thinks of Karen's trademark peppermint gum. That and his "Nos da, cariad" indicate that Gareth's move toward the purely spiritual is accompanied by a heightened appreciation of what is valuable in human affection. The paradox is that this is the more pronounced as he casts off the last vestiges of living by the flesh; the equation therefore becomes: spirit = insight = love, and this works out for each of the adolescents in *Moonwind*.

It also holds true for most of Lawrence's science fiction. *Star Lord* brings a highly developed space traveler into the lives of a poor Welsh family. Here too are the details that inspire repugnance for the flesh-connected details of human life (an outdoor toilet that stank) and a profound cynicism about human morality (Erlich is hounded by government officials and the army). But the final resolution revolves around the issue of love; it is love that impels Rhys to offer to meet the Mawrrhyn's price, so that Erlich may go home. *Calling B For Butterfly* follows suit. Four teenagers and two little children are the only survivors of a ghastly accident in space. As their desperation increases, so do the noisome details of their enforced companionship, complete with a reeking baby and chocolate-smeared hair. Yet, the shyest of the teenagers is roused from her lethargy by the baby's need, and in loving the child, she is herself redeemed. *Children of the Dust* presents us once again with the familiar paradox; on the one hand, in a post-nuclear-holocaust world, there is the inadequate commode and the festering flesh, but there is also the mutation of corrupted human nature into something much finer and infinitely more loving.

Given this clearly marked pattern, it should be obvious that *Moonwind* is not alone in drawing on themes with a marked resemblance to Gnostic tenets. But Lawrence does not revile flesh, or have her characters revile it, without offering something in its stead. In almost all of her science fiction novels, she frees characters from the limitations of human nature in order to indicate what we may become: Erlich, the Golden Boy, the advanced mutants, and Bethkahn are all superior creatures who have evolved beyond the physical and spiritual corruption of the flesh. And, in each of these works, there is a moment of choice when a character steps out of his or her framework into a more receptive state, impelled by the demands of love. The character who takes this step disassociates him/herself from what he or she has known up to this point, the bleared-seared quality of human existence. (This existence is not so much distorted by villains as it is marred by cumulative insensitivity. Destructive actions and policies seem to be the result of an inability on the part of most people to apprehend or respond to spiritual values. We are, according to Lawrence, not as bad as we are blind.)

What do youngsters make of these demanding, complex novels? Do the Gnostics after almost two thousand years, still exert an appeal? Do they still beckon the elite to a secret knowledge? Do young readers perceive that the negation of the status quo is always followed by mystical transcendence?

What ought to appeal to the young is that the mystical transcendence in these novels always beckons to a youthful, as opposed to an adult, character. Adults are not wicked in these novels, but they are too inured to deny promptings of flesh. This makes them powerless to help the teenaged protagonists. In *Star Lord,* the villagers promise help but cannot deliver it; in *Calling B For Butterfly,* the crew on Ganymede is unable to help the youngsters in the lifeslip unit; and the parents in *Children of the Dust* can not prevent the radioactive fallout from changing their children. Even adult characters whose portrayal is essentially positive, like Drew and J.B. in *Moonwind,* cannot alleviate Karen's fears or Gareth's despair. In a Lawrence novel, salvation, deliverance, and enlightenment are for the few and, invariably and not coincidentally, the young.

I wonder how much of Lawrence's negative treatment of the details of human needs reaches young readers and whether it is offset by her implicit promise that somewhere it can all be better? No one can definitely answer these questions. Day-to-day changes in society produce changing reader needs, but what would seem to be enduring about Lawrence's work is that she avoids the twin traps waiting for those who write for young adults. She does not minimize their pain, and she offers no easy analgesic resolutions to it. Instead, she asserts the primacy of spirit and indicates that the brave and the loving will find their way to its triumph—through a path the Gnostics trod long ago.

BIBLIOGRAPHY

Flowers, Ann F. Rev. of *Moonwind,* by Louise Lawrence. *The Horn Book Magazine* 63.1
    (Jan./Feb. 1987): 60.
Lawrence, Louise. *Calling B for Butterfly.* New York: Harper, 1982.
_____. *Children of the Dust.* New York: Harper, 1985.
_____. *Moonwind.* New York: Harper, 1986.
_____. *Star Lord.* New York: Harper, 1978.

15

Captain Kirk and Dr. Who: Meliorist and Spenglerian World Views in Fiction for Young Adults

Joseph O. Milner

"To boldly to go where no man has gone before...," the bold oath of the television series *Star Trek,* suggests a courage and a hope that new worlds will be better worlds. A comparable show, *Dr. Who,* is by title less bold and implies a question that never gets resolved. Doubt about any final goodness prevails in *Dr. Who,* whereas *Star Trek* makes a point of trying to find the ultimate goodness the characters think must exist in their well-ordered universe.

These two television series that adolescents (and adults) have doted on represent two contending views of creation that are constantly emerging in the events and characters of the two series. In the starship *Enterprise,* we have a searching voyage led by a noble, self-assured commander who is verging on an ideal of perfection. His crew, too, shares this ideal; the crew's very composition suggests a world order of rational cooperation by people representing the total spectrum of human life. The exemplary Mr. Spock himself profiles a mainstay of world order and brotherhood in his entirely rational life. The body of the crew, who live in a well-ordered society representing all races, genders, and nationalities, are an ideal microcosm, a picture of a perfectly ordered universe that *Star Trek* suggests could exist. This is the meliorist worldview.

Conversely, Dr. Who is not a model for future civilizations, but is instead an observer who accepts the typically mixed cultures he encounters. The technically advanced creatures he meets are almost always carrying some very heavy baggage from ancient primordial times, and the radically advanced cultures he observes are flawed by amazingly primitive vestiges of lost ages. Dr. Who, accepting all that he meets in a skeptical anthropological fashion, is almost always the victim of those prominent flaws. He would be extinguished but for his clever ways and their insidious foolishness. He lives only to move from one incredibly desperate situation to another. The worldview or rhetoric that shines through this series says there is no progress; everywhere we tread there is a throwback to the Dark Ages. Things get worse if anything. This is the Spenglerian worldview.

The Guardians, which was also British, was even more pessimistic and certain that entropy was at full throttle. The sardonic bumper sticker "Spengler was an Optimist" was a perfect appellation for that older series.

Television is obviously not fiction in the strict sense of textual prose, but it does build a fictive world that quickly illustrates the major argument I want to forward. The argument has three main lines of thought:

1. All fiction, like all analytic discourse, has a persuasion or rhetoric at its base,
2. The rhetoric of such fiction, particularly science fiction, wants most essentially to establish a world view or primary vision of existence,
3. The worldviews in science fiction for young adults split neatly into two contending visions: meliorist and Spenglerian.

I have argued elsewhere that all of children's literature's genres have a dichotomous nature (Milner, "Axiological and Metaphysical Polarities in Children's Literature"). Like science fiction, the other mainline genres have this polar nature, or at least are better understood by a dichotomous view. Because the rhetoric, as Wayne Booth makes us know, are persuasions to significant, essential matters, it makes sense that two of philosophy's centerpieces, axiology (social values) and metaphysics (worldview, concern with matters beyond the physical), would be likely given primary place in a writer's fiction. Fiction thus revolves around these two essential philosophical dimensions.

I will touch on some of these genre splits briefly to show the breadth and power of this approach and then return to the focus of attention, science fiction. Consider these dichotomies in five basic genres of children's literature:

1. Fantasy (metaphysical) secular/sacred
2. Historical Fiction (axiological) heroic/iconoclastic
3. Mysteries (metaphysical) resolved/confounding
4. Survival Fiction (axiological) supportive/subversive
5. Animal Stories (metaphysical) platonic/darwinian

I have written an essay delineating the first dichotomy in *Webs and Wardrobes: World Views in Children's Literature* (Milner and Milner). The different worldvisions of E. B. White and C. S. Lewis are so apparent that it seems strange to spell out the things that separate them. Interestingly, here as in the television series we have different cultural or national foundations that inform each of their visions.

Historical fictions like Esther Forbes's *Johnny Tremain* and Christopher Collier and James Lincon's *My Brother Sam Is Dead* illustrate the differences between the heroic view Forbes presents of the American Revolution and the more investigative examination presented in the Collier account of that same war. Joel Taxel has shown that the cultural foundations of these two writers was also very different. Both were Americans, but Forbes wrote at the time of World War II, while Collier wrote during the wrenching turmoil America suffered in the war in Vietnam.

Mysteries are typically an exercise in cognitive closure, a test of the rational process. Humans love to solve a mystery, vicariously taking part in the mental aerobatics of a famous detective like Sherlock Holmes or Father Brown. These are puzzles that in the case of a book like Ellen Raskin's *The Westing Game* are typically solved at the end of the story. Mysteries normally reach a practical resolution; yet there are mysteries that work on deeper levels of understanding and raise more questions than they can solve. They work as Alan Garner's *The Owl Service* does to confound the reader. They represent a world of complexities and contradictions rather than the orderly world of the resolved mystery. Robbe-Grillet's *The Erasure* is a powerful example of this contorted world in adult mysteries. His detective seems to turn out to be the murderer in a story that is so complex that it makes even the ironies and irrationalities of Scott Turow's *Presumed Innocent* seem straightforward and wholly rational.

Survival fiction is as ancient as Daniel Defoe's *Robinson Crusoe*. Sustaining the British culture, keeping the familiar alive, seems to be his primary task. In many ways, this wish for familiarity can be seen as driven by a colonial ethos. Expanding the empire, remaking any terrain so that it comports with mother England, is the underlying value system. William Steig's *Abel's Island* carries a more subversive message. The value structure and routines of Abel's Edwardian life are eroded; they are replaced by self-knowledge, self-sufficiency, and a rich aesthetic dimension new in his life. He focuses on living where he is rather than returning to his life of gentlemanly ease. And, most important, when he returns to Amanda and his comfortable life, he gives us a subtle clue to the depth of his subversion when he says his clothes felt a little uncomfortable.

The rhetoric of animal stories is also often polemic. Almost all of these stories are built on a Platonic world view in which a great chain of being extends from omniscient God to dumb stones. In the Platonic hierarchy, human creatures are placed above animal life and are responsible for being stewards of the animal world and all of nature. Therefore, the Platonic view requires that humans make difficult value decisions in that realm. So, in Marjorie Kinnan Rawlings's *The Yearling* and Fred Gipson's *Old Yeller* it is not surprising that the crisis of the story is centered on a young boy's need to accept the idea that he will have to kill an animal that he loves. The less common Darwinian worldview is not the same. Instead of a vertical hierarchy, it poses a horizontal continuum on which the entire animal kingdom is placed. Darwin's continuum—unlike Plato's clearly defined hierarchy—knocks down barriers between human and animal, sees the natural world as an inseparable progression. Darwinian theory questions what the Platonic hierarchy sustains in its clear separations. Do dolphins talk? Can apes solve complex problems? Do animals dread pain? How are humans different? Because all of these questions break down belief in a clear difference between humans and animals, they make it more difficult to kill or to make any decisions

for the other members of the animal world. Allan Eckert's *Incident at Hawk's Hill*
is one of the rare books that has a Darwinian rhetoric rather than a Platonic one.
Although this Darwinian rhetoric is rare in animal stories, we can sense in our
lifetime a huge shift in attitudes that will make books like *Incident at Hawk's Hill*
more ordinary.

I have taken the time to look at five other genres because it sustains the
possibility that the basic three-point argument can be applied broadly rather than
narrowly. Qualifications or nuances can be developed in every genre I've used to
explain the paradigm, but as a basic proposition it works well in each of these
mainline sets to help us explore and understand the works that fall inside them.

These popular television science fiction series, *Dr. Who* and *Star Trek*,
demonstrate the persuasiveness of the dichotomy in the genre, but it can be seen
even more vividly if we take a closer look at young adults' texts. Science fiction
is a complex genre that encompasses books of all levels of quality. Some offer
merely technological claptrap and attempt to wow the reader by assembling as
much gadgetry as possible. The core of most of these books, however, is redolent
with societal assessment that suggests an axiological position. Either the authors
exhibit a reactionary response to the tendencies of society and wish to call these
to their readers' attention, or they long for an ameliorating transformation of
mankind that leads toward a future utopia. The former are much more the staple
of this genre than are the latter; much of science fiction is reactionary. John
Christopher, William Sleator, and a number of other fine writers do a splendid job
of characterizing the foibles of their society in projecting a worst-case scenario for
our culture. Christopher teaches us in *The White Mountains* that ease and certainty
can all too easily replace liberty and will and that only a precious few Ozymandii
are abroad in our lives. In contrast, other science fiction writers, like Sylvia Louise
Engdahl in *Enchantress from the Stars,* point to a state of principled behavior in
which the oath taking leaders act only at Kohlberg's highest stage of moral
development.

The meliorist view, broadly defined, celebrates human progress and the
vision that civilization is generally moving toward an almost Edenic state. Jacob
Bronowski's *The Ascent of Man* is exemplary of this near-utopian vision of
humankind's journey. Conversely, the Spenglerian position is a skeptical view of
humankind's pilgrimage. It sees people as fundamentally flawed, unable to
progress, and forever caught in the tension between angelic and bestial natures.
Spenglerians see a human as similar to Shakespeare's character Bottom: appear-
ing to be angelic but with the head of an ass on his/her shoulders. This view
contains a basic uncertainty and fear of what the future might hold for mankind.

A host of books illustrate these opposing world views, but the dichotomy can
be seen most clearly in Engdahl's *Enchantress from the Stars* and Christopher's
The White Mountains. These authors differ on the four basic features common to
most works of science fiction:

1. a conception of human nature,

2. an understanding of history,
3. a perception of science and technology, and
4. a use of the formal and contextual elements of fiction.

Distinct conceptions of human nature most severely separate the two writers. Engdahl clearly feels that humankind has the ability to progress. Her array of full and believable characters urges her readers to higher levels of moral understanding. Engdahl is not ignorant of the viciousness that can lurk within all humans: Her story paints a picture of a culture that mechanically, rationally sets out to control and to drain other human beings. Yet even within this self-seeking culture something, we don't know exactly what, has impelled Jarel to rise far above his culture's moral norms. He has transcended his culture, and Engdahl is clearly pleased to let us know that such transcending is possible. She sets Jarel in bold relief against the simpler evils of his brothers: their thirst for power, wealth, and regal women. From the beginning of the story, Jarel possesses virtue far beyond his culture's, and in the course of his relationship with Elana, he moves toward a elevated level of moral thought and action.

The Oathkeepers represent the possibility that a civilization might draw near to moral perfection. From the first, Illura demonstrates wholehearted adherence to her oath, an analogue to Jesus' Golden Rule or Kant's categorical imperative. She consciously chooses to give her life to attain a distant and altruistic goal for another civilization. Elana's father is a near parallel to St. John's idea of a God who so loved the world that He gave His only child. Engdahl presents a vision of humankind that centers around the capacity to produce, under the right conditions, people who exemplify Niebuhr's standard of the moral person: self-sacrifice for a higher good.

In *The White Mountains*, Christopher projects a less hopeful view of humankind's basic nature. He is concerned that a basic evil in everyone threatens to draw us away from a spiritual world and into a bestial existence. In his story, the mechanical Tripods have slowly overcome the world and are lobotomizing its children. In this postmodern rural land, the triune gods have removed as much evidence of the past as possible. Watches and books are lost; all sense of who humankind was and what it might have been has been slowly eroded. This people's most precious means of retaining a sense of the past and of good and evil is irretrievably lost when they relinquish their wills upon being capped at age fourteen. From that moment, they float numbly through life as satisfied, well-fed beasts. They give up all sense of self and merge into the mindless collective. It is the fear of such a loss of individuality, along with a haunting sense that any understanding of the difference between good and evil will be forgotten, that drives Christopher's writing. He warns us of a time when humans could lose spirit and become like machines.

Such distinct visions of humans impose very different roles on characters who act as helpers or mentors. In books that have a meliorist view of humankind, the role is that of guide, one who helps the protagonist along the natural road to goodness. For example, with prompting and modeling by Elana's father and others, Elana can rise from her personal and selfish involvement in the Oathkeepers' mission to a higher level of moral virtue. With such protagonists the battle to be fought is an interior, moral one, rather than an external war. The meliorists' deepest insight and best hope is to show how individual growth can occur. The guides or mentors are generally a part of the preferred culture rather than outlanders or aliens. They are expressions of what humankind's best future might be.

In reactive books, characters like Christopher's Will Parker are encouraged and nourished by pariahs who search for one honest man to teach. These skeptical, questioning sorts, like Ozymandias, dwell on the outskirts of the culture and seek to turn their pupils away from the treacherous ease of the mainline culture, generally calling for escape from the predators who mean to collectivize them and their pupils.

This conception of the nature of people implies a particular view of human history. The differences between the meliorists and reactives become magnified here. Engdahl sees civilization moving forward through the ages with slow but steady progress. Marx Wartofsky has constructed a scheme based on the work of Piaget, which outlines humankind's movement toward utopia and which seems compatible with Engdahl's novel. She shares with other meliorists a developmental view of civilization's moral growth, leading to a "stage six" society: The three cultures in *Enchantress from the Stars* represent a child's, an adolescent's, and an adult's moral stance. Collectively they suggest Kohlberg's three basic levels of preconventional, conventional, and postconventional moral thinking. The fact that some of her characters inhabit the third stage affirms her belief that moral achievements are accessible to others.

The strange reversal of the cycles of time in *The White Mountains* makes us feel closer to a Spenglerian view of history than a progressive one. The history seems to center around entropy rather than growth. The forward thrust of technology in the achievements of the Tripods' world is undermined by their wholly dehumanized culture. The ruins of the old cities are evidence of the history's turnaround. Those cities, once embodiments of hope in humankind's progress, are now ruined. The present is bucolic and rudimentary, and the life people have attained seems barren. For the Engdahls of the writing world, the eye strains forward into history, searching for a time when the good life, if not the perfect life, will be enjoyed by all. The Christophers, however, fret about the future and yearn for the better days of past history.

Beyond presenting very different views of people's nature and humanity's destiny, these writers offer strongly contrasting views of science and its offspring, technology. The view of science presented by Engdahl may seem very strange to those who have a classical understanding of the field. It might, in fact, be seen by many to be negative. The villainous colonizers are grounded solidly in science and technology, whereas the Oathkeepers seem more akin to the Andrecians— mystical and almost irrational. They seem more inclined toward magic than technology. However, their civilization is built on the new science: deep structural advances rather than a concern with surface gadgetry. They understand and control gravity with their minds rather than resisting it with machines. Because their science is invisible, intangible, it is all the more powerful. The three civilizations Engdahl depicts seem, indeed, similar to Alvin Toffler's first, second, and third waves of history. The instantaneous transfer of information in the third wave, which Toffler opposes to the physical movement of paper or people in the second, is paralleled by Engdahl's machineless technology. Engdahl's is a science not to be dreaded or deferred, but one which is more the servant rather than the master of humankind.

Science is less palatable to Christopher. He sees technology as dehumanizing people. He wants it destroyed by his protagonists, who retreat from the marginal comforts of that machine-dominated terrain to a barren but preferable landscape. His humans ironically use the old war technology to demolish the despotic Tripods. Will's father's watch, a product of the olden industrial times, becomes a part of the rebellion against the projected horrors of advanced technology. So Christopher is caught in some ambivalence: The technological evil can only be destroyed by technology itself. Despite this apparent irony, Christopher seems to be quite repelled by technology's essential menace.

The feelings of these authors toward the materialism generated by science and technology are another expression of their attraction to or revulsion from science. For example, no opulence, gadgetry, or surplus of goods appears in the lives of Engdahl's star people. They always seem to have simply adequate stores for the basic needs of life. The Imperials, however, are always in search of raw materials; their exploitive colonization inevitably leads to crushing others. An important message about the connection between goods and goodness seems to be close to the surface of Engdahl's book. Such a connection is not farfetched; it is explicitly articulated by contemporary thinkers such as Abraham Maslow and Mortimer Adler, who argue that a democratic distribution of the essential goods is a basic step toward societal goodness.

Christopher, on the other hand, links luxury and a surplus of goods with indolence and capitulation of the will, which inevitably lead to mental imprisonment and mindless collectivism. The castle's plenty and the congeniality of Eloise almost lead Will to a willing capping after his earlier struggles to preserve his independence. Living in rags like Ozymandias removes the escapees from goods and ease and is their only hope for freedom in the world. One senses that though Christopher has a respect for goods and property, he rejects them when they are balanced against freedom. Unlike Engdahl, he does not accept the abundance of goods in a postindustrial/new science world as a given, nor does he believe that such plenty can help to eradicate greed and hostility.

The shape a science fiction novel takes is often a benchmark for the world view of its creator. *Enchantress from the Stars* takes on a shape that is quite complex: A first person preface and prologue frame a limited omniscient narrator who moves freely from one culture to the next but who can only enter certain minds. The very complexity of this varying structure beckons the reader to follow these protagonists in their paths of cognitive and ethical growth. The nuances underlaying each change of culture further suggest the complexity of life in that new world.

Christopher's novel has a far simpler structure: The story follows a clear linear patten and the narrator is first person rather than a complex one such as Engdahl's narrator. Christopher's unwillingness to enter the alien Tripods' minds is itself a statement about his own openness to any new forms of life. The particular perspective, first or third, does not matter so much as the general willingness or hesitancy to explore and understand incredibly different life forms. Here the self-centeredness of the narrative voice and the polarity of good and evil implicitly reinforce a point of view that is explicitly set forth in Will's story.

Setting offers an even more reliable means by which we can understand the worldview of its creator. Almost predictably, those novels which are set in a far distant time frame are written by meliorists. By moving great distances in time (and often space) authors can reshape humankind or the beings who populate their books and thereby startle us into new visions of ourselves as human beings. For instance, in all three of the Engdahl societies, we can recognize our culture, but we envision coming to be like the Oathkeepers. By setting the novel in a far future time, Engdahl forces us out of the familiar surroundings of today to see small reforms as mere tinkering. She projects the need for radical change.

The Spenglerian authors are far more likely to place their characters closer to the present. In *The White Mountains,* the ruined city, the watch, the other artifacts and geographic landmarks all demonstrate that the people the tripods are seeking to enslave are not much different from us. Characters of a time nearly contiguous to our own show us what might be changed to rectify our mistakes in the present age, to repossess what has almost slipped away. If time were too distant, if the culture had changed too much, the reader would lose the template by which such a realistic reshaping could be performed.

Each of the four features of these two authors' works presents a dichotomy that is strong and revealing: Humantity ascends or it is naturally ruined; civilization moves toward utopia or caves in upon itself; science and its offspring, technology, are means by which we enlarge and perfect ourselves or they turn, like Dr. Frankenstein's famous monster, upon us. Even in the author's fictive form we see a clear dichotomy: The story's structure is either challengingly complex or straightforwardly simple, and setting is either distant enough to force contemplation of radical reform or close enough to beg us to retreat to the golden days of yesteryear. We are forced to choose between distinctly divergent paths.

Young readers most often encounter various degrees of Spenglerian writing. For instance, Sleator's *House of Stairs* illustrates a reactive view of human nature and history, identifying science as the motive force in their decline. The novel shows people almost beaten into a ratlike state by science. Here, as in Christopher's novel, these dehumanizing forces work to erase the distinction between good and evil and to reduce the characters to animals rather than people. O'Brien's *Z for Zachariah* contains that same reactive message. Ann Burden, the main character, confronts technology in her bucolic world, a haven from the destruction science has brought upon the rest of humanity. There is some faint hope for survival at the novel's end, but Ann's dream of a new Eden has been forfeited by Mr. Loomis's conquest and control of her valley. Science, again, becomes the exploiter and destroyer of humankind. Mr. Loomis is like the Tripods; he is not as direct or blatant, but his actions imperil the most humanizing elements of mankind.

Occasionally, books like Monica Hughes's *Keeper of the Isis Light* appear, in which truly brave new worlds are foreseen as possible futures for us. Although Hughes's earthling, Mark London, cannot measure up to the good light keeper, Olwen, the fault seems to be a temporary shortcoming rather than a permanent fallen state. Concern with superficial features has not yet been put aside, but a clear hope for purity in relationships still exists. Hughes's faith in progress is clear. She joins Engdahl in hope for humankind's nature and destiny .

When we talk about books and television series we are looking at long spans of attention for students. Short science fiction, which they read more readily than novels, exhibits a similar pair of polar stories: "The Star" by Arthur C. Clark and "The Ones Who Walk Away From Omelas" by Ursula K. Le Guin speak quickly but eloquently for the Spenglerian and meliorist worldviews. In Clark's short tale we have an ironic Christmas story, a serious *Life of Brian*. The star many Earthlings celebrate is from the perspective of another civilization, a token of doom, not a sign of hope and deliverance. Clark looks at what appears to be superordinate events from a cosmic perspective that reduces Earth's spectacular events to a negative blip in the giant universal pattern. The same cynicism and doom is reduced to Earth scale in Ray Bradbury's "There Will Come Soft Rains." He represents a civilization (ours perhaps) through his automated house that is so technologically profound that it completely serves the needs of the people who dwelt in it. The doom, as Churchill predicted, comes dramatically "on the swift wings of science." That which comforts the people emulates them in an Earth holocaust of nuclear fire that burns the family's last leisure moments into the outside skin of the impermeable house. Le Guin does not assume the same posture with regard to the future. She uses the tainted utopia of Omelas not to eviscerate all perfect futures but to caution her reader that seeming utopias are short of the mark unless they provide perfection for every creature that abides in the land. She instructs us on the final step from democratic capitalism to a utopia beyond that which Spock's mind could organize for us.

BIBLIOGRAPHY

Adler, Mortimer. *Six Great Ideas*. New York: Macmillan, 1981.

Booth, Wayne. *The Rhetoric of Fiction*. Chicago: U of Chicago P, 1983.

Bronowski, Jacob. *The Ascent of Man*. Boston: Little, Brown, 1974.

Christopher, John. *The White Mountains*. New York: Macmillan, 1967.

Clarke, Arthur C. *The Nine Billion Names of God* "The Star." New York: Signet, 1967. 247-53.

Collier, Christopher, and James Lincoln. *My Brother Sam Is Dead.* New York: Four Winds, 1974.

Eckert, Allan W. *Incident at Hawk's Hill.* Boston: Little Brown, 1971.

Engdahl, Sylvia Louise. *Enchantress from the Stars.* New York: Atheneum, 1970.

Forbes, Esther. *Johnny Tremain.* Boston: Houghton, 1960.

Garner, Alan. *The Owl Service.* New York: Walk, 1967.

Gipson, Fred. *Old Yeller.* New York: Harper, 1956.

Hughes, Monica. *Keeper of the Isis Light.* New York: Atheneum, 1981.

Kohlberg, Lawrence. "Moral Stages and Moralization: The Cognitive-Developmental Approach." *Moral Development and Behavior.* Ed. T. Lickona. New York: Holt, 1976.

Le Guin, Ursula K. "The Ones Who Walk Away From Omelas." *The Winds Twelve Quarters.* New York: Harper, 1975. 275-84.

Maslow, Abraham, ed. *Motivation and Personality.* 2nd. ed. New York: Harper, 1970.

Milner, Joseph O. "Axiological and Metaphysical Polarities in Children's Literature." Philological Society Meeting, Charleston, SC, 25 March 1983.

Milner, Joseph O., and Lucy M. Milner, eds. *Webs and Wardrobes: World Views in Chidren's Literature.* Lanham, MD: UP of America, 1987.

Niebuhr, Reinhold. *Moral Man and Immoral Society: A Study in Ethics and Politics.* New York: Scribners, 1932.

O'Brien, Robert C. *Z for Zachariah.* New York: Dell, 1974.

Raskin, Ellen. *The Westing Game.* New York: Dutton, 1978.

Rawlings, Marjorie Kinnan. *The Yearling.* New York: Scribner, 1947.

Robbe-Grillet, Alain. *The Erasures.* New York: Grove, 1964.

Sleator, William. *House of Stairs.* New York: Scholastic, 1974.

Steig, William. *Abel's Island.* New York: Farrar, 1976.

Taxis, Joel.. "The American Revolution in Children's Fiction." Research in the Teaching of English 17.1 (1983): 61-83.

Toffler, Alvin. *The Third Wave.* New York: Morrow, 1980.

Turow, Scott. *Presumed Innocent.* New York: Farrar, 1987.

Wartofsky, Marx. "The Relation Between Philosophy of Science and History of Science." *Essays in Memory of Imre Lakatos.* Ed. R.S. Cohen, P.K. Feyerabend, and M.W. Wartofsky. Boston: Reidel, 1976.

16

Raymond Briggs's
When the Wind Blows:
Toward an Ecology of the
Mind for Young Readers

Millicent Lenz

Raymond Briggs's *When the Wind Blows,* a cartoon format satiric treatment of nuclear holocaust, appeared in 1982, first in Great Britain and then in the United States. Briggs was spurred into satire by the British government's publication of an inane pamphlet, *Protect and Survive,* which also provoked E. P. Thompson's *Protest and Survive,*[1] a justly angry exposé of the absurdity of thinking civilians might defend themselves from nuclear warheads by means of improvised shelters made of homely materials—unhinged doors, furniture, and sacks of grain. Reviewers have questioned the appropriateness of Briggs's book for children but generally agree on its visual artistry and adroit cautionary power; many have recommended it highly for those readers who are, in critic John Cech's well-turned phrase, "old enough to absorb the caustic parodies of *Mad Magazine*" (203). Its best-seller status in Great Britain, production as a play on the BBC and in a London theatre, and issue as a videocassette attest to its striking imaginative appeal.[2]

The nursery rhyme origin of the title—Rockabye baby, in the treetop, / When the wind blows, the cradle will rock—sets the ironic tone and helps characterize the Bloggses as infant-like in their helplessness against nuclear threat. An attentive reader will also remember the calamitous end of the nursery rhyme—When the bough breaks, the cradle will fall, / And down will come baby, cradle, and all—as prefiguring the Bloggses' doom. Their moon faces project childlike openness and terrible innocence, adding to the satirical sting in their victimization by the impersonal and uncontrollable forces of international politics and technological warfare (See Figure 1).

Looking beneath the deceptively simple satirical surface of Briggs's picture book to its implications, I find certain parallels, fortuitous but intriguing, with the thought of Gregory Bateson, the noted epistemologist, anthropologist, and theo-

rist of cybernetics, whose best-known essays are collected in *Steps To an Ecology of Mind: A Revolutionary Approach to Man's Understanding of Himself*. It would not be difficult to imagine, if one did not know better, that Briggs had Bateson's ideas in mind when he fashioned his satire. To those not yet familiar with Bateson's works, my comments may serve to show the pertinence of his ideas to nuclear criticism. As I shall demonstrate, Bateson is concerned with the urgency of adopting a new way of seeing reality, of achieving a transformation of consciousness, essential to preventing the destruction of civilization. The significance of *When the Wind Blows* lies, I believe, in its incorporation of the same concern in a work of art.

The link between Bateson's thought and nuclear criticism is their common ultimate concern with human survival. Nuclear criticism is aptly described by critic William J. Scheick as a mode of discourse diverging from the fashionable directions of contemporary literary criticism in its aim to redirect "critiques of cultural artifacts from the remote spatial void of poststructuralism to the apposite inner-spatial realm of human ethos." Nuclear criticism tends, Scheick continues, to be inherently ethical, seeking "to expose the one ultimate concern that has always mattered to humanity throughout history: the preservation of life" (5). By doing the unfashionable, that is, making *ethical judgments* of texts, it places an implied hope in "the capacity of the human mind to redirect itself," to achieve a revision of human consciousness, "an imaginative intuitive revision, a seeing anew" or "a neo-Romantic intuitive vaulting of mind" (6). Thus, its stress on the negative—the dark depths of the human unconscious—is but a "necessary prelude to an awakening of humanity to its potentiality for re-minding and re-vision" (8).

Unremittingly moralistic in its implications, Briggs's story features an unsophisticated and somewhat muddle-headed retired British couple, James and Hilda Bloggs, trying to cope in their commonsensical ways with the radio bulletins warning of an imminent nuclear attack. James ("Ducks" to his wife) has uncritically filled his head with the platitudes and euphemisms the bureaucratic vocabulary uses to camouflage the terror of mass destruction; his morning has been spent at the public library reading the newspapers, which Hilda dismisses as "full of rubbish" and refuses to heed. Her characterization of the news as rubbish has some validity; its effect on James, in any event, is to fill his head with a mishmash of scientific and political jargon, replete with malapropisms to signal his naivete to the reader. When Hilda ventures to ask him who will win, if there is indeed a war, he responds with this tirade:

Well, the Americans have Tactile Nuclear Superiority, due to their IBMs and their Polar Submarines, but in the event of a Pre-Emptive Strike, innumerate Russian hordes will sweep across the plains of Central Europe.[3]

Of course the U. S. Air Force and the Marines will come to the rescue—as in World War II; both Hilda and James are fixated on the past, imagine nuclear holocaust through outmoded images, and pin their hopes on such now-dead saviors as Churchill, Roosevelt and Stalin, "all good blokes," as James says. The result will be the triumph of Western ideals, in James' opinion:

One Man—One Vote, and women too nowadays of course, and thus the Communist Fret to the Free World would be neutrified and democratic principles would be instilled throughout Russia, whether they liked it or not. That's the World Scenario as I see it, at this moment in time.

The numerous verbal mistakes underscore his fuzzy thinking. Hilda tries to avoid any topic so unpleasant as war; cheerful to a fault, she assumes they will manage to muddle through, even without Winston Churchill to lead them.

To prepare for the blast, the two faithfully follow the instructions in the pamphlet James has found at the library. The dramatic irony is heightened by the reader's superior knowledge of their certain doom, confirmed by intervening two-page spreads showing nuclear warheads and nuclear submarines speeding toward their targets. The plot pulsates with a growing tension, climaxing with the moment of explosion, visually rendered by two blank pages of white tinged with rose around the edges.

The benighted Bloggses suppose they have escaped with their lives, oblivious to the silent, lethal, but invisible radiation that is killing them inch by inch. In the ensuing days, they slowly sicken and die, all the time expressing their trust in the eventual arrival of emergency services, their fragmentary, half-remembered phrases of religious comfort ("Thy Rod and Thy Staff Comfort Me/All the Days of My Life"), and even at one point, a fantasy of a New Eden arising in England, another Renaissance; now that the slate has been wiped "clean," James says, the world can begin afresh. The stark reality, visualized in the final cartoon frames, is their pathetic death in darkness and pain, wrapped in the paper potato sacks recommended by their now defunct civil defense agency as protection against the intense heat of nuclear incineration (See Figure 2).

This entire scenario, viewed from a perspective informed by Bateson's thought, is the result of "bad thinking." The central assumption of *Steps To an Ecology of Mind,* says Mark Engel in the foreword, is that we as human beings "create the world we perceive, selecting and editing 'reality' to fit our belief systems" (vii). To apply this assumption simplistically to the fate of the Bloggses and indict them for bringing doom upon themselves would, however, be a grave error, for Bateson's critique is pointed at bad belief systems. The Bloggses are caught up on a tangled web of what Bateson calls "virulent ideas," largely unconscious beliefs that have held sway in their most deadly form since the Industrial Revolution. He sums them up in "The Roots of Ecological Crisis," testimony dating from 1970, when Bateson appeared before a committee of the State Senate of Hawaii on behalf of the University of Hawaii Committee on Ecology and Man, supporting the bill (S.B. 1132) that (when it was later passed) established an environmental center at the university. Here are the ideas Bateson renounces in *Steps To an Ecology of Mind.*

> (a) It's us *against* the environment.
> (b) It's us *against* other men.
> (c) It's the individual (or the individual company, or the individual nation) that matters.
> (d) We *can* have unilateral control over the environment and must strive for that control.
> (e) We live within an infinitely expanding 'frontier.'
> (f) Economic determinism is common sense.
> (g) Technology will do it for us. (493)

These ideas have in common a hubristic, ego-exalting, and dichotomous mode of thinking, as well as an assumption that humans can stand *outside* nature and apart from it. Even if we could (which is rank nonsense), as Bateson remarks later, *"The creature that wins against its environment destroys itself"* (493).

The result of these ideas, ingrained in Western consciousness, is (on the microcosmic level) the death of the Bloggses and (by extension) of humankind. The most fundamental epistemological error, however, is identified in Bateson's "Pathologies of Epistemology." Critiquing Darwin's theory of natural selection and evolution, wherein the unit of survival was seen to be the species or subspecies, Bateson insists on his insight that instead, "the unit of survival is *organism plus environment"* (*Steps To an Ecology of Mind* 483).[4] He goes even further: *"The unit of evolutionary survival,"* he finally concludes, is *"identical with the unit of mind."* Our Western way of conceiving of the world, our whole frame of consciousness, rests upon an error. We have chosen the wrong "unit of survival" (*Steps To an Ecology of Mind* 483).

Bateson more fully explains his identification of the unit of survival with the unit of mind in "Form, Substance and Difference." Taking a "systems" view of survival, he points to two kinds of ecology, the "informational" or "entropic" and the "bioenergetic." A bioenergetic system (for instance, a person, like James or Hilda Bloggs) is mortal and dies, but an informational system, or system of ideas, has a kind of immortality. "Socrates as a bioenergetic individual is dead. But much of him still lives as a component in the contemporary ecology of ideas" (*Steps To an Ecology of the Mind* 461). Bateson's cybernetic epistemology expands *mind* outward from the individual consciousness; the individual mind "is immanent but not only in the body. It is immanent also in pathways and messages outside the body; and there is a larger Mind of which the individual mind is only a subsystem" (461). The larger Mind is "immanent in the total evolutionary structure," or at a lower level of systemic thinking, "in the large biological system—the ecosystem" (460). Viewing the fate of the Bloggses from Bateson's perspective, it follows that their lives have been forfeited to an error at the root of Western thinking, the misidentification of the unit of survival with a particular nation—a misconception setting technologically armed nations against one another with predictably disastrous consequences.

Bateson takes humanity to task for "arrogating mind to ourselves"—setting us "outside and against" the world, seen as mindless and not deserving of "moral or ethical consideration." This is the inevitable result of defining our survival unit as ourselves and our "folks," set against other social units, races, or "the brutes and vegetables." If we relate to nature in this way and additionally "*have an advanced technology*, [our] likelihood of survival will be that of a snowball in hell. You will die either of the toxic by-products of your own hate, or, simply, of overpopulation and overgrazing." Thus, he concludes, we must restructure our whole way of thinking (462). The premises of thought popular in the "precybernetic era" will doom us. Policy decisions, such as those governing the detonation of nuclear arms that destroyed the Bloggses world, must not be left to persons who lack the largeness of mind to see the survival unit as identical with the total ecosystem. Immanent mind, because it contains our "insanities," is itself subject to possible insanity: "It is in our power, with our technology, to create insanity in the larger system of which we are parts" (466).

Bateson does not claim, incidentally, mastery of this new cybernetic way of thinking. Under LSD, however, he did experience "the disappearance of the division between self and the music to which I was listening" (463). He places his best hopes in the way of thinking exemplified by artists and poets, who intuitively "bridge" complex levels of mental processes; artistic skill involves the synthesizing of thought and feeling, unconscious and conscious levels of mind, and holds them in an organic whole (464). Perhaps artistic ability, or at least artistic appreciation, should be a prerequisite for election to public office, as it once was in traditional Chinese society.

Bateson believes cybernetics offers us the way to understand systems of complex interrelationships, but this knowledge in itself can be put to destructive as well as constructive uses. He comments in "Versailles to Cybernetics" on the use of computers (James Bloggs called them "commuters") as a substitute for human thinking, as when governments use them to decide policy, thus "petrifying the rules of the game" (*Steps To an Ecology of the Mind* 474). Contrariwise, cybernetics can be the key to the attitudinal changes necessary to a new systemic, ecological way of thinking, helping us understand how complex systems work. He calls the science of cybernetics "the biggest bite out of the fruit of the Tree of Knowledge that mankind has taken in the last 2000 years" (474). It remains to be seen whether or not this bite may prove indigestible.

Significant historical moments are moments when patterns of relationship are dramatically changed—when "people are hurt because of their former values." As human beings, we value "patterns of relationship," we seek to know where we stand vis-à-vis other human beings, in relationships of love, hate, respect, trust, dependency, and so on (470). It is no longer enough for us or the Bloggses to value only the patterns of relationship in our personal lives, for cybernetic thinking tells us we belong to a much larger unit of survival; we ignore this larger perspective at our peril. If we as a species wish to forestall the fate of the Bloggses, we need to cut through the "rubbish" of the newspapers and of government pamphlets purporting to tell us how to survive and demand from our decision-makers a holistic perspective, an accurate use of language, and an ecological way of thinking—or as Bateson would say, an ecology of mind.

Readers who know nothing of Gregory Bateson, ecology, and the cybernetic model of thinking can be helped to understand the meaning of "an ecology of mind" through Briggs's story. Books, someone said, are lifeboats of ideas. To extend the metaphor, the story of the Bloggses' end, depicting the torpedoing of the ark of civilization by a bad belief system with its mistaken notion of the family or the nation as "the unit of survival," can awaken us to the urgency of our need to cleanse our perceptions, to start to think critically about our thinking itself. Much attention has been given of late to the need to teach youngsters from their early years how to think, to bring metacognitive awareness into our educational process in the early grades. We can, through informed critiques of texts such as *When the Wind Blows,* help young people realize that ignorance and unexamined premises can have fatal consequences.

Books can make a difference in the way we see the world; they help to shape our perception of "reality" for better or worse. We can choose texts that move us towards a perception of the unit of survival as the whole system of life on our precious and fragile planet. And as Buckminster Fuller reputedly remarked, "On Spaceship Earth there are no passengers; everyone is crew." If we fail in this realization, if we perpetuate our bad belief systems, we shall share the ignominious fate of James and Hilda Bloggs (See Figure 3).

NOTES

1. U. S. edition edited by E. P. Thompson and Dan Smith (New York: Monthly Review Press, 1981). Thompson's own contribution to the collection, "Overthrowing the Satanic Kingdom," was reprinted in *The Nuclear Predicament: A Sourcebook,* edited by Donna Gregory (New York: St. Martin's Press, 1986). For a U. S. government publication in the same vein as *Protect and Survive,* but designed for use with school children, see *Your Chance to Live,* published by the U.S. Civil Defense Preparedness Agency (Washington, DC: GPO, 1973), SM 3-12.

2. *When the Wind Blows.* Video. With the voices of Sir John Mills and Dame Peggy Ashcroft. Screenplay by Raymond Briggs. Dir. Jimmy T. Murakami. International Video Entertainment, 1987. 80 min. Reviewed in *The New York Times,* 19 June 1988, Art/ Leisure Section: 30.

3. *When the Wind Blows* is an unpaged picture book.

4. In another essay, he improves upon this by saying the unit of survival is the flexible organism in its flexible environment. See "Form, Substance, and Difference" in *Steps To an Ecology of Mind* (New York: Ballentine, 1972), 451.

BIBLIOGRAPHY

Bateson, Gregory. "Form, Substance, and Difference." The Nineteenth Annual Korzyliski Memorial Lecture, The Institute of General Semantics, 1970.

_____. *Steps To an Ecology of Mind: A Revolutionary Approach to Man's Understanding of Himself.* New York: Ballantine, 1972.

_____. "Pathologies of Epistemology." The Second Conference on Mental Health in Asia and the Pacific, 1969.

_____. "Versailles to Cybernetics." Two Worlds Symposium, 21 April 1966.

Briggs, Raymond. *When the Wind Blows.* London: Hamish Hamilton, 1966. New York: Schocken, 1972.

Cech, John. "Some Leading, Blurred, and Violent Edges of the Contemporary Picture Book." *Children's Literature* 15 (1987): 197-206.

Scheick, William J. "Nuclear Criticism: An Introduction." *Papers on Language and Literature* 26.1 (Winter 1990): 3-12.

Selected
Bibliography

Michael Levy

The items listed here do not include studies of individual authors and, for the most part, are in addition to the critical works listed at the end of each chapter.

GENERAL REFERENCE

Carpenter, Humphrey, and Mari Prichard, eds.*The Oxford Companion to Children's Literature.* New York: Oxford UP, 1984.

Collins, Robert A., and Robert Latham, eds. *Science Fiction & Fantasy Book Review Annual,* Westport, CT: Meckler, 1988-1989; Westport, CT:Greenwood, 1990-present.

Gunn, James, ed. *The New Encyclopedia of Science Fiction.* New York: Viking, 1988.

Lynn, Ruth Nadelman. *Fantasy Literature for Children and Young Adults: An Annotated Bibliography.* 3rd ed. New York: Bowker, 1989.

Magill, Frank N., ed. *Survey of Science Fiction Literature.* 5 vols. Englewood Cliffs, NJ: Salem, 1979.

Nicholls, Peter, ed. *The Science Fiction Encyclopedia.* New York: Doubleday, 1979.

Pflieger, Pat. *A Reference Guide to Modern Fantasy for Children.* Westport, CT: Greenwood, 1984.

Smith, Curtis C., ed. *Twentieth-Century Science Fiction Writers.* 2nd ed. Chicago: St. James, 1986.

Something About the Author. Ed. Anne Commire. Detroit: Gale, 1971-1990. Ed. Donna Olendorf, 1991-present.

CRITICAL AND HISTORICAL WORKS

Antczak, Janice. *Science Fiction: The Mythos of a New Romance.* Westport, CT: Greenwood, 1987.

Brians, Paul. "Nuclear War Fiction for Young Readers: A Commentary and Annotated Bibliography." *Science Fiction, Social Conflict and War*. Ed. Philip John Davies. Manchester, UK: Manchester UP, 1990. 132-50.

Crouch, Marcus. *The Nesbit Tradition: The Children's Novel in England, 1945-1970*. Totowa: Rowman and Littlefield, 1972.

Gunn, James. "A Basic Science Fiction Library." *Library Journal* 15 (Nov. 1988): 25-31.

Hannigan, Jane Anne. "Youth and Future Studies: Science Fiction Visual Images as a Source for Change." *Frontiers of Library Service for Youth*. New York: Columbia University in the City of New York School of Library Science, 1979. 43-56.

Hartwell, David G. "The Golden Age of Science Fiction is 12." *Top of the News* 39 (Fall 1982): 39-53. Rpt. in *Age of Wonders: Explaining the World of Science Fiction*. New York: Walker, 1984. 3-24.

James, Edward. "Yellow, Black, Metal, and Tentacled: The Race Question in American Science Fiction." *Science Fiction, Social Conflict and War*. Ed. Philip John Davies. Manchester, UK: Manchester, UP, 1990. 26-49.

Kennedy, DayAnn M., Stella S. Spangler, and Mary Ann Vanderwerf. *Science & Technology in Fact and Fiction: A Guide to Children's Books*. New York: Bowker, 1990.

Ketterer, David. *Canadian Science Fiction and Fantasy*. Bloomington: Indiana UP, 1992.

Lenz, Millicent. *Nuclear Age Literature for Youth: The Quest for a Life- Affirming Ethic*. Chicago: American Library Association, 1990.

Lynn, Elizabeth. "Women in, of, and on Science Fiction." *Top of the News* 39 (Fall 1982): 72-75.

Sammons, Martha C. *"A Better Country": The Worlds of Religious Fantasy and Science Fiction*. Westport, CT: Greenwood, 1988.

Shinn, Thelma. *Worlds Within Women: Myth and Mythmaking in Fantastic Literature by Women*. Westport, CT: Greenwood, 1986.

Svilpis, Janis. "Authority, Autonomy, and Adventure in Juvenile Science Fiction." *Children's Literature Association Quarterly* 8 (Fall 1983): 22-26.

Weber, Thomas J. "Children's Science Fiction." *The Twentieth Century*. Ed. William T. Moynihan and Mary E. Shaner. Masterworks of Children's Literature, Vol. 8. New York: Stonehill, 1986.

Tymn, Marshall. *Science Fiction: A Teacher's Guide and Resource Book*. Mercer Island, WA: Starmont, 1988.

Woolf, Virginia. "Feminist Criticism and Science Fiction for Children." *Children's Literature Association Quarterly* 7 (Winter 82/83): 13-16.

Index

About the
Editor and Contributors

MARILYN FAIN APSELOFF is a Professor of English at Kent State University where she has taught Children's Literature since 1968. She is past President of the Children's Literature Association (ChLA) and has served as a board member. She has presented papers at many meetings: ChLA, Modern Language Association, Midwest MLA, International Association for the Fantastic in the Arts, and others. In addition to numerous articles, book chapters, and reviews, she is the author of *Nonsense Literature for Children: Aesop to Seuss*, with Celia Catlett Anderson (1989); *They Wrote for Children Too: An Annotated Bibliography of Children's Books By Famous Writers for Adults* (Greenwood, 1989); and *A Critical Biography of Elizabeth George Speare* (1992).

K. V. BAILEY has contributed essays and reviews to *Foundation, The Wellsian, The Australian Science Fiction Review*, and other critical journals and symposia. He has been Senior Lecturer in History at Daneshill College, was Chief Education Officer at the British Broadcasting Corporation, and has worked extensively in the field of environmental education. His books include *The Listening Schools* (1976) and *Past, Present, Future* (1982); his verse collections include *Alderney, and Other Worlds* (1982) and *The Sky Giants* (1989).

THOM DUNN, a Professor of English at the Hamilton Campus of Miami University of Ohio since 1986, has published extensively on science fiction and other forms of fantastic literature from his perspective as a student and teacher of medieval and Renaissance literature and culture. He is coeditor, with Rich Erlich, of *Clockwork Worlds: Mechanized Environments in SF* (Greenwood, 1983) and *The Mechanical God: Machines in Science Fiction* (Greenwood, 1982).

PATRICIA HARKINS is an Assistant Professor of English at the University of the Virgin Islands, St. Thomas Campus. Her areas of specialization include Caribbean literature, mythology and folklore, and children's literature. She is a published creative writer and scholar who lives on a fantastically beautiful and culturally rich island where she teaches creative writing and literature.

HOWARD V. HENDRIX has published in a variety of formats and genres—short stories, novelettes, poems, dramas, and critical artricles. His experimantal story, "The Art of Memory," in the June 1989 **EOTU** was nominated for a Pushcart Prize that year, and several of his science fiction short stories have been nominated for the Nebula Award of the Science Fiction Writers of America.

KARL HILLER is a published writer of short fiction and a committed role-gamer. At present, he is pursuing a graduate degree in clinical psychology.

ELIZABETH ANNE HULL has taught science fiction at William Rainey Harper College for more then twenty years. With her husband, Frederik Pohl, she co-edited *Tales from the Planet Earth* (1986). She has served the Science Fiction Research Association as editor of the *SFRA Newsletter*, Secretary, and President; and she has been active in World SF (as editor of *World SF Newsletter*), the International Association for the Fantastic in the Arts, the Popular Culture Association, and the Midwest Modern Language Association. She has contributed articles to *Extrapolation, Locus, Science Fiction Chronicle*, and various anthologies and encyclopedias; her story "Second Best Friend" appeared the December 1986 *Aboriginal SF*.

RAYMOND E. JONES is an Associate Professor in the Department of English at the University of Alberta. He is coauthor of *Canadian Books for Children: A Guide to Authors and Illustrators* (1988) and Associate Editor of *The HBJ Anthology of Literature* (1992). He has written a teacher's guide to Madeleine L'Engle's *A Wrinkle in Time* (1991) and published articles on Canadian arctic fiction for children and on such writers as Philippa Pearce, Maurice Sendak, Julia Cunningham, Monica Hughes, Janet Lunn, and Kevin Major.

MILLICENT LENZ is presently on the faculty of the University at Albany, SUNY, School on Information Science and Policy, where she conducts classes in literature for youth. She co-edited *Young Adult Literature: Background and Criticism* (1980), with Ramona M. Mahood, authored *Nuclear-Age Literature for Youth: The Quest for a Life-Affirming Ethic* (1990), and has contributed essays to *ChLA Quarterly* and a variety of other jounals. She is presently at work on a reference book devoted to the selection of literature for young adult readers.

MICHAEL LEVY is a Professor of English at the University of Wisconsin—Stout, where he teaches science fiction, children's literature, and technical writing. He is the author of the critical study *Natalie Babbitt* (1991) as well as articles on topics as diverse as *Paradise Lost*, feminist science fiction, and *Dr. Who*.   A frequent contributor of book reviews to a variety of journals, he was recently named coeditor of the *Science Fiction and Fantasy Books Review Annual*. He is married to Rhysling Award-nominated poet Sandra Lindow and has two children.

JOSEPH O. MILNER serves as Chairman of the Department of Education at Wake Forest University and is the Director of the eight-site North Carolina Writing Project. He is a member of the National Faculty, is editor of *North Carolina English Teacher*, serves on the Editorial Board of *Children's Literature in Education*, is the past Chairman of the International Assembly of NCTE, is Vice Chairman of the Conference on English Education, and has been NCTE's nominee to the National Board for Professional Teaching Standards. He has authored books and essays on English education, children's literature, aesthetics, linguistics, and American literature. He is now completing an English Method text, *Bridging English*.

JUDITH N. MITCHELL is a Professor of English at Rhode Island College. Her work has appeared in *The English Journal, ALAN Review, VOYA, NEATE Leaflet*, and *The Journal of Popular Culture*. She has written research essays, and she was a contributor to the NCTE *Books for You* (1986). Anticipating ordination as an Episcopal priest, Dr. Mitchell lives in Providence with her husband; their four children live close by.

FRANCIS J. MOLSON is a Professor of English and the Chairperson of the Department of English Language and Literature at Central Michigan University. In addition to nineteenth-century American literature, his specialization is children's literature, in particular children's fantasy and science fiction. He is the author of *Children's Fantasy,* the chapter on children's and young adult science fiction in *The Anatomy of Wonder*, the chapter on young adult fantasy in *Fantasy Literature: A Reader's Guide*, and many articles. He is currently working on a history of American children's science fiction.

ROGER C. SCHLOBIN is a Professor of English at the North Central Campus of Purdue University. He has authored six books and has edited over fifty. His various other publications include over one hundred essays, various poems, fiction, reviews, and bibliographies in such varied topics as fantasy literature, pedagogy, science fiction, medieval literature, linguistics, and microcomputer hardware and software. He is one of the founders of the International Association for the Fantastic in the Arts and is editor of *The Journal of the Fantastic in the Arts*.

M. SARAH SMEDMAN is a Professor at Moorhead State University in Moorhead, Minnesota, where she teaches graduate and undergraduate courses in children's literature. Currently President of the Children's Literature Association, she has published numerous essays on children's literature in major journals and reference works. She is especially interested in eighteenth-century British literature, girls' series books, and contemporary writers who write of children confronting spiritual challenges.

C. W. SULLIVAN III is a Professor of English and Director of Graduate Studies in English at East Carolina University. He is the author of *Welsh Celtic Myth in Modern Fantasy* (Greenwood, 1989), coeditor of *Herbal and Magical Medicine: Traditional Healing Today* (1992), editor of *The Children's Folklore Review*, and current President of the International Association for the Fantastic in the Arts. His articles on medieval Welsh literature, mythology, folklore, fantasy, and science fiction have appeared in a variety of anthologies and journals in Great Britain and America.

J. R. WYTENBROEK is a Professor at Malaspina College in British Columbia, Canada. Her areas of major academic interest include fantasy and science fiction together with children's literature—a frequently happy combination. She has written a book on science fiction writer Madeleine L'Engle, due out soon, and several articles in the fields of science fiction, fantasy, and children's literature. She also reviews for journals in these three fields.